GENUINE VALIDATION

GENUINE VALIDATION

COMPASSIONATE COMMUNICATION THAT TRANSFORMS DIFFICULT RELATIONSHIPS AT HOME AND WORK

CORRINE R. STOEWSAND, PH.D.

ISBN 978-987-86-0725-2

Ciudad Autónoma de Buenos Aires : Corrine Rhesa Stoewsand, 2019.

1. Autoayuda. 2. Relaciones Interpersonales. 3. Familia. I. Título. CDD 158.2
1. Self help. 2. Interpersonal Relations. 3. Family. I Title.

GENUINE VALIDATION

COMPASSIONATE COMMUNICATION
THAT TRANSFORMS DIFFICULT RELATIONSHIPS
AT HOME AND WORK

----

by Corrine R. Stoewsand, Ph.D.

Foreword by Pablo Gagliesi

Edited by Andrea Rosenberg

Cover design by Cynthia Cravero Klinsky

Chapter top paintings by Catharine Cary

Illustrations by Angery Palm

Diagrams, charts and graphs by Corrine Stoewsand

Back cover photo by Valeria Mondino

AMARSE PRESS

CARRBORO, NC, AND BUENOS AIRES, ARGENTINA

This book is dedicated to

my father, Gilbert Stoewsand, whose generous love gave me the courage to take a path less traveled,

Marsha Linehan, a brilliant psychologist, teacher, and living bodhisattva,

all my patients and students from whom I have learned so much,

and to Jose Omar Vega whose suffering touched my soul and awakened me to this path.

CONTENTS

ACKNOWLEDGMENTS

I have been inspired and accompanied on my journey, sharing the path of compassionate communication with families whose pain and suffering is so often invisible to others as they accompany a loved-one with a mental illness. I would like to thank especially my long-time companions on the path of genuine validation, including Carola Pechon who helped me to understand that validation is much deeper than just words. I also thank Pablo Gagliesi who is spreading this practice throughout South America. Pablo believed in me when I was having trouble believing in myself. I want to communicate my deep appreciation for everyone on my "mindfulness team" who supported my study and encouraged me to write and teach, especially Natali Gumiy, Maria Costa, Catalina Moiseeff, Pilar Solanas, Lorena Llobenes, Paula Rautenstrauch and Juan Pablo Restrepo. Also thanks to Paula Jose Quintero has been teaching side-by-side with me for the past few years since Carola moved to Bariloche.

I want to thank all the psychologists and other mental health professionals who attended my courses on mindfulness and compassion over the years. I am bound and committed to live my life fully consistent with what I teach thanks to the presence and the lessons that I have received from my students.

I am deeply and profoundly indebted to the generosity of friends and strangers who donated to my crowd funding campaign to get this book off my computer and into the world. Thank you Fabian Fiorito, Titti Erksell Barker, Alfredo Lhullier, Owen Lawlor, Dean Borg, Eduardo Martinez, and Chuck Bruzee. Infinite gratitude goes out to Joe Tuana and Kevin and Marcela Dennehy. Thanks to Josie Trueblood, her mom Elena, and her whole family for supporting me in the final steps of getting this out to the world. Thanks to the hundreds of supporters who 'liked' me and my work and shared my campaign on Facebook. It has been so validating!

This book would never have been finished without Andrea Rosenberg, a genius who polished the manuscript and tipped me into the world of independent publishing. Also thanks to Emilio Casares and Tatiana for their editorial insights and Samuel Warde for his proofreading.

I stand on the shoulders of my teachers with infinite gratitude and joy for each one of them, and to their teachers, and their teachers' teachers. Attending their workshops and retreats around the world and studying their writings, lectures, and podcasts, I somehow found my own words emerge from their teachings. Only a small handful of my teachers are included here and each one is a true Bodhisattva and a profoundly dedicated practitioner of mindfulness and compassion: Richard Davidson, Paul Ekman, Seizan Feijoo, Paul Gilbert, Sandra Gonzalez, Marsha Linehan, Donald Ninestine, Toni Packer, Carl Rogers, Marshall Rosenberg, B. Alan Wallace, and Shinzen Young. And a very special thank you to Valerie Porr who first taught me the power of validation and made me re-do my homework over and over until I finally got it! Thank you, Valerie.

Finally, I want to thank the thousands of parents, siblings, grandparents, sons and daughters, aunts and uncles, best friends, neighbors, and even the housekeepers who attended my classes for families and loved-ones of persons with emotional dysregulation and impulsive behaviors. You are all truly the unsung heroes. Your love, your pain, your persistence, and your courage have taught me so much. I am deeply honored to have walked this path with every one of you.

PREFACE

Learning to validate has made me a better person and a happier person. I will not kid you; the level of deep personal and interpersonal transformation that I am teaching is not fast and easy. It requires persistent practice, self-inquiry, and an openness to making mistakes and learning from them. Within this book, I map out a path that is transformational for communication and relationships, including your relationship with yourself, through practices that develop presence, acceptance, empathy, compassion, wisdom and respect.

I lived in New York City for 25 years, going to graduate school until I earned a doctorate degree, and working in urban economics, planning, and management. Life was good. I had work I loved, financial stability, and a weekend cabin in the woods. In addition, I was also studying psychology and doing weekly volunteer work teaching stressed out families what I was learning, as I was learning it.

However, I was really exhausted and burned out. I decided to take a break and move to South America to directly experience different cultures and to study Spanish—a sort of sabbatical. In Argentina I was fortunate to be offered the opportunity to co-teach classes for family members of emotionally vulnerable persons when my Spanish was barely coherent. These classes were based on Dialectical Behavior Therapy (DBT), developed by Marsha Linehan and first taught to me by Valerie Porr back in New York, who insisted that I get trained in DBT. The essence of DBT skills is training in emotional and social intelligence *par excellence*. Validation is one of the most transformative of all DBT skills.

I have been teaching these classes to family members every week for the past 12 years and it has been some of the most meaningful work in my life. Then I began teaching psychologists, counselors, and other professionals at health and human service organizations, and then finally in business environments (where emotional reactions also occur, difficult conversations take place, and conflict emerges.)

Validation is one of the most important skills that I teach in these classes. Genuine validation fosters profound changes in individuals and families. It is a powerful form of compassionate communication that can be effective at improving our ability to communicate with others, especially those relationships that are difficult for us, and helps us and others move out of emotional suffering—or at least not make the situation worse. Validation helps us at home, at work, and in all areas of our lives. There is another side effect of genuine validation—we help not only ourselves, but we can also help others to experience less emotional suffering.

It is not always easy, however. In the hundreds of workshops on validation that I have conducted over the years, invariably someone speaks up and says something like *"This is all just theoretical; it's really impossible to do in actual practice! You don't live in my house!"* Or another common response is, *"How can I validate when everyone is invalidating me all the time? (or when my boss is a ¡$%*#!)."* Or the most common reaction is, *"I need people to validate me!"*

The first answer to these types of problems is *"You are correct. I don't live in your house (or I don't work at your company) and I can't imagine how difficult it must be for you. It is true that genuine validation can be really hard to do sometimes, even impossible if we are facing difficult emotionally charged situations."* It is not easy to change our habitual ways of automatically responding, especially when we are in 'emotional mind' ourselves or facing someone who is experiencing intense emotions. It is a skill that can be developed through practice and experiential learning. This book is filled with exercises to develop skills necessary for compassionate communication, such as focus, mental clarity, and self-compassion.

The world can be an invalidating place. As we learn to recognize our own emotional state, we learn to validate ourselves. This is integrated into the practice of becoming centered and grounded. Then we are far more effective at communicating in ways that validates the experience of others, reduces their distress, and builds trust.

I have seen thousands of people make a shift in how they respond when confronted by someone who is angry, anxious, sad, or ricocheting between all three. I know from personal experience how painful it is to live with anxiety and fear and also how difficult it is to live with, work with, or love someone who is emotionally volatile. As a human being, I also know exactly what it is to experience the pain of an emotion that just doesn't go away as much as I might try to suppress, ignore, or escape it. And I know how validation can sometimes, somehow, ease the burden of suffering for everyone involved.

Each chapter of this book builds upon the previous. The first part of each chapter is both theoretical and practical. It defines and explains a fundamental aspect of validation. It offers exercises and practices to develop specific skills around each fundamental aspect. The second part of each chapter then explains how to apply both the understanding and the skills to genuine validation. Examples, stories and vignettes based on real experiences of real people bring the concepts to life. Each chapter has a summary to review each of the teaching points.

Today we are losing interpersonal connection. Even as we sit together with friends and family at our sides, we are on our cell phones, tablets, and laptops ignoring our loved ones around us. According to the World Health Organization, we are living in an era of increasing anxiety and depression.[1] Direct, honest, and compassionate communication may just be the most effective prevention. The commitment to actually do the practices is up to you, dear reader. If you decide to embark on this path, if you follow the instructions and do the practices, you will experience how genuine validation improves your level of comfort with yourself and your ability to build and maintain solid relationships with others, which is according to scientific studies, the top predictor of a long, healthy, and happy life.[2]

FOREWORD

DR. PABLO GAGLIESI

I met my friend and colleague, Corrine, many years ago in an intensive training for Dialectical Behavior Therapy (DBT). She was helping a group of families of persons with borderline personality disorder in New York and I was a psychiatrist, disoriented in the treatment of these clients in Buenos Aires. The wind rises up, with luck, sometimes, selecting people for their values. Corrine decided to try her luck with us in Buenos Aires and became part of our DBT team. It seemed that Argentine tango spoke to her and she remained. Since then we have worked together on many projects. Mindfulness was still an unknown concept in Latin America and she has poured herself into teaching and disseminating mindfulness, an activity to which she continues to be committed.

DBT is a psychotherapy that was created to help severely disturbed persons. In the implementation of standard behavioral therapy, researchers systematically found clinical problems that left clients desperate and therapists confused. There were many questions: How to help these people who suffered so much and avoid therapy being terminated? How to help them change and build a life worth living?

The history of these clients was a story of mismatches, of an imperative need for connection and, dialectically, of a deep learned fear of being hurt, justified by their own history. The question of how to sidestep this fear and connect was a challenge.

Marsha Linehan, the researcher who developed DBT, observed that some interventions used in session created this connection and sometimes change occurred. Fewer clients abandoned therapy and they felt more understood and less alone in a place where they were new intergalactic arrivals. It was a type of psychological intervention that had no name within the repertory of behavioral therapy.

This intervention is generically called *validation*. Validation consists of two movements. In the first movement I adopt a principle that says what the other person feels, thinks, or does always makes sense, even if I cannot find it. And the second involves a visible, public action in which I communicate that validation to the other person.

These may seem like easy, natural movements, but I can assure you, they are not. We do not take this approach naturally. On the contrary, we are sometimes more attentive to asymmetry than to symmetry, to the anomalous than to the regular, or to what is lacking than to what there is. We can be more attentive to defects than to virtues.

While this is neither simple nor natural, I can assure you it is a trainable skill that can become simple and natural. This book tries to move closer and cultivate this particular form of communication, central in DBT, and bring it to other intervention models, not only in psychotherapy, but outside the consulting room in daily life.

The power of validation has never ceased to amaze me. Recently I met a client who had lost the love of her life and she felt that she was going crazy from the pain. She was alternating between agony, uncontrollable crying, desolation, and despair. Everyone had been telling her that she should be strong, that nobody goes crazy from sadness, or that she just needed treatment for depression. While she was talking, I realized that she lost someone that she truly loved and she was possibly afraid of losing her mind. I just said to her directly "the same thing happened to me." She immediately took my hands, her crying quieted, and she looked me in the eyes for the first time in the session. For many years validation has permitted me to connect with the clients who suffered the most and to resolve relationship problems in my personal life that I believed had no remedy.

Corrine has worked for many years with families and friends of persons with intense emotional dysregulation and this experience has made her an excellent validation trainer. Her study and practice of mindfulness and compassion have allowed her to go beyond and reflect of validation not only in psychotherapy, but also as a valuable tool that can both change the course of a relationship and heal people.

1

INTRODUCTION

Performance obsession can lead to insensitivity, impatience, and even arrogance toward other people, especially when we perceive them to be not up to our standard.

— THUPTEN JINPA

"Too many children live with the feeling that they are not accepted for who they are, that, somehow...they don't "measure up." How many parents...focus on the ways in which their child is "too this" or "too that," or "not enough of this or that"? Parental disapproval, in the form of shaming, humiliating, or withholding...might result in obedience; but at what cost to the child, and to the adult that child becomes?"

— MYLA KABAT-ZINN

Why *genuine* validation? Genuine validation comes from the heart. It is sincere. It is not just a recipe for what to say or a "strategy." It is a deep and intimate human connection with one's self and another person. It is an expression of acceptance, empathy, compassion, and wisdom that arises from being profoundly present with another person. It's not just words.

This book is for anyone who wants to have better relationships and healthier communication. Although this book is especially useful for people who have a conflictive interpersonal relationship with one or more persons, it is clear that everyone needs to feel that their inner experience makes sense. The more effective we are at validating, the better we can manage our social interactions and even the relationship we have with ourselves. Developing validation skills increases our emotional intelligence and the level of satisfaction with our own life.

Validation is useful at home, at work, at school . . . in any interpersonal relationship where we often jump to giving advice or focus all of our attention on resolving problems, or worse, react automatically out of our own frustration or stress. Validation is a strategy which goes inward and outward. Going in, we pause and take time to recognize what is the internal experience, what is authentic, and what is true in the present moment. It may be simply noticing: *This is hard . . . I am really trying to understand . . . I am hurting inside . . .* Going out, we put ourselves in the other's shoes, trying to understand from the most empathic and compassionate perspective what the other is experiencing. This does not entail trying to make everything all better for another person. It is recognizing, accepting, or corroborating emotional pain, stress, wants and needs of another—and leaving the problem where it belongs.

When we validate the feelings of others, it helps them manage their emotional reactions more effectively and, at the same time helps us manage our own frustration or anxiety that arises when we find ourselves "hooked" by what another person says or does. Conflict and misunderstandings can be prevented or resolved with the help of validation. Difficult conversations are made easier. Relationships flourish.

It should not be surprising that mindfulness and self-compassion are an important first step in order to help others, to be kind to others, and to connect with others. If we are centered and calm, we are much more effective. This book offers information and practices for the inward practice of self-validation, including fostering self-acceptance, reinforcing personal limits, and caring for one's own internal resources, vitality, and resilience—all of which allow us to be more present and more patient for others. We are able to respond with empathy, understand deeply, open our hearts with compassion, and communicate in validating ways that are not possible if we are afraid or angry.

Genuine validation is sharing a path of mindful compassion. We develop it for ourselves from within and then we share it with others. Practicing validation can make an enormous difference in one's own life and in the lives of those whose we touch. Those in a leadership position may find it difficult. It can be a new and even more effective leadership style. It may be a shift from instructing others to allowing them to find their own solutions—and learning from their own mistakes. Moving away from control and toward validation can be an enormous challenge, but this change can represent a path toward deeper relationships and important long-term benefits for everyone.

If you have family members, friends, peers, colleagues, supervisors or subordinates at work, or anyone in your life who can be difficult for you to interact with, then genuine validation will be especially helpful. If you find it hard to cultivate and sustain interpersonal connections, this is a guidebook to effectively nurture relationships over the long term. If you beat yourself up with self-criticism and perfectionism until you are stressed and anxious, then self-validation may be the antidote.

2

—————

WHAT IS GENUINE VALIDATION?

Fundamental to our human experience is a need to feel that I am understood, others care about me, and my feelings matter.

∼

It was mid-afternoon, and Carla, 8 years old, was still in bed. The night before, lightning had hit a tree in the backyard of her house. Carla was afraid and crying throughout the next morning, so her mother had decided to go to work late. By this time however, her mother was losing the whole day, along with her patience. "Carla, you're just being silly and dramatic. The tree fell during the storm last night. Everything is OK now. The sun is out. Your friends are getting out of school now." Carla started to cry again. "Get up right now! Don't be ridiculous." At this point, Carla started crying louder and kicking from deep under the covers. She screamed, "Go away! Leave me alone! I hate you!" Frustrated, anxious, and not knowing what else to do, her mother threw up her arms and left the room.

A while later, mom's sister, Cathy, stopped by and visited her niece. She sat down next to Carla and said softly, "I heard about the storm last night. It must have been really scary when the lightning hit the tree." Carla looked out the window. "I would have been terrified if I were there. In fact, just thinking about it makes me feel a little afraid." Carla looked her aunt and Cathy continued, "Were you scared when it happened?" Carla's eyes were big and, staring at her aunt, she ever-so-slightly nodded her head. Her aunt touched the back of her hand and asked her if she could take her to outside to see the fallen tree.

Carla was silent for a couple of minutes and her aunt patiently sat beside her. Eventually Carla spoke up, "OK. I'll show you."

In contrast to her mother, her aunt validated Carla's emotions. She learned that her feelings were normal, that they made sense, and she found the strength to go out and face what she feared. Carla's mom knows that her daughter is sensitive, and she just wants Carla to be happy. But Carla didn't come with instructions that explain that she needs extra validation and patience compared to her siblings. Mom needs to skillfully validate Carla's feelings in ways that will help herself to be more patient and empathic with her daughter, which will also help Carla develop more security and self-confidence.

Validation is not something we should do just for children. We will see many examples throughout this book in all kinds of situations for all ages. Instead of triggering emotionally charged responses, we can learn to validate. We learn to not make the situation worse . . . and sometimes we may even be able to defuse an emotional explosion or prevent an emotional implosion. Validation may enable us to help a loved one, friend or co-worker bear the fury, fear, shame, or hopelessness they are already experiencing. It can help us to get through our own difficult moments. Couples who genuinely validate each other's feelings and behaviors are probably more likely to be happier with their relationship. Families who learn to validate are forever transformed. In the workplace, validation eases stress, improves communication, and makes for better working environments.

Clark and Janet were on the faculty at a university. One day, Janet was clearly tense and frustrated. A senior colleague who was working with her on a research project was dragging his feet on following up. Clark heard the anger in her voice, listened carefully and patiently to what she was saying, and then spoke up, "Janet, that must feel so unfair. I would be totally frustrated if I were in your shoes. And I know you are under a lot of pressure to publish." Janet let out a dramatic exhale and her whole body visibly relaxed. She rolled her eyes and responded, "Yeah, but I get it, I get it. I am the junior one in the department right now and I have to do all the work."

Clark could have tried to explain to Janet how the system works, and in fact, he almost did! The moment that Clark decided not to give advice—but instead to listen deeply—that moment changed the course of their interaction. Clark understood where Janet was coming from and validated her perspective with words, which created the space for Janet to see her situation from a broader perspective.

There is a magic moment when we decide to not say or do anything. That gives us a moment to breathe, to calm our own anxiety to speak, to connect more deeply with the other, and to put ourselves in the other person's shoes. As a result of Clark's decision not to speak, but to listen and validate, Janet got out of her emotional state of mind and she connected with her own inner wisdom about her situation - a much more valuable experience. Just as important, Clark experienced a happy surprise and a level of satisfaction over his interaction with Janet. He walked away feeling better about himself, just like Janet.

Genuine validation is a useful and effective way to strengthen all of our interpersonal relationships. It opens communication, builds trust, and maintains healthy relationships. It helps us deepen our compassion for others and ourselves and reduces conflict in our relationships with others. So what, exactly, is genuine validation?

If something is *valid*, according to *Webster's Dictionary*, it is *well grounded or justifiable, being at once relevant and meaningful.* Validation does not create relevance and meaning. It affirms that which is already well grounded in relevance and meaning. *Valid* is also defined in the same dictionary as *appropriate for the end in view, effective.* Thus, validating something confirms that it is effective or appropriate in terms of goals and objectives.

Validation affirms that a subjective human experience is important, authentic, understandable, or that it makes sense. This is more than just finding the right words to assert validity—although that is an important aspect that we will cover. We can validate with words, with tone of voice, with facial expressions, with posture and movement, and with deeds. We can even validate with thoughts, with attitudes, and with silence. **Genuine** *validation is heartfelt and sincere.*

In order to verify validity—that is, to validate—we have to begin by learning to observe in a new way. One has to learn to be a scientist, observing and accepting experience with curiosity and without prejudging or interpreting the experience. Genuine validation requires presence. We may cultivate new ways of being present and accepting while we practice new ways of using language in our thinking and speaking. We learn to communicate that others are important to us and that we accept them for who they are. When we communicate through words or through silent expressions that we care about how they feel, we validate their feelings are normal, not to mention relevant and meaningful. Telling a loved one that he or she shouldn't feel embarrassed in a given situation is like insisting that the rain should not fall. We validate to help others effectively reduce their suffering and to reduce our own suffering, and this requires a new flexibility and personal discipline. We have to unlearn our automatic reactions.

Keith was the director of a social services agency with a lot of responsibility for individuals and families with complex problems and few resources. He had hired Mark, a young social worker whom he thought would be very promising, but turned out to be very nervous about his job responsibilities. Keith really needed staff and he could not afford to let Mark go just because he was anxious.

At work Mark asked lots of questions about how to handle his cases, speaking very quickly and insisting that he needed solutions urgently, but then he interrupted his advisors or brushed off their suggestions as unworkable! In these moments Mark would sometimes stutter or stumble over his words or repeat himself several times. It seemed as if he was insecure about making decisions and also embarrassed and anxious about asking for advice.

Keith found himself irritated when he was in a meeting with Mark. However, Keith was getting some coaching on validation and he decided to try to see if he could improve his uncomfortable relationship and difficult communication with Mark.

Keith tried to be a patient listener and reflect back what he understood. "Mark, that's a good question and I can see that you are really worried about getting this right." Keith tried ask more questions of Mark instead of giving advice—even when Mark wanted help. "What solutions have you been considering?" He tried to describe what he thought Mark was feeling. "I know the system here can be very frustrating" or "I can tell you are very worried about this case and you want to help." Keith rarely had as much time as Mark seemed to need, so he ended conversations by offering to talk later (and keeping his word). "That is an interesting question, and I know it's important to you. Maybe you could give some more thought as to possible solutions. I have about 10 minutes at the end of the day and I would be happy to help you think through the pros and cons of your alternatives."

Within a few months, Keith's patience and validation began to pay off. His relationship with Mark dramatically improved and it even seemed that Mark's relationships with others were also smoother. He experienced Mark to be more calm and confident, able to solve many of his problems effectively. Communications were more concise. Keith gained a long-term and committed employee and most importantly for Keith, he became a better supervisor.

Validation is acceptance. We accept another as he or she is in the present moment. This does not mean that we approve of everything that another does. Others do many things that annoy us. In spite of that, we can also recognize their emotions as authentic to their experience and their desires as legitimate. We can corroborate the importance and relevance of their feelings. We are not giving advice; we are not asking the other to change; we are not stubbornly resisting them in any way. We are accepting, we are empathic, and we are open to understanding and confirming the importance of their experience.

Validation is an act of compassion. As we will see in future chapters, compassion and caring are fundamental self-protection systems. Compassionate communication is calming. Feeling loved gives us a greater sense of safeness. It soothes our fears. From birth we are programmed to feel calm when we hear kind words, a soothing voice, or a tender touch. A common response to validation is a sense of safeness that allows an opening for more dialogue and greater understanding.

Why can't we just learn a few magic validating words right away? Well, we need to understand exactly what it means to be present and fully conscious of the other person and of our own internal experience. Then, our communication must be consistent and congruent to communicate the acceptance and compassion that we genuinely feel. Our words, tone of voice, gestures, facial expression, and body language all say together: *You matter to me, your feelings are important to me, I care about you, and I really want to understand your experience as best as I can.* Such validation is something that we must learn to authentically think and feel. Just saying the right words will most likely fail because our facial expression and tone of voice come from the heart and communicate a lot more information than just words.

If we are trying to communicate validation when we are emotionally activated, it may backfire. It takes a calm and open heart to be compassionate and tolerant of others rather than criticizing and condemning people. It's easy to react automatically to an angry coworker or family member, or to be cynical and distrustful of their "overreactions." As human beings, we are programmed to defend ourselves when we are being attacked, not to validate the anger that our attacker is experiencing. We can all fall into that trap, even after years of practicing validation.

Sara worked hard to make ends meet as an administrative assistant for a large corporation. She had been working in her current job for almost a year, but she felt that others were disrespectful and even contemptuous toward her. It was a competitive environment that made her feel insecure and defensive. Often she was convinced that others wanted her to quit her job.

After learning the basics of validating, she felt she was at least able to go in and just be present and listen fully, even if she did not say much of anything. She did just that as best she could, but some days she ended up feeling more resentful than ever. That's when she realized that she needed to feel validated and that her workplace was an environment where there was not much going around.

Sara learned and practiced lots of mindfulness, self-compassion, and self-validation. Eventually she was more grounded and centered and she could step back and see the big picture, not taking everything so personally. With more mental space and clarity she could then get closer to others, put herself in their shoes and understand when they were feeling pressured and anxious to meet their goals. She felt less dependent on the need for validation by others, and yet somehow she felt she was more accepted. She was gaining more and more respect from her colleagues by listening, asking questions, and validating their needs and feelings. She ignored the blame game and took responsibility for just doing the best that she could, mindfully validating her own feelings and caring for herself when the going got rough.

Sara needed to recognize and stabilize her own fear and insecurity with lots of emotional self-validation in order to be consistent and effective at recognizing and accompanying someone else's emotional state. This was not easy for Sara and to be honest it took her a year of hard work and practice with coaching to get it right. We all need to see our own habitual or conditioned responses arise and see them for exactly what they are—conditioned responses, automatic behaviors, and habitual ways of acting out our fear, sadness, or righteous anger and defensive posturing. This book offers information and recommendations that are useful in protecting ourselves from the stress and reactions of facing yet another crisis of a loved one, a colleague, or even a boss. It includes inner-directed practices of self-compassion and, of course, self-validation, prerequisites for effectively responding to others with genuine validation.

Cultivating validation is a process. We have to develop mindfulness and acceptance, apply empathy and compassion, learn and practice new skills, and let go of old ways of thinking and doing. We have to rise above our own anger, fear, shame, and guilt. We cannot worry about feeling foolish or controlled by others. When we are truly present, fully compassionate, and genuinely validating, we strive to treat others not in ways that are worthy of them but in ways that are worthy of *ourselves* and aligned with our own values. We do not treat others "meanly" when they are mean to us because *we are not mean*.

Thus, the practice of genuine validation not only changes our relationships with our loved ones but also our relationships with ourselves. Validating ourselves is key to having a sense of inner security and emotional stability. We are more accepting of ourselves just as we are in the present and able to let go of our internal judgments and self-criticisms. We practice self-compassion and self-care by validating ourselves and our negative feelings, desires, and frustrations as well as our own strengths and successes. We all need to be validated and nurtured, and there is only one person always present and available for the job—oneself.

WHAT, EXACTLY, DO WE VALIDATE?

We cannot create validity; we can only confirm that which is already legitimate. We corroborate that which is real, observable, logical, based on sound principles . . . or simply makes sense. We may compare something to an authority, to general knowledge, or to our own private experience to verify whether it is understandable and reasonable. So what exactly do we validate?

Emotions. Our emotions and feelings are <u>always</u> valid. Emotions are the product of evolutionary development; they are biological responses that improve our rate of survival. There are neither "correct" emotions nor "incorrect" emotions. Friends, family, society, and religions may judge and label emotions as "good" or "bad," but if we consider that these are biological responses to internal or external events in combination with mental interpretations and thoughts about these events, then we can see that the emotion is neither good nor bad. It just is. Thus, all emotional responses, including feelings of anger, envy, or even feeling grouchy are indeed valid. The behavior that results from an emotion may or may not be valid, but the emotion itself is certainly an essential and valid part of our experience as human beings. When we validate emotions, we confirm and corroborate that the emotion is normal, natural, caused, and perhaps painful if that is the case.

Needs, wants, and desires. Human needs and desires are universal. For example, we all need and want autonomy and choice over our own lives, connection and interdependence with others, recreation/play, and physical nurturing. We want to feel good about ourselves. We don't want to suffer. All of these needs and desires are valid. While it may not be valid or even possible to satisfy our endless desires or meet all of our needs all the time, we can recognize and validate needs and desires as legitimate. We want what we want. Even if we can't have it, we can feel the desire itself or we can experience a need as a need.

Opinions and beliefs. Each person has the right to their opinion—likes and dislikes, whether something is attractive or unattractive, the best way to solve a personal problem . . . Each person has the right to their own spiritual, religious, political, and social beliefs, moral codes, and beliefs. And no one has the right to force their opinions and beliefs on others. We can validate opinions and beliefs simply for what they are in the present moment. Opinions are valid as <u>opinions</u>, not as truth!

Behavior. While we may consider all emotions, all needs and desires, and all opinions to be valid, authentic, and/or based on sound principles, not all behavior is valid. For example when we act impulsively our behavior may not be based on valid reason or good judgment. We can validate the feeling of anger (the emotion makes sense given the circumstances), but we would not generally validate behavior such as throwing things, threatening others, physically attacking others, or even yelling insults and profanity (the behavior is not reasonable nor effective.) Of course, this is not universal; it is dependent on the situation. If someone were really threatening to kill a loved one, for example, physically attacking that person to prevent such an action would be valid behavior. Behavior that is effective, responsible, respectful, and considerate of others is valid behavior.

(A note about "behavior": in this context "behavior" is commonly understood as observable behavior, such as gestures, verbal expressions, and actions.)

Thoughts or reasoning. Not all thoughts and reasoning are valid. Without getting into the analysis of formal logic, valid reasoning has true premises, logical validity, and true conclusions. In everyday usage, this means that we need to be conscious of our interpretations and we need to separate observations from interpretations. For example, the statement "She always does things to me to make me mad" expresses an interpretation that the other intentionally wants me to feel angry. This may or may not be valid (true)—we have no evidence that allows us to know whether that was her intention or not. On the other hand, "I felt angry after she did that" is a valid description of events if the speaker did, indeed, feel angry after she did that.

So, just to be really clear here, any human experience can be validated, although we want to avoid validating the invalid! It would not be very effective to corroborate someone's thoughts, opinions, or predictions as facts, for example, "Yes it is really true that your boss is always unfair to you and he is even-handed with everyone else" or "We have to accept that this situation is never going to change" or "You are correct, you have the worse mother in the world." Distorted thoughts, generalizations, and blaming are types of thinking that are not valid. We do not want to validate opinions as if they were facts nor ineffective and harmful behavior as if it was worth repeating. Sometimes we really have to look hard to find that which is valid and temporarily ignore the rest.

Genuine validation is sometimes confused with saying yes, agreeing, approving, giving in, or doing whatever others ask. It is sometimes confused with giving compliments, praise or flattery. It is none of these things. As we will see later in more detail, we can validate someone's experience AND say no.

TEST YOUR UNDERSTANDING

These concepts are fundamental. Try to respond and then click on the number after each for the answer or go to the endnotes.

1. What is always valid and why? [1]

2. What is sometimes valid and sometimes invalid?[2]

. . .

It is useful to learn a little more about what is invalidation in order to better understand validation. A response is experienced as invalidating when one communicates one's feelings and receives a response that is erratic, incoherent, inappropriate, or extreme. These may include responses that ignore, judge, or reject one's internal experience. ("You're being overly dramatic." "It's not that bad." or "Stop being a cry baby.")

It can also be invalidating when someone's expectations are dashed or when good intentions and effort is minimized or ignored. ("You made cheesecake? Do you know how fattening that is? I can't eat that." or "Were we proud of you for your high grades and sports achievements? No, we expected it from you.") Sometimes these types of invalidating responses may be offered with the intention of helping another person to feel better, work harder, or be stronger, but they unwittingly trigger an even stronger negative reaction.

Invalidating responses can be impulsive reactions that any of us might do if we get suddenly get hooked into an emotional and impulsive reaction. Regardless of the intention, such responses are invalidating and can be hurtful to anyone. It may be easy to underestimate the suffering of someone who is emotionally sensitive, vulnerable or volatile. Many people may trivialize, criticize, or even attempt to punish such emotional responses instead of validating them.

Beth, a senior in high school, knew all along that her boyfriend Shaun was going to return to his home in New Zealand at the end of his six-month visit. She had never pretended that the relationship could last longer than six months, and she believed that she was mentally prepared for his leaving. Two weeks after he left, she found herself having trouble getting out of bed in the morning, crying during the day, and missing classes. She was not even going out with her friends. Her mother, who was getting worried and anxious over Beth's behavior, tried to help by saying, "Beth, you knew all along he was only here temporarily. You need to stop moping around and snap out of it. You can't get all depressed now that he is gone. You'll feel better if you just forget about him."

Albeit with good intentions, Mom denied her daughter's experience and made Beth feel a lot worse. Her invalidating comments arose from anxiety and worry—not from a place of kindness and compassion. If Beth could "snap out of it" and forget about Shaun, she would. But she can't, and her mother's comments made her feel ashamed and angry on top of feeling sad and missing Shaun.

Invalidating responses do not corroborate the desires, opinions, behaviors, or ideas that we experience. An invalidating environment rejects our basic feelings on a regular basis. It communicates again and again that our responses are inappropriate or incorrect. Invalidating responses ignore the importance of our experience instead of trying to understand or at least recognize the authenticity within the message. Invalidating responses do not teach us to label our internal experiences nor to modulate our emotions. They do not teach us to tolerate distress nor to focus on realistic goals, both of which are necessary for effective problem solving. Without sufficient validation at an early age, one may be left with few skills in these areas, which may exacerbate emotional vulnerability. Genuine validation, on the other hand, may effectively reduce such vulnerability and teach acceptance and compassion.

Invalidation is all around us. It can be subtle or profound. If others do not recognize and respect us as deserving the same respect as themselves or others, if they deny or dismiss our feelings as unimportant or incorrect, if they don't allow us the right to have our own opinions or beliefs, it may be an invalidating experience. The world can be an invalidating place. On the other hand, perhaps surviving in an invalidating environment validates that we are in fact, strong, competent, and not so fragile. Therein lies the wisdom inherent in genuine validation, which we will see more of later in the book.

Invalidation from the people who are closest to us is the invalidation that hurts the most. We need to have emotional steadiness and a sense of internal stability or equanimity to face an invalidating environment, and these qualities can be cultivated by the validation of those who are closest. Emotionally sensitive or temperamental persons may be particularly vulnerable to invalidation and benefit enormously from emotional validation in their daily lives.

How might Beth's mother have validated her daughter's feelings? She might have sat down and just breathed for a minute. Or ask herself what was she needing in that moment or inquired into her own feelings. Then, a bit more centered and grounded, aware of her desire to help her daughter feel better, she would be more likely to ask Beth if she wanted to talk and then listen fully without interrupting. She might ask a few additional questions. She might reflect that it is often painful when a relationship ends and communicate how it makes sense that Beth is missing Shaun and feeling lonely—even if she knew he was going to move.

Among our family, friends, or colleagues, we all probably know someone who seems to generate a lot of conflict or who might be over reactive, temperamental, or generally grouchy—in other words, someone who is emotionally volatile. Or perhaps we know someone withdrawn, timid, sad, or fearful, someone who avoids social interactions or is afraid of some types of situations. Validation will be surprisingly effective at helping us manage our relationship and our communication with both of these types of people. If one of these types describes the person looking at you when you look in the mirror, then you should become an expert on self-validation!

1. Genuine validation opens communication, builds trust, and maintains healthy relationships.

- Genuine validation is something that we must learn to authentically think and feel—not just say.
- Genuine validation changes not only our relationships with our loved ones but also our relationships with ourselves.
- We have to practice self-compassion and self-care by validating ourselves and our negative feelings, desires, and frustrations as well as our own strengths and successes.

2. What, exactly, do we validate?

- Emotions: Our emotions and feelings are always valid.
- Needs, wants, and desires: Human needs and desires are universal. For example, we all need and want autonomy, interdependence, play, and physical nurturing.
- Valid behavior: While we do consider all emotions to be valid, not all behaviors are. To be valid, behavior must be respectful and/or effective.
- Valid thoughts or reasoning: Valid reasoning begins with true premises or descriptive observations. Interpretations are clearly identified as such and not presumed to be facts. Conclusions, thus, are hypotheses based on interpretations. A rigid attitude based on an interpretation that is presented and repeated as if it were a fact is an example of distorted and invalid thinking.

3. NEVER validate that which is NOT VALID.

- Distorted thinking: "Yes, your co-workers are always so unfair to you."
- Generalizations as if they were concrete facts: "You are right. Nobody ever cleans anything around here."
- Excessive blaming: "Yes, I know, he always screws up."
- Opinions, judgments, or evaluations as if they were facts: "It is true that they are perfect and we don't measure up to them."

- Ineffective or harmful behavior: "Yeah, just kick the soda machine if it doesn't work." or "I know how much better you would feel if you went shopping so take my credit card and buy yourself some new clothes."

4. Invalidation

- An invalidating response occurs when we communicate our thoughts and feelings and receive a response that is erratic, incoherent, inappropriate, incongruent, or extreme.
- Invalidating responses include responses that ignore, ridicule, minimize, judge, or reject one's experience.
- The world can be an invalidating place.

Validation is most important from the people who are closest. It helps build resilience and emotional stability to comfortably make one's way in an invalidating world!

3

UNDERSTANDING EMOTIONS

Our emotions have energy and wisdom and they can guide our values, goals, thoughts, and actions. Unfortunately our emotions can also lead us awry, which they do far too often.

ric's parents were internationally renowned scholars; they were brilliant and they were often invited to speak and to teach in many different countries. They had been working abroad extensively since Eric was an adolescent, leaving him alone in the house (a block away from his grandparents). During college his parents arranged for him to live in a religious center and upon graduation he worked for several years as a financial analyst.

Eric felt his mother was an emotional mess and his father was impenetrable. He had learned that indifference was his safest response. His mother sometimes ended up crying and begging him to tell her what she could do for him. This only pushed him away further and made him even colder toward her. She was swimming in her own emotional sadness and remorse, unable to be open to or curious about her own feelings, much less what was going on with her son. Meanwhile, his father was caught in an angry and futile struggle with Eric, telling his mother how Eric was to blame for the poor relationship between father and son.

Eric's parents could not see through their own emotional states and missed countless opportunities to reconnect with their son. Eric secretly applied to graduate school abroad and told his parents about his plans to move only three weeks before he was scheduled to start classes.

Everyone in the family was intellectually brilliant but with low emotional intelligence. Understanding our emotions can go a long way toward helping us respond effectively. Emotional intelligence is the ability to recognize and effectively manage one's own emotions as well as the emotions of others. Genuine validation invites us to invest the time and practice to cultivate this skill.

Few people are able to modulate their emotions through "will control." It is rarely effective to tell a guy to "just calm down" when he is emotionally activated. He would if he could, but he is in emotional mind and he can't. On the other hand, a woman who is disconnected from her emotions, who is in denial of an emotional experience is not going to be convinced that she is feeling something, when she is not.

Emotional mind

Marsha Linehan describes an emotionally charged state of thinking as "emotional mind."[1] To put it another way, the emotion is directing the experience. The rational part of the mind is pretty much working in service to the emotion. We might describe this as "mental hijacking." Reasoning may be clear and logical . . . and also distorted. When we are sad, we remember just the things that disappointed us. When we are angry, we remember all the injustices that we experienced. In emotional mind, it is probably very difficult, if not nearly impossible, to think about the short- and long-term consequences of our actions.

Usually we want to escape such this emotionally-charged state of mind as quickly as possible. We might find ourselves ruminating over our problems or generating negative thoughts (which sometimes distracts attention from the sensations and urges of the uncomfortable negative emotion), though such thinking ultimately sustains the emotion. Negative thoughts and negative feelings can spiral around each other, making the situation much worse, even when that kind of brooding is the opposite of what such a person intends to do. Of course we can also experience low-intensity, fleeting emotions. Being sensitive, accepting, and aware of both intense and subtle emotional responses is at the heart of emotional balance and emotional regulation.

Practice 1. Observe your emotion

Take a little time to observe your mental state in the moment. Practice this daily when you are in a low-intensity emotional mind. (The more we practice recognizing a small wave of emotion, the more skills we will have at stepping back from a bigger wave or allowing an emotional tsunami to wash over us without making the situation worse.)

Notice your breath and feel the rise and fall of the lower abdomen. Count five to ten exhales as you feel the movements in the abdomen.

Sitting still and in silence, observe whatever physical sensations enter into your awareness for a minute or two.

Look for any emotion(s) that you are feeling in the present moment. It may be helpful to scan for feelings in your stomach and chest as you look for emotions.

Check to see if there are any urges or impulses to move or do something. Observe the urge without acting.

Count another five to ten exhales and continue to feel sensations that arise in your body. Notice how the feelings change from inhale to exhale and from one breath to another, and how your attention jumps around (or is called) from place to place.

PROFILING EMOTIONAL REACTIONS

Once triggered, the chemical released by my brain surges through my body and I have a physiological experience. Within 90 seconds from the initial trigger, the chemical component of my anger has completely dissipated from my blood and my automatic response is over. If, however, I remain angry after those 90 seconds have passed, then it is because I have chosen to let that circuit continue to run.

— DR. JILL BOLTE TAYLOR

We each have a unique emotional profile in a given situation.[2] An emotional profile has three main characteristics. The first characteristic of an emotional profile is the *threshold* at which an emotional response is triggered. Some people have a low threshold for anger and others have a high threshold, for example. The threshold may also interact with the mood of a person or other vulnerability factors. For example, if someone is in an irritable mood, this will probably result in a lower threshold for triggering an angry emotional response. A person who is overtired because of lack of sleep may be more vulnerable to feeling sadness and may cry more easily.

The second characteristic of the emotional profile is the *intensity* of the emotion. An emotion can be mild and hardly noticeable or it can be extreme and powerful. Some people habitually over-control their emotional responses. They may minimize their internal feelings or totally ignore them by distracting their attention from their feelings to their thoughts or actions. For example, one may identify stiffness in the neck and shoulders or loss of appetite, but not be aware of the frustration that is the cause of these sensations. Other people may experience an intense emotional reaction and have little ability to regulate their feelings, fully acting out all of the urges and impulses that an emotion unleashes. For example, upon feeling frustrated a person may act out anger with insults, swearing, threats, and other loud verbal attacks.

The third characteristic is the _duration_ of the emotional response. Sometimes the emotion goes away immediately, and other times it seems to stick around for hours before returning to baseline. One wave of a single emotional response will last 90 seconds from the full release of electrical charges, neurochemicals, and hormones until a return to homeostasis. The emotional response lasts longer when thoughts, speech, or actions continue to evoke the emotion.

Some people tend to be emotionally sensitive and temperamental. An emotionally sensitive person generally has a low threshold at which emotions are provoked and a high intensity of emotional response. The emotions tend to linger, often including a pattern of thinking or ruminating that can sustain an emotion for as long as the ruminating continues. An emotionally volatile or temperamental person experiences _under-control_ and may react with high emotional drama and impulsive behaviors. An emotionally distant or stoic person exhibits a pattern of _over-control_ and may ignore the presence of an emotion. Both types may be emotionally sensitive to what others say and do. These represent two different ways to cope with unpleasant emotions that have been learned and reinforced over time. (There are also genetic factors that influence these patterns of emotional responses.)

The challenge of emotional intelligence is to wholeheartedly experience the vulnerability and the distress of the emotion, even inquiring into the information and motivation of the physiological response, without acting out every impulse that arises. It is not suppressing or avoiding the emotion; it is feeling the wave and allowing it to arise and pass while appropriately communicating to be as effective as possible in the situation.

If one is furious with someone, "acting out the impulse" might mean loudly insisting or yelling. Allowing the emotional wave to arise and pass might be for example, leaving the situation to get some fresh air and resuming the conversation hours later. If one is embarrassed, the impulse might be to avoid or hide. Feeling the shame wholeheartedly, with a sense of humor even, might connect us to our shared humanity. If one is worried about a problem with no solution, the impulse is to ruminate. What would it be to fully experience the feelings of anxiety and not the worry thoughts (and perhaps to relax and let go of tension, allowing the wave to pass)? Emotional intelligence is the flexibility to experience the emotion without grasping or rejecting, to inquire into the experience, and to respond effectively. In fact, the science shows that just naming the emotion that is experienced reduces the intensity of brain activation and we might feel a little reduction in our discomfort.

Effectively balancing one's own internal emotional responses and being supportive to help others regulate their emotions is a lifelong challenge for most of us. Our emotions give us information about ourselves and the world, and we need to tune in to this information. Our emotions give us energy and creativity and we need to take advantage of them appropriately. Connecting with the wisdom of an emotion without impulsively or immaturely acting out the emotion is an elusive and priceless ingredient in personal happiness, well-being, and success.

We cannot change our emotional reactions without regular practice aimed at modulating habits that have been conditioned and reinforced over many years. Immediate changes to habitual patterns of emotional reactions are not likely. Focusing on a single response that occurred at a specific moment and triggered by a specific event can reveal a lot of information about how to change patterns of behavior. This also begins to cultivate greater emotional intelligence.

Intense and frequent emotional reactions are most likely to occur in interpersonal situations, especially with coworkers, family members, and loved ones—the very people we interact with every day and especially those we love. These are the people who tend to provoke our emotions most frequently. It is less likely, but of course can also occur, among strangers or people for whom we don't feel strong emotional bond.

Like radar, our brains are constantly scanning the environment for the possibility of threats. If a threat or danger is detected, our entire nervous system sends electrical-chemical signals that alert us to the threat and we feel fear or anger. If safety and security are registered, we feel relaxed, comfortable, and probably even loved.

Every emotional response has a profile. The emotional profiles of two different persons in the same situation might vary by baseline, intensity, and duration. In the next diagram, the larger curve illustrates an emotional reaction of a person with greater intensity and a longer time period as compared to the smaller curve. A person who is emotionally sensitive may frequently experience emotional responses that follow the pattern of the bigger curve.

Some people may experience one or two specific emotions intensely and for a prolonged period (for example, difficulty in regulating anger, sadness or fear), and others may experience any and all emotions intensely.

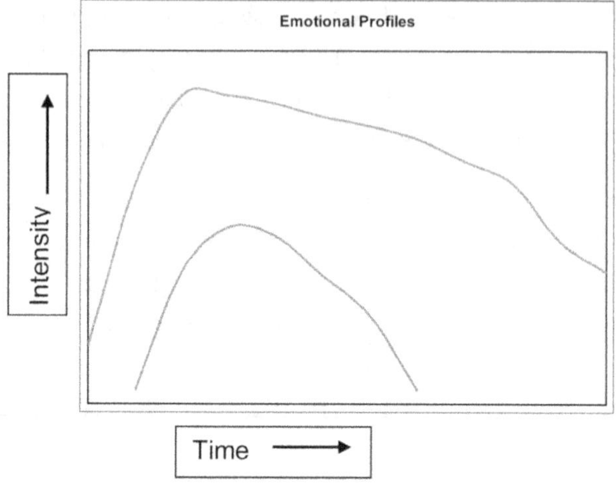

Profiles of emotional responses.

Let's imagine a vary logical woman whose emotional response to a situation is represented by the smaller, lower curve, whereas her husband's stronger emotional response is represented by the larger, higher curve. It would <u>not</u> be helpful for her to think that her husband should be less dramatic. It would be invalidating to tell him that he is "just exaggerating." It would also be invalidating for him to tell her that she "is cold or without feeling." Every emotional reaction is valid and unique.

Primary and secondary emotions

When we are in an emotional state of mind, our thinking and our behavior can lead us down an unpleasant path. Emotions can have powerful energy that pushes us into engaging in impulsive behaviors and damaging actions such as yelling and insulting, overeating, consuming alcohol or drugs, or isolating oneself at home in bed. These impulsive behaviors can often evoke other emotions, such as guilt, shame or anger.

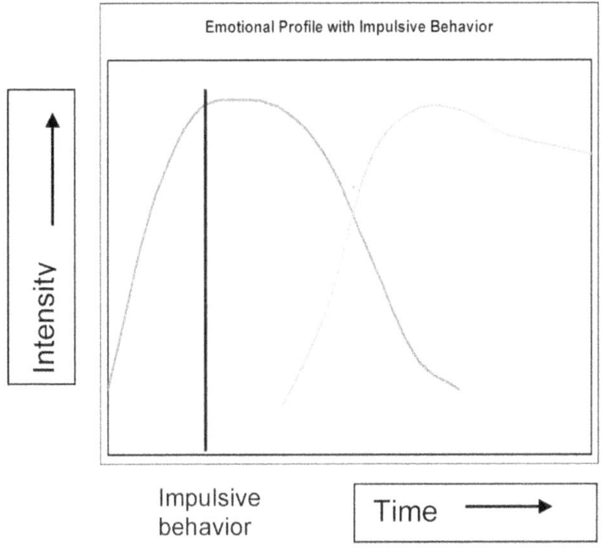

Profile of primary emotion with impulsive behavior,
leading to a secondary emotion.

In a highly charged emotional state, a person may engage in an impulsive behavior that has the effect of reducing the emotional discomfort very rapidly but sets off2`11Ish another emotion. As a result of the impulsive behavior, the first emotion is defused, but often a second emotional response arises as a result of the first emotion. Sometimes these sequences of emotions can become repetitive patterns that result in acute emotional discomfort, chronic stress or anxiety, sleep problems, interpersonal conflict or avoidance, or a roller coaster of pain and confusion until the emotions and behaviors seem completely unmanageable. Below are a couple of concrete examples—see if any of these resonate:

Primary emotion ➟ **Behavior based on primary emotion** ➟ **Secondary emotion**

Anger ➟ **Yelling** ➟ Guilt

You become angry and speak harshly or even yell at another person.

The anger is relieved, but then an uncomfortable wave of guilt or shame arises because you yelled at someone.

Shame ➠ **Hide** ➠ Sadness. You are embarrassed in front of others so you quickly slip away from the situation, which reduces the sensation of embarrassment, but then a feeling of sad loneliness arises.

Anxiety ➠ **Eat** ➠ Anger

You are feeling anxious and worried and cannot seem to sit still. Impulsively you find something to eat, and you wolf down half the container of ice cream or a bag of potato chips. Shortly thereafter, you are no longer anxious, but instead angry at yourself for overeating.

In these examples, one emotion provoked an impulsive behavior and this action provoked another emotion. There can also be a direct interaction between emotions without any intervening behavior, and this kind of interaction is common but often overlooked. In this case a primary emotion is provoked and immediately a secondary emotion arises as a result of experiencing the primary one. For example, when some people feel fear, anger over the feeling of being afraid may arise automatically. On the other hand, some people may feel angry, and then immediately feel fear of their own anger.

Some of us develop patterns of experiencing secondary emotions. For example, a person who is often irritated, frustrated, and angry may not allow himself to feel other emotions. Anger becomes practically the only fully expressed emotion, perhaps because it can feel empowering. Other emotions such as sadness, shame, or fear may feel like weaknesses. Escaping an emotion and connecting with a secondary emotion becomes a habit. Over time such a habit can result in overlooking the facts of a situation, misinterpreting and misunderstanding the situation, and losing touch with reality—effectively dissociating from the primary emotion and its causes.

Some say that anger is always a secondary emotion. Someone may respond with anger that is secondary to the sadness of an important loss. Or rage is the consequence of (or a strategy for avoiding) the feeling of shame that was evoke by a humiliating situation. Irritation can be the result of anxiety over a potential threat. Intense anger can effectively divert one from feeling fear when there is a real or imagined danger. It may seem like some people respond to almost everything with anger, and in these cases it is especially important to look for the underlying primary emotion.

Sadness is also a common secondary emotion. Feelings of hopelessness, helplessness, emptiness, loneliness, and so on may all be products of feeling another emotion. Feeling nervous or anxious about something, one might think "I can't do anything right," which converts the anxiety to sadness. Someone may have been raised in a family where they were not allowed to express anger or other emotions. The primary emotion may be swept away by feeling sad and powerless. Sadness may not only be more acceptable, it may even provoke gestures of concern from other family members, thus reinforcing the expression of sadness instead of the primary emotion.

It is not always easy to recognize the primary emotion. It may help to consider the emotional trigger and question whether the triggering factor and the resulting emotion make sense, or whether there might be another step that we missed. Once the primary emotion is identified and experienced, the secondary emotion instantly dissolves.

Sarah, the mother of a 25-year-old son, described her emotional response when her husband told her that she should start discussing with their son the need to move out and into his own apartment. She felt a surge of hot anger. A few minutes later they got on an elevator and she was still steaming. To distract herself, she began a conversation with the two young women there. They were the same age as her son and they were in medical school.

Sarah and her husband walked out of the elevator and went to their car, where Sarah began to cry. She realized that she had not been angered by her husband's comment; she was deeply saddened. Their son had barely finished high school and had spent the previous seven years on psychiatric medication, depressed, sometimes violent, and addicted to computer games. It was a stark contrast between these cheerful young medical students and her son. As impatient as her husband was, the reality was that her son was still in no condition to move out and live alone, and she was deeply *sad* about her son's condition.

Once a person connects with the primary emotion, the secondary emotion is no longer the problem. Sarah's anger dissolved into sadness. If our goal is to validate emotions, we have to learn to experience the primary emotion and to recognize it in others. A word of warning: It may be obvious from an outside perspective that someone is "really" sad or afraid and not angry. But a person in angry mind may not be open or willing to connect with a primary emotion, and it would be invalidating to tell them to do so.

Why do we have emotions, especially when they seem to make life painful? Why can't we live without fear? Why is life so complicated?

We are hardwired at birth to experience emotions. They provide us with information about our environment and energy to respond in the moment as needed. Our emotions also communicate something to others through our facial expressions, tone of voice, gestures, actions, and words. Emotions served the human population well for hundreds of thousands of years of living in primitive conditions where life spans were much shorter and life-threatening conditions were more common. As Daniel Goleman points out, however, "in the ancient past a hair-trigger anger may have offered a crucial edge for survival, [but] the availability of automatic weaponry to thirteen-year-olds has made it too often a disastrous reaction."[3]

In today's society, our senses are over stimulated and the speed of communication and travel is exponentially more intense than it was for our ancestors. Our emotions are invalidated and our attention is bombarded with all kinds of thoughts and sensory experiences. Most of us do not hunt, fish, farm, prepare food, nor do craftwork by hand every day. Such activities require prolonged attention and patience. They may have also contributed to balancing emotional responses even when living conditions presented more threats to life and health. These kinds of activities foster resilience—a faster return to a baseline of calmness after the threat has passed.

The next few sections describe a few basic emotions including the types of things that are is most likely to trigger the emotion and the physiological response that we feel in our bodies. Seven of these emotions have universal facial expressions (according to Paul Ekman in his groundbreaking research showing that aboriginal people with no contact with the modern world exhibited the same facial expressions for these seven emotions as persons living in modern societies).[4] Since emotions are biological and innate, nobody has to learn how to "put on an angry face," consciously tensing the face in a way to get others to feel fear or otherwise control them when angry. Universal facial expressions are unconscious, preverbal expressions of feeling, and even babies will communicate their emotions with their faces.

Emotions energize and motivate us in ways that are necessary for our survival. For example, imagine that it is late in the evening. You are at home, tired and hungry. Then you hear the sound of an unknown person moving around in your home. You might instantly go into a state of high alert and all awareness of being tired or hungry instantly disappears. Your reaction is useful in this case. On the other hand, imagine feeling fear every time you are alone in your house. The fear may make rational sense based on past history, but it is not helpful to experience fear when there is no real threat or imminent danger. First, it is useful to understand the function of each emotion to help us identify what we are feeling, or what others might be feeling. We can keep in mind that sometimes the emotions are "justified" (feeling fear when there is a thief in the house) and sometimes they are "not justified" (feeling fear when one is alone in the house.) In other words fear when one is alone in the house is understandable, but it is not justified because there is no real threat to one's health or one's life.

ANGER (FRUSTRATION, IRRITATION, FURY)

Anger may arise when we are attacked, hurt or threatened or if we have a goal that is blocked. There is an increase in blood flow to our arms and hands, making it easier to fight with hands or strike with an object to defend ourselves. There is an increase in heart rate and a rush of hormones such as adrenaline that generate energy and temporary strength. We often feel powerful and strong when we are angry. Our attention may be clearly focused on the best attack or the strongest defense against the threat.

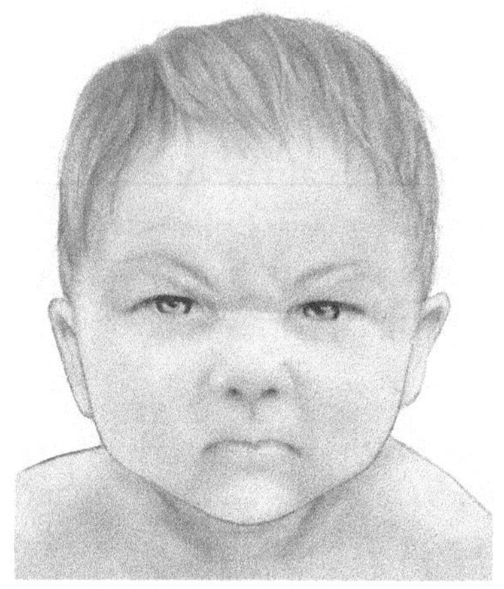

When someone is angry, the brows move down and together, and in fact many of the muscles in the face draw toward the center. The lower lids of the eyes move up and the eyes stare out intently.

Our "angry mind" may <u>feel</u> clear and accurate, even as we remember only that which supports our attack/defense system and forget that it is a partial, limited, and distorted view of the world. It is almost impossible to be nonjudgmental with beginner's mind when we are clouded by anger. In other words, if I am angry because someone has treated me unfairly, I am likely to remember all the injustices that the other has committed and the anger may even block my memory of those moments when the other was generous, kind, impartial, or even neutral. As clear, focused, and strong "angry mind" may feel, it is usually quite distorted. If we find ourselves irritated, frustrated, or furious, it is a sign that we need to attend to ourselves and give a bit of time and space to the thoughts and physical sensations of our anger before proceeding with any interaction.

The physical sensations of anger often include tension in the face, especially around the eyes or the mouth. We may feel tension in the jaw or we may notice that our teeth our clenched. It is common to feel tightness in the neck, shoulders, arms, or even clenched hands. We may feel our hearts beating faster. We may feel stronger or our biceps may feel pumped. There may be an urge to attack or hurt another person's feelings or defend ourselves. We may want to yell, insult, swear and we may even have the urge to physically harm another person or thing, even if it is something that we would never actually carry out. The urge to act can feel strong but we can have total control over our behavior and never engage in that action. (For example, that feeling of wanting to strangle somebody, but we would never really do it.)

JOY (*DELIGHT AND HAPPINESS*)

The universal smile of the mouth along with a slight rising of the cheeks just below the outer corners of the eyes is the expression of genuine joy.

Joy occurs when a situation is pleasant or beneficial to well-being. It releases an empowering increase of energy and inhibits negative feelings and worry thoughts. Joy often opens attention and is accompanied by an internal feeling of spaciousness. It also accompanies more effective and flexible responses to challenging situations.

Joy, delight, and happiness have a beneficial effect not only on our mental health but also on our physical health. Studies have shown that happier people have fewer health problems, live longer, and have shorter periods of illness in their old age before dying. Obviously, our quality of life is better when we experience joy.

Joy is something that we can nurture and promote. The human brain easily falls into noticing and remembering the negative (perhaps owing to the need to be alert for predators, remember where they have been, and how to escape them). We can actively attend to positive things that inspire gratitude, connecting and communicating with others, and the beauty of what we see, feel, hear, taste, or smell. Nurturing joy, happiness, and well-being is a relatively recent subject of research in the field of positive psychology.

FEAR (ANXIETY, NERVOUSNESS, PANIC)

Experiencing a threat or danger to life or health can generate fear. The response often includes an increase in heart rate, an explosion of electrical energy in the nervous system, and a flood of hormones that create a state of alert and readiness for action. There is an increase in blood flow to the legs, making it easier to flee. Fear can also cause a decrease in blood flow to the face and a momentary freeze in the body, creating an instant to decide whether to flee or hide or remain

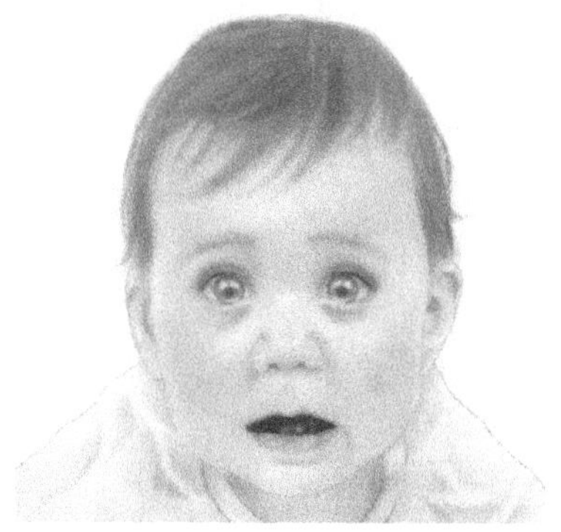

Fear is expressed when the eyebrows move up and closer together and both the upper and lower eyelids move upward. The lower lip may be stretched back and the whole head may move back a little.

frozen to avoid detection. The attention tends to fix on the threat, the escape, or both. Very intense fear may result in collapse and loss of consciousness.

The sympathetic nervous system activates the "fight, flight, or freeze response." When the sympathetic nervous system is totally overwhelmed with fear, the parasympathetic nervous system activates a different response—fainting, that is, losing consciousness in the face of fear.

From an evolutionary perspective, fear has to be one of the first and oldest emotions. A reptile, an insect, even an invertebrate marine species may respond to predators or other threats with a surge of energy to move away and escape or to remain absolutely still and therefore unseen or hidden. This response overrides most other needs and urges. For example, no matter how hungry one is, hunger disappears if there is an imminent threat to one's life.

In my own opinion, fear is the most powerful and ancient emotion with the most intense physical sensations. A friend of mine, Cheryl, was 40 years old when she described in great detail all the physical sensations in her body when she awoke one night, 20 years prior to telling her story, to the feeling of a snake around her legs in her bed while sleeping in a cheap rooming house in India. It was a region known for the cobras. She was frozen, sweating, tingling and tense from head to toe. She was unable to move from the intensity of her fear. She was also terrified that she would wake up her partner, who was sleeping with her, because he might move and rouse the snake and cause it to attack. An even more poignant and painful example of the potential intensity of the fear response is the schoolchild who stood frozen in front of a terrorist reloading a semiautomatic and then fainted just as the attacker lifted the weapon to shoot.

Fear can be experienced at a low intensity. Anxiety is a form of fear— fear of the future. Stress is also the same neurochemical response as fear. Anxiety and stress may be considered to be mental states, rather than emotions, but a mental state can also be broken down to waves of increased intensity and decreased intensity. Chronic anxiety and stress are implicated in serious health problems. A life free of excess anxiety and stress is possible and leads to improved health and well-being.

. . .

When something unexpected occurs that is not threatening (that does not startle us with fear) the emotion that arises is surprise. Surprise directs our attention to novelty. We tend to pause, to be still and fully present. Our attention expands and our interest increases. Our eyes and mouth open as if to receive information. "Surprise" is a short-lived emotional response, while awe and wonder are longer-lasting versions of that feeling. We are fully alert and wide-awake when we feel surprise, astonishment, awe, or wonder.

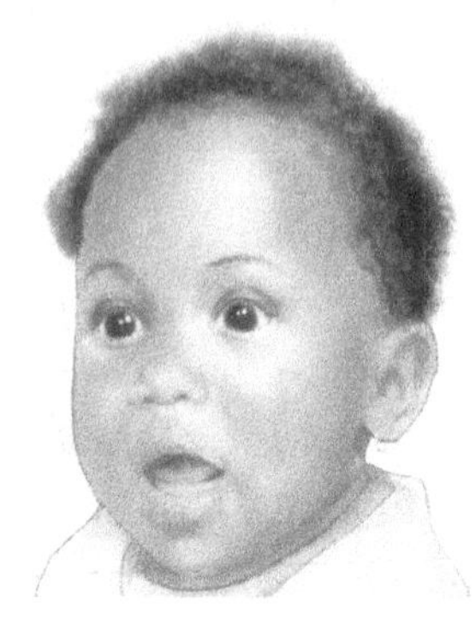

The universal facial expression of surprise includes lifting the eyebrows and opening the upper and lower eyelids to offer more information about the unexpected event. Often the jaw relaxes and the mouth opens.

Awe and wonder are the feelings of being humbled or shaken by the vastness, the mystery, or the beauty of nature or the universe. The capacity to inspire awe in others is what makes good leaders great. Awe can be associated with curiosity, humility, inspiration, and insight. When we are feeling surprise, awe, or wonder, time may seem to slow down and the feeling of a deeper connection with the universe, the supernatural, or the spiritual may arise. Physical sensations may include feelings of relaxation, physical expansion of the face, chest, or the entire body or the feeling of stillness or peace.

Scientists have just begun to study awe and wonder. The consequence of experiencing awe is a deep and profound connection with the present moment that opens up the desire to connect with others and increases generosity and compassion. (Honestly, it sounds like mindful presence!)

. . .

DISGUST *(REVULSION, REJECTION, DISAPPROVAL)*

The facial expression of disgust shows the nose lifted and wrinkled as if to block out a smell, and the lips either closed or with the tongue sticking out as if to eject something from the mouth.

Disgust may be triggered by being in contact with something poisoned or contaminated, or being touched by somebody disliked or being around a person or group whose behavior or thinking could be harmful. We can find others morally disgusting just as we can feel disgust for spoiled food. It generates the energy and urge to push away, block, or eject noxious odors, poisonous food, or offensive sights.

Disgust can generate discomfort in the stomach, nausea, or, when it is extremely intense, actual vomiting. It may be experienced as disapproval and critical thoughts. We want to push away, block, or move away from that which triggers disgust. The world seems to be more and more polarized, with disgust for people of differing race, political parties, class, religious beliefs, sexual orientation, or any other difference that one may evaluate as morally corrupt or socially toxic.

Linehan notes that persons who have been released from prison after serving their time for pedophilia may have to register their places of residence for the rest of their lives long after serving their prison term. This is not required of murderers or others who have committed other heinous crimes. It may be that the crime of pedophilia generates so much disgust that people want to know where these ex-offenders live so that they can stay away. [5]

LOVE *(INTEREST, ATTRACTION, COMPASSION)*

Love is not something that mysteriously drops out of the sky while harps are playing. It is an emotion, and it can be evoked and reinforced like any other emotion. If we get to know someone with valued characteristics or admirable qualities that enhance our life or help us reach our personal goals, this can generate feelings of love, interest, or attraction.

There are many types of love, including the feeling of "falling in love" with another person, the love of a mother for her baby, for a sibling, a close friend, or feelings of love for a pet or for a place or thing. Love is a feeling of interest and connection associated with the "relaxation response" of the parasympathetic nervous system, which generates a state of calm, contentment, and cooperation. We may get a feeling of warmth or spaciousness in our chests or around our hearts. An urge arises to pay attention to or move toward that which we love. It may generate a sense of being safe and protected, a sense of belonging, a desire to care for, to help, and to protect another, along with feelings of happiness or joy.

While I noted above that fear is one of the oldest emotions on the evolutionary chain, love has to be up there as well. In most species, two members must move toward each other and have physical contact to procreate. While we may not define insects or reptiles moving toward each other and copulating as having feelings of love, this behavior may signal an evolutionary precursor to the emotion of love, just as the impulse that an insect has to run away from a threat may be a precursor to the emotion of fear.

Love is an emotion that sustains families and communities in support of child-rearing, caring for the sick and elderly, and sharing the production of shelter and food. It is the glue that holds tribes together so that its members live happier, healthier, and longer lives.

Sadness (*disappointment, grief*)

Sadness arises after losing something important or someone irretrievable, not reaching a goal, or having things not be the way one wanted them to be.

The face of sadness has the corners of the mouth turned down and the chin pushing the center of the lips upward. The center of the eyebrows lift together and up (and sometimes create a horseshoe shape in the wrinkles of the forehead).

When experiencing sadness there is a lack of energy, a heaviness in the chest or in the whole body, and a tendency to isolate oneself or avoid social interaction. Sadness is almost always associated with ruminating and negative thinking. There is a saying that "sadness loves sadness" which means that when we are sad, we tend to think sad thoughts, remember disappointing events and failures, and perhaps even feel hopeless about the future. Depression is the phenomenon in which a person gets stuck in the thoughts and feelings of sadness without being able to break free of this negative state.

It seems that the reduction in energy, lack of enthusiasm, and slowed metabolism experienced in sadness keep humans closer to home, where they may be safer. Sadness allows for reflection to accommodate life adjustments after a loss or disappointment. It also seems to have another function. When we see a friend or loved one sad, we will probably attend to this person and offer help. The facial expression of sadness, with or without tears, can be a nonverbal way to ask for help or attention or comfort.

THE SOCIAL EMOTIONS

Our most basic physiological needs for survival are food, water, and shelter. But human beings also need love, connection, and belonging to others or they will most likely die. Living in a family, tribe or other social group is necessary for evolutionary survival. Humans don't run very fast or climb very well to escape predators. The evolutionary success of humans came from their ability to band together to protect and help one another: to build shelter, watch for predators, tend the fire, care for young and old, and communicate with one another.

The social emotions probably emerged long before speech. (A hypothesis based upon observations of my cat, who comports himself with jealousy when his brother gets too much of my attention!) Our need to belong, fit in, and feel accepted is part of being human. Being perceived as different means a risk of rejection. Contempt, jealousy, envy, and shame are four basic emotions that involve interpersonal connections. These feelings are not triggered in relation to objects. We could also include love as a social emotion, but in the broadest sense of the word we care about, like, or desire things, places, or even ideas, not just other people. Compassion and kindness, however, are forms of love that we feel only toward other sentient beings.

CONTEMPT (*SCORN, DISDAIN, AND EVEN SOME TYPES OF DISRESPECT*)

Essentially contempt is an emotion that arises from being near a person or group that is perceived as inferior to oneself or one's own group. Contempt may also arise if being around a person or group could result in oneself being scorned by others. Contempt has a lot in common with disgust, but it also includes a feeling of superiority over an "inferior" person or group or particular beliefs or behaviors.

Contempt can communicate to others "I am above that," or "I am not that type of person," or "I won't get sucked down into that." It is an urge to move up and back or push the other down and away. Some people can actually enjoy the feeling of contempt, as it includes the sense of being superior in some way. A smirk or a sneer may appear to be an awkward half smile.

Contempt can be subtle and seem unimportant. For example, an aficionado of classical music may express a subtle level of contempt for a young hip-hop fan. However, contempt may be at the heart of "tribal psychology"—an intolerance for others who are different —which is part of our evolution and biology. Contempt can be linked to widespread and dangerous antisocial behaviors such as adolescent bullying, sexual abuse, hate crimes, war, and even genocide. We all must look deeply within ourselves, see where contempt resides, and be fully aware of our own shadows. Contempt is insidious. Two people can get together and validate each

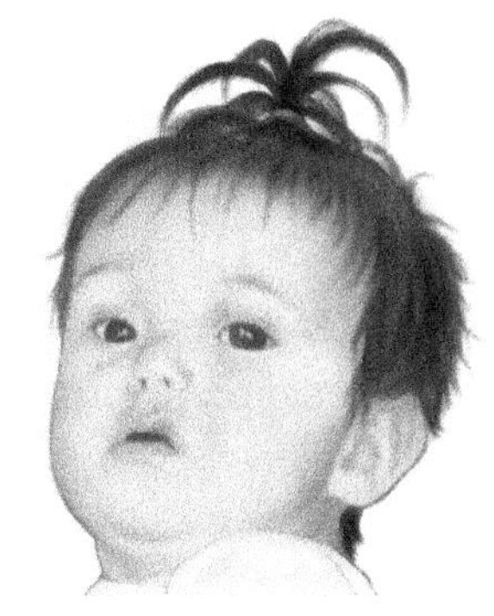

Contempt is the only facial expression that is asymmetrical. One side of the mouth is lifted, sometimes one eyebrow is raised and the head is usually lifted giving the sensation that the person is looking down their nose.

other's judgmental thoughts and feelings of superiority and further set themselves apart from and above others. This is the first step to racism, nationalism, homophobia, anti-Semitism, misogyny, and all other forms of tribalism.

JEALOUSY

Jealousy arises from not getting enough attention from another person or from losing the attention of a loved one to someone or something else. Siblings can be jealous of each other over a parent's attention and care. Pets can be jealous of each other for their owner's attention. And obviously an intimate sexual relationship is fertile ground for jealousy to germinate.

Jealousy does not have a universal facial expression or a specific physiological expression. It causes a feeling of distress and possibly discomfort in the chest or stomach. The energy that arises from jealousy is an urge to control the other, to bring the person closer, or to put the person under surveillance, including stalking another on social networks. The fundamental impulse that jealousy sets off is to step in the middle to receive attention that is being given to another.

Most of the research on jealousy has been focused on couples. Jealousy arises and a partner acts in a way intended to strengthen the relationship. From an evolutionary perspective, jealousy in men serves to ensure paternity confidence—that is, the procreation of one's own genes. In women jealousy serves to ensure shared child-rearing.

Jealousy may trigger anger, contempt, or disgust as secondary emotions. In some places it has been shown to be the leading cause of domestic violence against women. Jealousy can also trigger self-blame, shame, and depression. An interesting bit of anthropological and historical research revealed high rates of suicide because of jealousy that were reported in the late 19th century in Fiji, where jealousy was described as a "racial trait of Indian men" that was evoked when European men slept with their women.[6]

Envy

Envy is a feeling of discontent and longing for something that someone else has. That *something* might be an object, but it could also be a character trait, skill, achievement, recognition, or anything that someone else has. Like jealousy it does not have a universal face or specific physiological response, although there may be tension in the chest or stomach. It is the urge or the energy of desire, want, or hunger for something that another has, and this energy can be used to get that thing in prosocial ways (working hard to earn it) or in anti-social ways (stealing it or injuring another).

Envy can be quite intense if one strongly desires something that another person has and feels that one deserves it just as much as, or even more than, the other person. There is a social comparison involved in envy. When someone else's happiness, skill, or good fortune generates envy, that results in judgmental thinking, distress and possibly antisocial behavior. Probably for these reasons envy has a bad reputation in spiritual and religious contexts. Nevertheless, envy can also spawn healthy competition and constructive energy. The longing of envy can have the flavor of resentment toward another, or it can have an empathic joy for the other's achievement while inspiring us to work even harder to obtain our desires.

SHAME (HUMILIATION, EMBARRASSMENT, REJECTED)

Shame does not have a facial expression. The urge to hide or disappear may cause someone to look down or to cover their face.

Shame is an emotion that touches on our need for social acceptance, connection, support, and love. It is a deeply unpleasant feeling that arises from being socially rejected, and it can be triggered by just the (real or perceived) possibility of being rejected, observed, or judged. It can be a feeling that we are fundamentally flawed and unworthy of love, that we will not obtain the kind of social connection that we need, or that we do not belong. Christopher Germer calls shame the "mother of all emotions," because at its most fundamental level, shame is the dreaded feeling that we are *unlovable*.

Sensations of weakness throughout the body may arise with the urge to hide, disappear, withdraw, cover the face, or just remain completely still. Sometimes the face feels hot (and among some fair-skinned persons it appears red) or any other part of the body may feel hot. There might be a feeling of nausea in the stomach. Interestingly shame may cause smiling or giggling, clearly an evolutionary response to avoid social rejection and even turn it into social attraction and receive love, which is at its essence, just what shame wants.

(Shame is an emotion that I describe as the "invisible emotion," and it is addressed in further detail later in this chapter.)

"The Big Wave of Kanazawa" by Katsushika Hokusai.

An emotion is like a wave that rises and passes.

Before an emotional response occurs, there may be *vulnerability factors* that reduce the threshold at which an emotion is provoked or increase the intensity of the emotion. Examples of emotional vulnerability may include: hunger, fatigue, stress, menstruation, illness, or personal history in similar situations.

1. Provoking event - There is always something that provokes or triggers the emotion. *An emotion does not arise without a provoking event!* This may be an internal event (thought or feeling) or an external event, a "hook" that evokes the emotional response. *(Were it not for this event, the emotion would not have occurred at that moment.)*

2. Interpretation - At the moment that something provokes an emotion, there is usually an interpretation or evaluation of the event. These are *thoughts*, and can include mental stories, internal dialogue,

mental images, beliefs, judgments, etc. Thoughts influence which emotion is triggered and the intensity of the emotion.

3. Physical sensations - The brain sends out electrical charges and neurochemicals that result in physiological activation such as changes in: heart rate, blood pressure, muscular tension, hormones, digestive chemicals, etc. Physiological changes generate physical sensations in the body. If the emotion is intense, there will be some type of energy or impulse to act.

It is important to differentiate a thought from a feeling. Sometimes we might say "I felt like that was unfair," for example, but *technically "that was unfair" is a thought, not a feeling.* The feeling might be tension in the neck and shoulders or it might be the emotional feelings of frustration that accompany thoughts about unfairness.

4. Behavior - Voluntary behavioral responses can be separated from the emotion. For example, we can separate the feeling of anger from the act of insulting someone or the feeling of fear from the act of moving away.

Some behavioral responses are involuntary and cannot be separated from the emotion, such as the feeling of fear cannot be separated from sweating palms. We may even communicate the emotional experience in unconscious and nonverbal ways, such as facial expressions, gestures, or tone of voice.

The emotion can also evoke words and actions that are (theoretically!) under our conscious control. Many times we don't even realize what the emotion is until the emotion is acted out—even if it is our own emotion.

5. Consequences - As a result of the emotional experience, there are often clear and identifiable consequences, such as lingering physical discomfort, ruminating, or a secondary emotion.

Let's see how the waves of emotions arise and pass. One day I was walking in the crosswalk of an intersection to get to the other side of the street with the green light in my favor. A bus coming toward me was about to turn left into my path. I glanced at the bus driver and made eye contact. I just assumed that he was going to wait and kept walking. A moment later the bus was within inches of hitting me. A flash of fear exploded through my body. In the next second I experienced a thought, "that was on purpose" and my fear turned to fury. I hit the side of the bus with my hand and yelled at the bus driver. I realized that passersby and shopkeepers could see and hear my behavior. I was struck by shame and I looked around, hoping that none of my meditation students were around to witness my behavior! I was quite shaken. I was aware of my distress, of the sharp pain in my hand from hitting the bus, and of the soreness in my throat from yelling at the bus driver. After this event, I did some intentional walking (and stomping), breathing, and concentrated self-compassion practice for at least ten minutes before I was back to a reasonable state of calm.

The entire sequence of emotions can be summarized as follows:

Fear

1. Provoking event: I suddenly saw a bus moving very close to me as I crossed the street.

2. Interpretation: It is going to hit me.

3. Feelings: The sensation of electricity exploding throughout my entire body—FEAR.

4. Expressions/actions: A split-second freeze, a moment of shock.

5. Consequences: Remembering the second before in which my eyes met the driver's eyes.

Anger

1. Provoking event: Remembering the second before in which my eyes met the driver's eyes.

2. Interpretation: He did that on purpose.

3. Feelings: Tension in my hands and an urge to attack physically and verbally—ANGER.

4. Expressions/actions: I hit the side of the bus with my hand and yelled an insult.

5. Consequences: Sharp pain in my hand and a sore throat.

SHAME

1. Provoking event: Seeing other people around looking at me from the sidewalks when I was in the street.

2. Interpretation: Everyone is looking at me. I thought, "I hope none of my students are here to see me!"

3. Feelings: The sensation of physical weakness and helplessness, hoping others did not see my angry behavior, and wanting to appear calm—SHAME.

4. Expressions/actions: With my head down looking to one side, I saw someone scowling toward the bus driving away while slowly shaking her head.

5. Consequences: The shame went down and a slight feeling of relief emerged.

This is a good example of three separate emotions, one after the other with no rest. The entire sequence probably lasted no more than fifteen seconds - although it took a lot more time for my mind to stop racing and my body to feel relaxed again.

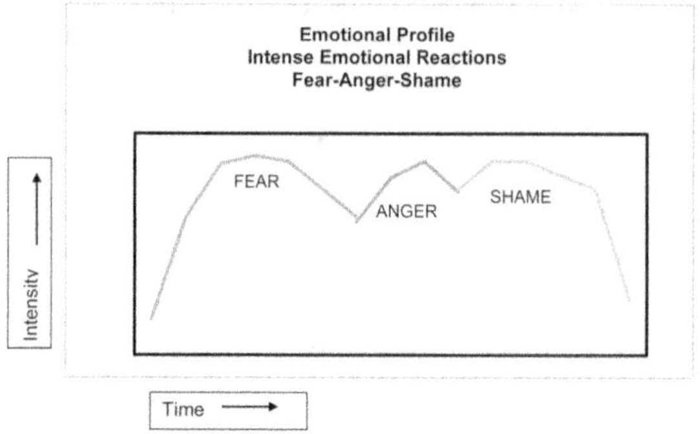

An emotional roller coaster of fear, anger, and shame.

There is no better way to understand your own emotional experience than to actually write out what happened step by step. Remember a moment when you felt hooked by something that someone said, when you felt tightness in your stomach or a sensation in your chest. Figure out what the emotion was and see if you can take it apart.

Practice 2. Deconstruct an emotional reaction

You will need pencil or pen and paper for this exercise.

Select a recent emotional reaction. It is often more useful to select an emotional response that is not extreme or intense. Answer as many of the items below as you can. If the triggering or prompting event for the emotion was a secondary emotion, then fill out another worksheet for the primary emotion. It is critical to identify one wave of one specific emotional response. (Remember, Dr. Jill Bolte Taylor says this lasts a total of 90 seconds!) This exercise should be a description of thoughts, feelings and events that lasted over a period of 10 minutes, maximum. It is not a description of internal experiences that last for hours. Select the moment when the emotion was first triggered or when it was at it's maximum intensity. NOTE: It is usually easier to select an emotional response that was of low to moderate intensity. Our memory is usually better and it is usually easier to sort out the thoughts from the feelings.

Name of the emotion:

Intensity when it was at it's maximum (0-10):

Approx. date and time of the reaction:

Place where the emotional response occurred:

1. Prompting event or emotional hook – What got you hooked?

2. Thoughts and interpretations – What did you think?

3. Physical sensations in the body – What did you feel and where?

4. Urges to say or do something, even if the urges were not acted upon - What did you feel like doing?

5. Verbal response – What did you say?

6. Actions – What did you do?

7. Consequences – Thoughts, feelings or actions that occurred as a result of the emotion or the behavior:

Shame, the "invisible emotion"

I am going to give shame (embarrassment, humiliation, mortification) some special attention to really understand it a bit more. Unlike many other emotions, shame is not easy to recognize, so it can be very difficult to understand what is going on and how to validate it. If we know someone who is sensitive to experiencing shame, we can dramatically improve our relationship by practicing validation. Plus, *the more vulnerable we are to feeling shame, the more we need to under-*

stand validation, to validate ourselves, and to learn how to recover from invalidation.

These days shame is everywhere, in all the ways that we criticize ourselves and find that we don't measure up. That dreaded feeling that we are unloved or unlovable is in our sense of insecurity, our low self-esteem, and our fear of being judged, rejected, or not appreciated. Shame can feel like a big empty hole that nobody and nothing can fill. The need to be loved is absolutely primal to our existence. Upon being born, a baby needs love; it will die without it. This need never goes away, although as adults we may not open ourselves to it. We may have even forgotten our need to be loved by focusing upon our work, our desire for success, or things that we buy, make, or own.

Deep and chronic shame can be linked to a traumatic event or events, childhood loss, neglect, or abandonment, bullying, or other types of invalidating environments. Shame is misunderstood and often overlooked, even when it becomes an intensely paralyzing and negative assessment of one's self as a person. Therefore, I describe it as the "invisible emotion" and it is invisible in many different ways.

Shame does not have a universal facial expression associated with it. As we saw pictured at the beginning of this chapter, anger, joy, fear, surprise, sadness, disgust, and contempt have associated facial expressions that are biological. Shame, however, does not have a universal expression. In fact, we might wear a neutral face or even a smile when we are feeling shame. Sometimes someone may even giggle or laugh from being embarrassed. This may serve to deflect the probability of social rejection, which is exactly what shame wants to do. So the first way that shame is invisible is in the eyes of others.

The second way it is invisible is that the energy of shame is the urge to become invisible—to others and also to ourselves. We might hide just our face by looking down or covering part of our face with a hand. If the emotion is more intense we may want to melt into the floor or escape from our own body.

The third way that shame is invisible is that it can be unspeakable. Shame can be so uncomfortable that many people cannot even describe it. It is linked to our deepest darkest secrets. It can be the feeling that we have when we believe that we would be rejected or excluded by others for our physical flaws, our human shortcomings, our inherent undesirable characteristics, whatever we have said or done that would lead to social rejection or exclusion, "if only they knew."

The sense of shame may be so powerful, it may feel like it is all the evidence that we need to prove that are not worthy of acceptance, respect, or love. So we will not even speak of it.

Finally, shame can be invisible because it is hard to detect for a number of reasons. We ignore the undesirable feelings of an unnamable emotion that is triggered by our darkest secrets. Shame can also provoke secondary emotions—"shame escapes" that are frequent ways to avoid the experience of shame. Some people habitually escape their feelings of shame by moving into another emotion. Some even jump from one shame escape to another, instead of experiencing the full range of physical and emotional feeling that shame evokes—with self-validation and self-compassion if necessary.

Some people totally deny that they experience shame. Perhaps it is a normal and natural aspect of shame to dissociate from the experience, at least a little. I have often heard this denial and I laugh to myself every time I hear it. I was once traveling with five psychologists when I mentioned—exhibiting both cavalier self-confidence and an astonishing naïveté—that I had not really experienced much shame or embarrassment since I'd become an adult. I'd suffered a lot of shame as a teenager, but I thought I had "outgrown" it. In spite of the snickering and sideways glances of my friends, I remained insistent. Over the next five days of our trip, five psychologists took every opportunity to embarrass me! It was not long before I was literally *humiliated* into admitting that yes, indeed, I was sensitive to shame and had not outgrown it at all! I know exactly how uncomfortable it is and how the urge arises to do anything to escape it.

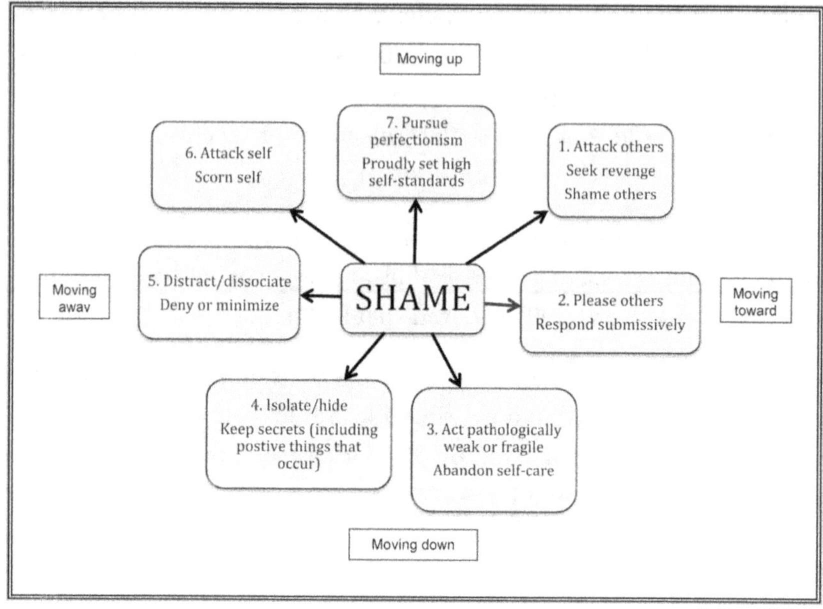

"Shame Escapes" are usually ineffective at genuinely escaping the "prison" of shame.

The diagram above describes seven responses to the experience of shame. These may be unconscious and impulsive reactions that immediately reduce the physical discomfort of the feelings and thoughts related to shame, although the may result in other negative consequences.

1. **Attack others:** Contempt and anger lift one up from the feeling of being ashamed. One is overwhelmed with the desire to seek revenge or shame others, blame others, insult others, and even use obscenities. Negative thoughts and feelings result in anger, toward one's self or others. The dreaded fear of being unlovable is replaced by the feeling of strength and energy of anger.

2. **Please others:** Shame may send forth the energy to please

others to avoid criticism or rejection. Pleasing others may include offering help, giving or loaning money, or giving gifts, which may provoke even more shame for being weak or submissive. Note: Some highly shame-sensitive persons perceive interpersonal relations in terms of domination/strength/no shame vs. submission/weakness/shamefulness—essentially the options are to shame or be shamed.

3. **Act pathologically weak or fragile:** The feeling that one is truly unlovable or deeply flawed may result in difficulty or resistance to making decisions to improve one's situation. One may even abandon self-care such as grooming and bathing, healthy eating, physical activities, and housekeeping activities because one feels unworthy of self-care or simply avoids these activities which trigger self-criticism or reminders of their flaws. These behaviors can be mistaken for depression, which may accompany this shame escape. However, it is useful to recognize that the primary problem is shame and the secondary problem is depression.

4. **Isolate/hide:** This shame escape minimizes the experience of shame by avoiding interactions that can evoke the feeling. One may avoid others, hide, keep secrets, excessively control or cut off communication with others, or stay at home in order to reduce the experience of shame. It is possible to simply perceive that it is more comfortable to be at home alone than to interact with others and not be aware that the discomfort of human interaction is shame.

5. **Distract/dissociate:** Shame is fundamentally the urge to disappear or escape. It may create a sense of suspension in time and space or mental confusion that makes us feel unreal and, perhaps, not seen. Some level of dissociation may be the inherent nature of the "invisible emotion." One may further deny, minimize or ignore the emotional experience and engage in behaviors that distract oneself

from one's feelings with compulsive behaviors or obsessively ruminating about specific problems or events.

6. **Attack self:** One of the most dangerous shame escapes can be behaviors that arise out of anger, disgust, or contempt toward oneself. These may include self-injury or obsessive smoking, drinking or eating, etc. These may appear to be forms of self-punishment for feeling flawed. In reality, these behaviors are effective shame escapes because the consequence of these behaviors is almost always instant, immediate relief of the intense unpleasant emotion. Even if the shame returns later with even more intensity, the immediate relief is enough to sustain these types of behaviors.

7. **Seek perfection:** Many people are intelligent, talented, and ambitious *and* highly vulnerable to the experience of shame. If one could compensate (for that fatal flaw that makes one unlovable) with achievements in school, sports, or work, then one will deserve admiration, respect, or love. Setting difficult or unreachably high standards for oneself, such trying to be the perfect child, friend, or parent; the most successful at school or work; or a high achiever in sports or other endeavors—can result in abandoning the activity when high standards are not met. On the other hand, achieving such goals rarely fills the black void of shame.

8. **Extreme jumping among all (1 to 7):** One may be highly vulnerable to shame, moving quickly or intensely from one strategy to another (often leaving others confused or angry and resulting in the social rejection that the ashamed person most fears.) One may also be unable to regulate thoughts and emotions in general, and jump from thought to thought and from one emotion to another.

It is useful to keep an eye out for the "invisible emotion" in oneself and in others. This feeling does not want to call attention to itself.

Brené Brown, a leading shame researcher, describes how shame does not withstand the light. Paul Gilbert, author of compassion-focused therapy, a treatment developed for persons with high levels of shame, would probably add that shame withers when exposed to love. Together Brown and Gilbert tell us to manage our shame with light and love—in psychological terms that would be exposure and compassion.

Exposure might include doing things that evoke shame—very small steps at first, slowly increasing the intensity over time. (It is important that we do this with others who will validate us and respond with empathy and not when the shame will be reinforced!) For example, speaking openly about those painful secrets. Perhaps they are stories of neglect, abuse, or bullying. Perhaps they are linked to physical aspects of one's body, one's status, heritage, likes or dislikes. Shedding light on these secrets, is knowing them, listening in and inquiring deeply into feelings around them, and sharing our pain, our secrets, and our vulnerabilities with others. As we put light on our suffering, it is useful to remember this is a human experience, our inner secret is not unique, and we are not alone in the world.

Compassion is seeing the pain and suffering of shame and responding with kindness, caring, and love. If it is our own shame, we soothe ourselves with kindness, compassion and love directed toward our inner selves. Chapter 10, Deepening Self-Validation is filled with antidotes for shame. If we see that shame arises in another, we can soften and validate. We respond in a nonjudgmental way and with kindness. Remember, shame is an "innocent emotion" that "just wants to be loved."[1]

The practice of exposure and compassion for our own feelings of shame may be one of the most important steps toward effectively validating shame in others. As we understand our own shame, we begin to be able see this emotion in others when it slips in between the cracks. Otherwise, we may not see that another is experiencing "the invisible emotion" or jumping from one shame escape to another. In fact, being around someone who is jumping from one shame escape to another can trigger rejection and anger if we don't understand what is happening, and it becomes very difficult to validate such confusing behavior. Self-validation may be a step toward experiencing shame under the light and the love in which it dissolves.

Shame, like all emotions, is not always intense and unbearable! Let me describe a simple example of a small, short wave of shame. One day as I was sitting in meditation looking out the window, I felt the movement of my arm as my hand moved toward my forehead. Upon noticing that my arm was moving, I realized that a memory had arisen—a mental image of a situation that had occurred in my early twenties: I saw myself sitting on a couch when I had just realized that I had fallen asleep in the middle of a party. Upon waking up, I felt my whole body awash with shame for having fallen asleep there.

Experiencing that mental image 30 years later provoked a very small wave of shame. The movement of my hand toward my face to cover my eyes was an automatic response to the feeling of shame. First I noticed that my hand was halfway toward my face, then I realized what I was thinking and feeling. The whole wave from start to finish lasted a few seconds. At that moment, my thoughts were clearly just thoughts and the emotional reaction was just a set of physical sensations including the movement of my arm. I was no longer experiencing this mental image as if it were reality. I smiled gently, lowered my hand, and put my attention back on my breath.

"MANIPULATION"

When we understand emotional responses, especially the physiological strength of intense emotional urges, we can begin to let go of thinking that a person acting in emotional mind is being "manipulative." The definition of *manipulative* in the online *American Heritage Dictionary* says "shrewd or devious management, especially for one's own advantage." This implies a combination of dishonesty and selfish intent, combined with intelligence and skill. In reality, the behavior of someone who is really angry or intensely insecure may be anything *but* skillful; there may not be any devious management or dishonesty involved. "Especially for one's own advantage" implies that manipulation is selfish. We all want to escape from intense negative emotions as rapidly as possible, so who's to judge that it is selfish?

There are a whole lot of negative judgments and assumptions made when describing someone's behavior as manipulative. It is pejorative interpretation that is rarely useful. Worse, it will likely increase the emotional arousal of both the person who is feeling manipulated and the other who is accused of being manipulative. If we are going to make interpretations about behavior, it is useful to do so from a position of empathy. Understanding that an intense emotional experience is a state of discomfort, even pain, puts us in a position to be much more effective at responding appropriately and with validation.

Thus, it is very helpful in cultivating genuine validation skills to erase this word from our vocabulary when we describe our loved ones and people who are suffering and just want to escape their pain or insecurity. We can, instead, acknowledge that, at some point, we all want to "selfishly" eliminate our emotional pain and we might have to enlist the help of others. Maybe, it really is easier sometimes to ask for help than to change one's feelings.

IS HE MANIPULATING ME?

Consider the young child who asks for candy when he is with his mother in line at the supermarket. Mom lets him select what candy bar he wants. The next week she says no, not today. The child is disappointed and starts to cry. Mom gives in and lets him have a candy bar. The next time, Mom is a bit firmer and the disappointed child cries a bit longer and louder. Mom can't take it anymore and she lets him have a candy bar, but "this is the last time." Each time this scene repeats itself, Mom is doing an excellent job of "training" her son to whine and cry by "rewarding" him with a candy bar each time. Who is "manipulating" whom?

By the way, how can Mom get a handle on the situation? Let's get a preview of validation. "Honey, I know how much you like those candy bars. They really are delicious. I know you are mad at me for not buying one for you right now. It is really frustrating. You might even get madder at me because the answer is going to stay 'no' today." Validating her child's desires as much as possible, Mom might mix this in with changing the subject and distracting her child. She might offer to give him a candy bar if and only if he is calm and quiet until he gets home and give him the candy bar only *after* he is calm and quiet all the way home. Or she might just have to ignore his crying and attend to her own needs to remain as calm and centered as possible by taking a moment to care for herself. There is no one right answer and validation may be the wisest action for the long term, but both mother and child have to get through the present situation as best as they can.

Let us consider one final shift in perspective regarding the child's temper tantrums and the mother giving him candy. What is Mom feeling? As her child begins to cry and scream in public, she may be worried about her child's distress. Or she may be feeling embarrassed that others are watching, perhaps worried that the tantrum is going to get worse. She may feel guilty that she is not a good mother. Whatever distress she is experiencing, she feels relief after giving her child the candy because his temper tantrum stops! Keep in mind that the child is not plotting and scheming how to make his mother suffer and then relieve her of her suffering in order to get candy. *That* would be manipulation. This kid just wants his candy and does whatever works to get it. Mom wants relief from her anxiety or shame so she gives him candy. The reinforcement for their emotional behaviors is transactional.

～

Human emotions have been of great service to our survival. There are basic emotions shared by all people in all cultures, including people living in the most simple as well as in the most complex conditions. Our emotions are biological, and we are all born with the capacity to experience them.

Being in an activated emotional state, or "emotional mind" is experiencing that moment when we are in the refractory period of an emotional response. Understanding the unique nature of what evokes an emotion and the profile of the "wave" of an emotion can help us accept different emotional responses in ourselves and others and regulate our emotions. We all experience emotions with differing intensities, durations, and thresholds. Through accepting our own experience, we can begin to accept the internal experiences of another to be authentic. An intense emotional response is not about pretending or exaggerating; the emotional experience is real, and may not be a pleasant experience. Behavior that can be described as impulsive or damaging is probably an attempt to escape, discharge, or reduce this emotional pain. While many impulsive behaviors are very effective at achieving that objective, they may work for only a short period of time and may have long-term negative consequences.

Understanding emotions

1. An emotional profile is unique to each person and each situation. It has three variables:

- The *threshold* at which an emotional response is triggered
- The *intensity* of the emotion
- The *duration* of the emotional response
- Some people have a pattern of *under-control* and react with high emotional intensity and impulsive behaviors. Others are more emotionally distant or stoic, exhibit a pattern of *over-control*, and regularly exhibit flatter emotional profiles.

2. Primary and secondary emotions.

- One emotional experience can evoke another emotion, for example, when one feels anxious and frustration arises just for feeling anxious, the anxiety is a primary emotion and the frustration is a secondary emotion.

3. All emotions have a purpose and a function.

- Human emotions are an evolutionary product of natural selection that helped support human survival and reproduction.
- Emotions energize and motivate us.
- Emotions communicate information to one's self and to others.
- There are a few basic emotions (or families of emotions) that are generally considered universal, such as anger, joy, fear, surprise/awe, love, sadness, disgust, contempt, shame, jealousy, and envy. Each emotion is triggered by certain types of internal or external events, and each emotion motivates a specific type of response.

4. Shame is a challenging emotion for validation as it may be "invisible." Fundamentally shame is the dreaded fear of being unlovable, a rejection of one's self as unlovable, and/or the urge to erase the observer of one's experience.

- There is no universal facial expression or voice tone.
- The primary impulsive actions of shame include movements to hide, to cover one's face, and to smile or giggle.
- Shame can be chronic and result in many behaviors and secondary emotions that effectively result in an immediately escape from shame (although they may not be effective and mature responses to the experience of shame).
- "Shame escapes" can include feelings and actions of

domination or attack, submission to others, abandonment of self-care, isolation, distraction, or dissociation.

5. An emotional response can be described as a process that includes the following components:

- Evoking event or "hook" – Internal or external
- Interpretations – Thoughts, memories, worries, etc.
- Feelings – Electrical and chemical activity in the brain, physiological changes, physical feelings, urges to act
- Emotional expressions – Facial expressions, body posture and movements, verbal expressions, and actions
- Consequences – Reinforcers, inhibitors, and secondary emotions

6. Intense emotional responses are rarely a form of manipulation.

- The term "manipulation" is used in a pejorative way and implies that someone is calculating, cunning, and skillful, and that the behavior is premeditated. This word is generally not a useful description of behavior that is part of an intense emotional response, nor is it likely to be an accurate interpretation of behavior, especially behavior that is impulsive or unskillful.

4

PRESENCE

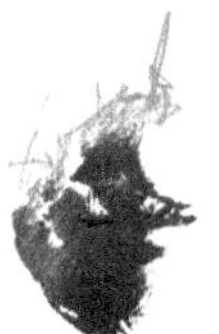

The greatest gift we can make to others is our true presence. "I am here for you" is a mantra to be uttered in perfect concentration.

— THICH NHAT HANH

One Saturday morning during breakfast Mary, a single mother, asked Martin, her teenage son, to put his dirty clothes in the washing machine. He tried to ignore her. He was already irritated because she had woken him up early by entering his bedroom without knocking, something that he had asked her not to do many times.

Of course his silence frustrated Mary and she repeated her request louder and insistently. Martin reacted, "Why do you always have to nag me? Why can't you just leave me alone?" Mary exploded and yelled, "What are your talking about? You never do anything around here! I'm the one who cooks and cleans and washes the clothes! I can't even get you to go to the store for me when I need something!" At that point Martin pounded the kitchen table, got up, and left the house without saying anything. Mary began to cry.

Mary needs to practice mindfulness. Perhaps she would have been more effective if she had been more aware of her frustration and anxiety before she spoke, perhaps even before her son woke up that morning. She might have noticed how impatient she was feeling and then paused to consider the most skillful means to ask her son to start the wash. On the other hand, she might have also been more open to her son, willing to learn what was going on in his mind or to carefully observe his experience that morning. The entire conflict could have been avoided if she had mentally inquired about what was going on right there in that moment for herself, for him, and between the two of them.

Had she paused and knocked on the door in the morning before she entered her son's room, he might have been in a better mood. At breakfast she could have asked him if he needed clean clothes, instead of swimming in her critical thoughts about what Martin should be doing to help her and then giving orders. Clinging to her own thoughts and criticisms of her son, of what he should do and shouldn't do, she invaded his privacy, insisted that he begin washing his clothes, and verbally attacked him—hardly aware of her son's experience.

In chapter 2 we learned what to validate and what not to validate. In chapter 3 we learned the basics of our emotions. Now we turn to *presence*—that is, paying attention to what we are doing, while we are doing it, to be aware of what is going on around us, and to see clearly our own internal experience. This is also known as mindfulness. It is the act of consciously and intentionally being fully awake and aware of what arises within our experience. Our attention is in the present moment and we are open and curious about what is happening. We may have to actively bring intention to the practice of letting go of the automatic criticisms and value judgments that frequently arise as we experience things that we don't like and want to push away, escape, or avoid. We are attend to the present without being judgmental, but we don't forget about our goals and our values.

Martin's mom, Mary, is not a bad mother and this type of situation is not unique. All of us can be stuck in our own thoughts, deluded and blinded by our frustration. These are not the moments in which we learn to practice mindfulness. These are more likely to be the moments from which we learn that we need to practice mindfulness!

To get started, we should find a moment when we are already fairly calm. Notice how we can connect to the present by direct experience through our sense perceptions. For example, we can see and hear only in the present. We know the difference between a song in our minds and the sound of music that we really hear in the present. We also see, feel, taste, and touch in the present. Pause for about five minutes, just listening to whatever sound arises. You never know what exactly the next sound will be, so pay attention. Notice how your ears just accept whatever sound enters and you hear it. When your mind wanders into the realm of thoughts, plans, ideas, worries, or any mental discourse of image that takes you away from listening to sound, simply bring it back again to *hearing*. Put this book down, close your eyes and for the next five minutes, just attend to sound—<u>now</u>.

There, you just completed your first mindfulness practice—allowing and accepting what arises, moment by moment. You may have noticed other things, like a physical sensation. You may have noticed thoughts arise. You have even found yourself completely distracted with thinking (and possibly abandoned the practice before five minutes was up). Mindfulness just notices all that.

We can direct our attention to the present by either focusing on one particular thing or by opening our awareness to the whole range of input from moment to moment. Focusing on one particular thing in the moment might be most accurately described as a repetitive, but gentle act of directing attention to the same thing over and over. Each time we realize that our attention is on something else—a worry thought, a memory, or running an analysis of how things should be—we lightly and gently guide our attention back to the object of our focus. We try to be kind and compassionate with ourselves in this process and let go of judgmental thoughts about how we are doing in the practice, what's good or bad, better or worse.

We can practice mindfulness by focusing our attention on one thing for an extended period or time—such as the sound of a musical instrument playing, the visual sight of an object such as a candle, or physical sensations such as the feelings that arise as we breathe. This is attentional training and it is very useful for building a greater capacity for concentration. We can also practice mindfulness with more openness in which we remain an impartial observer without actively choosing where our attention goes. We observe everything that emerges in our awareness with an attitude of interest and kindness. We are knowingly aware of what we see, what we hear, and what we feel or whatever arises in our consciousness, including thoughts.

We can mindfully see thoughts as thoughts, without getting caught up in the content. We can be aware of our mental activity without getting trapped in automatic responses, without getting caught up in judgments, and without ruminating about the content of our thoughts. We can be mindful of thoughts—as thoughts. We remain aware that our thoughts, worries, and memories are just mental events, not to be confused with reality. (For many of us "worry warts" our attention tends to go to negative thoughts about what might go wrong and cause our lives to become filled with problems and disasters, most of which never even occur. It can be tremendously useful to recognize these worries as merely mental movement without becoming swept up in the content of this mental activity.)

The effects of practicing mindfulness are being studied more and more by researchers (creating a new field called contemplative neuroscience). While this field is in its infancy and there are innumerable specific mindfulness practices and types of formal mindful meditations, there is evidence that these offer specific benefits which arise in direct relationship to the amount of practice. Some of the findings show that regular, formal mindfulness practice results in stress reduction, better concentration and mental clarity, increased capacity to regulate one's emotions, improved interpersonal relationships, and a stronger immune system. Many people describe how, beyond what we can independently and scientifically measure, mindfulness practice increases their sense of contentment and personal satisfaction with their lives, independent of external circumstances.

Being fully present is something we can bring to any activity at any time of the day. In an informal mindfulness practice, attention is paid to body postures, movements and sensorial perception in the routine acts of everyday living. In an informal mindfulness practice, we direct our attention to the task at hand aware of what we are doing and how we are doing it. For a few seconds or a few minutes, we intentionally connect to the present using any of our five senses or our "sixth sense"—sensations inside our bodies. For example, when we are in the shower, we notice the feel of the warm water, the vapor in the air, the smell of the soap, the color of the shampoo, the sensation of scrubbing our scalp with our fingers, or the chill of the air on our wet skin as we step out. If thoughts about the things that we have to do during the day arise in our minds, we just notice them and observe them as thoughts—images on our mental screen or words we hear within our minds. We practice letting go of thoughts and return our attention to where we are and what we are currently doing. No matter how obsessive our thinking mind is, we let go over and over to pay attention to what we are doing when we are doing it.

Mindfulness in daily life is central to most Buddhist practices, and presence, silence, and contemplation are practiced in some way in nearly all of the world's religions. "Deliberate attention to routine acts," (sampajañña) also translated as "knowing" or "introspection" or "clear comprehension," was among the most fundamental instructions that Buddha gave to his monks. "Deliberate attention" includes three aspects: understanding the purpose and the appropriateness of a task, being aware of one's own mental activity, and being aware of present reality, all while being engaged in a routine act. Jetsuma Tenzin Palmo, a well-known American nun in charge of a Tibetan nunnery in northern India, says it is like "spying" on your own mind, checking to see if you are mindfully present, if you are tired and your mind is dull, or if you are distracted.[1]

I often get asked by people how much of the time they should really practice being present. I think that the following passage is a good response:

"A monk, said Buddha, "should act with clear and deliberate attention when walking forward and back; when looking ahead and to the side; when stretching the limbs out and drawing them in; when wearing clothes and carrying his coat and bowl; when eating, drinking, chewing or tasting food; when at the toilet; when standing or sitting; when falling asleep or waking up; and when speaking or remaining silent."

Being mindfully present is probably not the normal way of being for many of us in today's busy and stressful world. Almost a whole day may pass while we are thinking about things other than what we are doing. We may go through a significant portion of our lives on autopilot by multitasking and trying to respond to the demands of work, family, school, etc., while at the same time we try to meet our own high expectations. We are often worrying about what we are going to do next instead of appreciating the very moment in which we are living. Whether we are at work or at home, with a co-worker or a with loved one, we may be likely to make split-second assumptions and evaluations about what they are doing or saying—even before listening and observing!

Investigations into the brain and multitasking shows that it is not actually possible, it is really single tasking in rapid fire, and there is a high cost to switching from activity to activity. It drains the energy of the brain, increases the stress response and decreases the brain's capacity for resilience. Heavy multitaskers perform worse on tests of task-switching ability than do light multitaskers, possibly because they have greater difficulty filtering out irrelevant information. Multi-tasking has a negative impact on learning and test scores in school. People with great capacity for concentration (such as surgeons) report a pleasant experience of being calm and centered during long periods of concentration and those with little capacity for concentrated single-tasking report more stress, anxiety, negative emotions, and maladaptive impulsive behavior.

Practice 1. Mindfully Walking

with the attention focused on the soles of the feet or open to seeing, hearing, and feeling

Mindfulness can be practiced anytime, anywhere. When you are walking you just walk. Observe the feeling of pressure on the soles of your feet, or the action of your knees and legs, or the passing scenery, or anything that you perceived as you are experiencing the walk. As thoughts enter your mind about the future (where you are going and what you will do when you get there) or about the past (where you've come from and what happened when you were there), you might observe such a thought as a "thought in the present moment" and then kindly and gently bring your attention back to the act of walking and the things that you can see or hear or feel as you are walking.

Practice 2. Observing and Describing

Labeling experiences as "see, hear or feel"

Sitting with your back straight—in a chair or on a cushion on the floor—whatever position allows you to remain comfortable with your back straight and your head as if it were floating upward.

Remain still while observing the breath and feeling the movements of your abdomen with each breath. Once you are settled into your breathing, you begin to watch what emerges within your consciousness or your attention. Notice each sensorial event as it arises into awareness - whatever you see or hear or feel:

- You might *see* what is in front of yours eyes, or the back of you eyelids if they are closed, or you might even *see* a mental image in your mind.

- You might *hear* a bird, or sounds of traffic, or a nearby motor, the sound of ringing in your ears, or you may even *hear* your thoughts, such as a mental conversation in your head.

- Physical sensations may arise in this open awareness, and you may *feel* such an itch or stiffness or an urge to move, or even an emotional feeling may occur.

You do not cling to anything; you just watch. Label each mental and sensorial event according to the categories "see" or "hear" or "feel." Remain an impartial observer of each mental event as it happens.

At first, you practice observing and noting for no more than three to five minutes. This requires complete attention and it is usually not effective to do this for long periods of time without practice. *If* you find it difficult to pay attention, speak the labels out loud "see", "hear" or "feel" in a slow and regular pace. Perhaps at the beginning of each exhale, just notice and label that which is predominant in the field of awareness at that moment.[2]

WHAT DOES MINDFULNESS HAVE TO DO WITH GENUINE VALIDATION?

Validation is, at its essence, a combination of personal mindfulness and interpersonal mindfulness skills. These are fundamental to validation in four specific ways: 1) we must be mentally present; 2) we focus attention on the other person; 3) we open our attention to our own experience in the present moment and we develop awareness of, patience for, and acceptance of our own feelings and reactions; and 4) we respond effectively and with integrity, such that our words and feelings and beliefs are congruent.

Heather's daughter, Chloe, was complaining for months about how fat she was and how she did not want to be in any photos at her brother's wedding. Heather habitually responded to her daughter's self-criticism by saying that she was beautiful and she would look just fine in the photos (invalidating Chloe's experience of feeling too fat). One afternoon her daughter began to talk about the wedding and her weight. Heather's impulse was to tell her she looked fine. This time she caught herself and decided to just be fully present. Heather looked at Chloe, listened deeply, and was completely open to her words, her tone of voice, her facial expression and her gestures. Chloe slowed down her self-criticism. She remembered how flattering the dress was that she had bought for the wedding and how much she liked her shoes. Heather secretly felt astonished and delighted. Just being present to what she was feeling and what her daughter was saying changed the course of the conversation. In fact, Heather's other daughter had observed the entire conversation and later she commented to her mom how surprised she was that her sister just seemed to "talk out" her own worries and calm herself when her mother just listened.

That magic moment that Heather decided to not speak changed the course of the entire conversation. Presence can be deeply validating. It communicates a deep respect for that which another is feeling, thinking, wanting or needing. Heather remembered that she did not want to invalidate her daughter, so all she did was listen deeply and remain fully present. As we practice being more mindful, we become more validating.

We are generally more effective if we are calm and centered than if our minds are racing around in fear, confusion, anxiety, anger, embarrassment, or any combination of emotions. In such an emotional state, our impulse is to do *anything* to escape our emotions; sometimes this might even manifest as trying to calm the other because we are afraid of their response. But such an anxious response is not likely to be effective. It will probably intensify the emotional reactions of everyone. It may reinforce a spiral of negative feelings, negative thoughts, ineffective resolutions, aborted communication, and damaged relationships.

Mindfulness of our own emotional state may inform us that we need to attend to ourselves before we can help someone else. Mindfully being present and aware of another's internal experience—without reacting out of anxiety—is the first and last step to genuine validation.

On the other hand, our normal mode of responding to someone else's emotional hurricane might be to remain rational and logical. A logical response may intensify the emotional reaction in the other person if it is interpreted as cold, uncaring, unloving, or invalidating in other ways. This could evoke even more anger, anxiety, or shame in an emotionally sensitive person. If we response from a place of pure logic, we might be masking our own fear or anger with a form of passive aggression.

The mindful response integrates the emotional response and the rational response. We can begin to integrate emotion and reason when we pay attention to our breathing. We take a mental step backward and observe everything. Then we respond as skillfully and effectively as we can. As we will see in subsequent chapters, a mindful response may be warm and compassionate or abrupt and irreverent—but it tries to be appropriate, wise, and effective.

Below we review and expand upon each of four qualities of mindfulness that are so fundamental to genuine validation: being mentally present, focusing attention on the other, opening attention to our own experience, and responding effectively and with integrity to others.

Being mentally present

We are present and we sustain our attention on trying to understand the other's experience. If our mind wanders off to other things, we guide it back to the present moment. It's pretty obvious that it can be invalidating to another if we are "listening" to them while watching TV, reading the paper, chatting on the telephone or surfing the web. It may be less obvious that we are not mentally present if we are thinking the things we have to do while nodding and looking at the other. Or perhaps we are looking at them and not really listening, but just waiting for the first pause in the other's dialogue so that we can speak.

Presence is open-minded and accepting of the other person, especially of their feelings. Presence is actively attending without being judgmental. That is not to say that we cannot make judgments or evaluations. We must be fully aware of our interpretations, exaggerations, and evaluations and not confuse them with observations and descriptions. This is much more challenging than it sounds. Being nonjudgmental involves being without prejudice and letting go of assumptions, predictions, and presuppositions. While we practice letting go of automatic judgments, we can (and should) actually apply mindfulness to discern the difference between what is safe and wholesome and what is dangerous or unhealthy.

Nonjudgmental awareness is essential and often difficult to achieve in a face-to-face conversation, especially when one or the other is insecure, strongly attached to their thoughts and ideas, anxious, rigid, or in any emotional state of mind. We focus on connecting to the other person and their inner experience. People often carry expectations, presumptions, and interpretations about what others say and do, instead of being open to listening, observing, and understanding. We want to be present with "beginner's mind," as if it were the first time we were having this experience—which it really is!

Practice 3. Mindfulness of a Loved One.

Pick a time when you can be alone for a few minutes, but also when your loved one is not too far away. Sit quietly with your eyes closed and begin to imagine that you are as open as the universe. Imagine that you can experience and hold all, just as the ocean experiences a wave and holds the rain. As you breathe imagine opening yourself to kindness and love freely flowing in and out of the body with each breath. After a few minutes, gently bring yourself back and find your loved one. From this loving perspective, let yourself be mindfully aware of him or her. Just notice gently; let go of any intention to shape the experience. Simply be aware of your loved one from this open place.[3]

FOCUSING ATTENTION ON THE OTHER

The most fundamental way to make another feel valued is to mindfully listen. We listen with our whole mind and body to the words that the other is saying. We observe the spaces between words, we listen to the silence, and we allow the other to think without pressure.

This is the point of departure to sharing the path of mindful compassion.

We give full attention to the tone of voice, facial expressions, body language, behaviors, and actions. These factors convey more information than the actual content of what is being said. Voice tone alone can be broken down into loudness, inflection, pitch, and word speed. Imagine saying the words "Oh, really?" How can you say these words and communicate authentic interest and curiosity? How can you say the same words with sarcasm and ridicule? Or say them and communicate a complete lack of interest?

Facial expressions also communicate a lot about the internal emotional state of another. It is useful to remember that many aspects of facial expressions are biological—that is, intercultural and universal. For example, a smile in any culture reflects a pleasurable state and pursed lips and furrowed brows communicate anger. The eye gaze communicates important information. Is the other person looking at something with interest or with anger? Is she talking to someone with a blank, dissociated stare or is she intently observing the person to whom she is speaking? Body language is much subtler and complex than it was thought to be in the 1970s, when it first became a popular topic. It is worth being mindfully observant of the gestures, posture, body position, and body movements of another, making not automatic interpretations, but rather thoughtful and empathic hypotheses about what these say about their internal experience, feelings and needs.

When we are in dialogue, we can also be observant of the other person's need for personal space—the distance they maintain from others and the space they perceive as belonging to them. If someone is angry and we enter their personal space, it may increase their anger. If we back off and sit down, it may lower their anger a notch. If someone is sad or afraid, their sadness or fear may become less intense if we move closer, perhaps even physically touching them on the hand or shoulder or even with a hug.

Behavior and actions (including what we say, how we say it, and our facial and body expressions) may be driven by emotional energy and acted out, or may be fully inhibited in spite of emotional and physical urges to the contrary. When we are in an emotional state, it is all too easy to engage in impulsive behaviors that are driven by the energy of the emotion. For example, anger may provoke aggressive behavior such as swearing, insulting, or even more threatening actions such as throwing things, breaking things, or physical attack. On the other hand, one may be steaming with anger on the inside but simultaneously deny the emotional state perhaps using sarcasm, stonewalling, or other forms of over-control or self-invalidation. Some people learn to respond to emotional dysregulation with apparent stoicism but privately engage in self-directed injury or secretly act out their vengeance toward others. We need to be mindful of our friends as well as strangers with all of our senses to integrate what we perceive in their tone of voice, facial expressions, body language, behaviors, and actions. Keen observation is necessary.

We want to go beyond listening and observing; we try to fully connect with the inner world of the other person. We actively seek to understand and clarify their inner experience: feelings, desires, thoughts, and needs. This helps us better understand the how and why of the views of another. When understanding occurs, a sense of calm may emerge on both sides, even if no point of agreement is reached. Once this understanding and calm is achieved, respect and trust for one another are possible, and there is a greater sense of freedom to open our minds and widen the scope of potential solutions.

Listening mindfully is a healthy activity for both parties. Studies show that when we listen mindfully, our heart rate and oxygen consumption are reduced and our blood pressure decreases. We develop patience. Having a "sounding board" who is genuinely listening promotes wellbeing and self-expression. By being good listeners, we promote the health and wellbeing of ourselves and others; we help to reduce stress in ourselves and others; we let go of having to solve the problems of others at the same time that we empower them to solve their own dilemmas.[4]

When we open our awareness to ourselves, we listen to the words that we are saying and we become aware of our own feelings, but we do not necessarily act on them. We recognize our thoughts as just thoughts, our feelings as just feelings, and our urges as urges. The practice of being present to the full flow of energy without avoiding or escaping or acting out is the challenge of mindfulness. We can feel the urge to react, judge, criticize or give advice, but we do not have to follow these urges. We observe our impulse to respond automatically, but without reacting. We try to suspend criticisms of the situation for the moment and be open to the present. We are not jumping to conclusions nor trying to think about the "correct" or appropriate response. We may even sit in silence with another without acting on an impulse to fill the silence.

We are aware of our own vulnerabilities and emotional reactions, and we practice experiencing our own feelings with patience and acceptance. If we are afraid of setting off an angry reaction in the other, we want to be aware of our feelings, appropriately communicate them, and effectively manage them. We want to keep our objectives and priorities in mind in each encounter. If our own emotional reactions are triggered and we cannot be effective in the moment, perhaps it is most appropriate to take a time-out to refocus on the present. We must learn to observe everything in the other and in ourselves with a good amount of patience and acceptance.

If we are mindful of our own feelings and attitudes in the moment, we will avoid incongruent communication. For example, if a person is experiencing a feeling of annoyance toward another person but is unaware of it or trying to inhibit the feeling, then their communication will contain a contradictory message. This happens all the time.

Incongruent messages are likely to be confusing and invalidating to others and may trigger an emotional arousal such as distrust or anger in the other person who is receiving the message. Our mood, our facial expression, tone of voice, body posture, and so on must be consistent with the words that we are saying if we are to communicate in a clear, honest, and authentic way.

Another example particularly important for parents to be mindful of is the feeling of disapproval. We all know full well when our parent does not approve of (or did not approve of) our actions. If someone disapproves, but pretends that the disapproval does not exist, the result is incongruent communication. It would be more truthful to acknowledge our disapproval to ourselves and to see how it may be related to our desire for their success. If we are mindful of our feelings of disapproval, we will take into account our automatic judgments, our frustrations, our fears, and our interpretations. By observing and describing such feelings within ourselves, we can regulate our emotions and our judgments. It is a little hard to believe, but observing and describing our own feelings has a calming effect. We take a step back. We gain a bit of equanimity in the face of our emotional reactions, desires, judgments, and urges to give advice.

Huh? How does that work? Perhaps we notice our own anxiety and take a deep breath and refocus our attention on observing and listening to the other. This might have a calming effect. Or we might say to the other, "As I listen to you, I am getting more and more nervous." Or, if we sense that a growing anger is becoming an obstacle to mindful listening, we might take a break to get a glass of water from the kitchen or we might excuse ourselves to go to the bathroom. Or we might say directly "I am feeling angry right now and I can't continue this conversation if I am angry. I want to take a break now, and we can talk later when I'm calmer." If we are in a conversation with another who is in an extreme emotional state, we should not expect that they will be able to calm down within a few minutes. Such expectations may result in another bout of feeling disappointment or anxiety or anger if our expectations are not met.

Stepping back and listening to ourselves, observing our mental events, and attending to our emotional state without acting on it takes practice. We can practice observing the urge to give advice before opening our mouths. We can practice observing our emotional state instead of focusing on whatever evoked the emotion or trying to make it end. We must be emotionally sturdy if we are to be effective at genuine validation. A few minutes of mindful meditation each day is one way to cultivate these skills.

RESPONDING EFFECTIVELY WHEN EMOTIONS ARE HIGH

It is important to be aware of our ultimate objective in an interaction. If we are with someone who is in an emotionally intense state, our top priority may simply be to stay as calm and relaxed as possible and to help the other person to calm down. However, it is all too easy to get caught up correcting what the other is saying, untwisting the emotionally distorted interpretations, defending ourselves, or explaining the actions of others. All of this will probably maintain or increase the intensity of the other person's emotional response as well as the intensity of one's own emotions. As this scenario unfolds, we are more and more likely to cling to the need to be right or to prove our point while we move further away from our top priority of being calm and empathic.

We must practice letting go of trying to prove a point or becoming distracted by illogical interpretations and attending to less important issues. When do we respond slowly, thoughtfully, and reflectively? When is it more useful to respond spontaneously and intuitively in an honest, direct way? If we practice mindfully focusing on the experience of the other while being open to our own feelings, we will recognize those moments. Thoughtful responses to a request, for example, might be, "Hmm, what you are asking makes sense, but I have to check on some things to see if it is possible" or "I want to sleep on it and get back to you tomorrow" or "I can see how important this is to you, so let me think about it." On the other hand, we might respond directly and intensely, "Right now? I can't, it is impossible!" or "I honestly don't feel like it after what happened earlier" or "Sure, no problem, I'd love to!"

We act as skillfully as we can. We keep our eye on the ball, as the expression goes, not losing sight of our objectives so that we can really be effective. If we need to practice regulating our own emotions during our interactions with our loved ones, we can practice being mindful of our own emotions and feelings through the day. Brief, but intense and focused practices of being mindful in daily routine activities can have a big payoff over time. It is not quantity, but quality that counts. We can take just a few minutes two or three times each day to observe our breathing and become centered in the present.

The formal practice

What we have seen up to this point is how to be more present in our daily lives. We can further refine our attention through a regular, formal practice. This increases the benefits of mindfulness in direct proportion with the cumulative amount of time spent practicing. We do engage in a formal practice to be better meditators. We do a formal practice to have more concentration, mental clarity, and emotional balance in our daily activities!

Formal practice can be done sitting, lying down or standing. We keep the body still with the back straight, the chest open, and the head balanced over the shoulders. We decide where to focus the attention, such as the movements in the abdomen with each breath, or the feeling of air entering and leaving the nose. Once we bring our attention to the breath, we could anchor the attention even more by counting the breaths.

The diagram, "Mindfulness: A process of training the attention," illustrates each step of the formal practice, although it can be applied to the informal practice -- and also just about any endeavor that requires our attention.

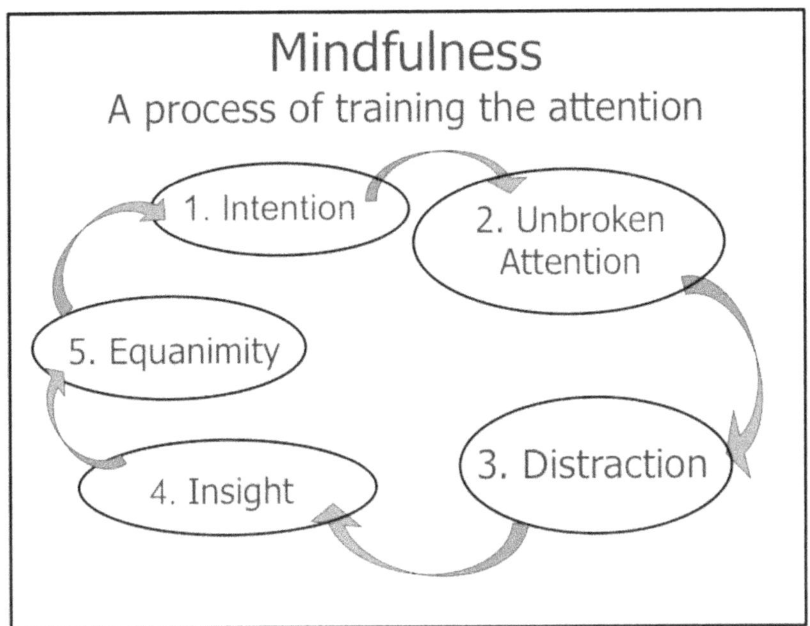

Step 1. Intention. Just try to put your attention on one complete breath. Inhale and exhale. Great, let's suppose the "intention" was clear and you successfully oriented your attention on your breath.

Step 2. Concentration. Did you sustain all of your attention on one breath from start to finish? (Try it again if you did not the first time.) We all get to Step 2 and most of us can attain unbroken concentration during one breath. If we continue this practice we will automatically move to step three.

Step 3. Distraction. We continue attending to the breath, but sooner or later the mind wanders away to something else. It is normal and it happens to everyone. We are no longer attending to our breath, we are in the "simulator," that is, in our heads relating to our thoughts as if they were reality. At this moment we are no longer connected with our breath nor with any other sensorial experience.

Step 4. Insight. This is the moment when we realize that our minds have wandered. It is not clear exactly how this happens but it seems that some type of sensorial experience arises and pulls us out of our heads. It could be a sound, a feeling, or something catches our eye and we are present once again.

Actually, in Step 4, two very important things happen almost simultaneously. The first is that we realize we were thinking. We see our thoughts as thoughts and we cease to experience them as reality. At the same time we remember our intention. We realize we are distracted and we remember what we wanted to be doing. This is a moment of clarity and insight. So mindfulness may be simply remembering over and over again to be present, to pay attention according to our intention.

Step 5. Equanimity. Now most people start out thinking that Step 2, Concentration, is the most important. Then they conclude that Step 4, Insight, is the most important. However, in my own experience, Step 5, Equanimity, is really the most important step in all of the practice.

At the beginning, the most frequent reaction to the insight that one is distracted from one's intention is usually frustration or self-criticism. This is a priceless opportunity for developing an awareness that holds whatever arises in our experience with acceptance and friendliness. At first we may have to accept self-criticism has arisen. We hold the self-criticism within our friendly awareness and we may have to really apply kindness and compassion to ourselves. Eventually we find that we can openly accept that we were lost in thought with a friendly awareness, without the slightest rise of frustration or self-criticism, and observe how our attention returns to the object of intention. This is one way to develop the calm centeredness of equanimity even in the face of something we don't like or don't want to happen.

After step 5, we go back to step one and, once again, we reorient our attention to the object of our intention. Each step engages our brains in a different way. The more we practice, the more we are rewiring our brains to put our attention where we want it, to bring it back when we are distracted, and to respond to ourselves with kindness and equanimity when things go differently than we intended.

Practice 4. Mindfully Sitting

with the attention focused on the breath and the posture

Sitting in a chair, relaxed, with the body in a symmetrical position and the back straight, let your attention rest on the movements of your abdomen as you breathe. Feel the expansion and relaxation of the abdomen with each inhale and exhale. When other thoughts enter your mind, observe them and bring the attention back to the breath and the movements of the abdomen. With an attitude of gentleness and acceptance of your mental activity, you return your attention to the breath each time you notice that it has wandered.

If it helps, you may count each inhale and each exhale from one to ten and begin over again at one when you reach ten. Whatever judgmental or critical thought comes up, try to let it go and observe your breath and your counting with kindness and compassion for yourself. Try this for at least ten minutes and no more than twenty-five minutes.

Validation is mindful dialogue

The formal practice helps us be present and centered in our daily interactions. How do we communicate mindfully? We pay attention with our eyes and ears. We observe them while they are talking without looking around or attending to other things. We are also fully aware of our own emotions without acting on them. We respond out of presence and wisdom. When we speak, we speak slowly and clearly. We are open to experiences as they arise without reacting to resist or change them. Every time we realize that we are distracted, we bring our attention back.

Being fully present helps us to notice the urge to speak. Before opening our mouths we have the opportunity to check if others are still speaking and, if so, to let go of that urge and return to fully listening. We do not talk over others or interrupt them. When we speak, our words are precious and truthful. We describe without being judgmental or pejorative. We are fully present with our inner experience and with the others.

Being mindful trains us to *listen more effectively* and *respond more reflectively*. We will find mindfulness to be a skill that is useful in reducing conflict and developing a more stable and empathic relationship with our friends and family. This is the foundation of genuine validation.

～

CHAPTER SUMMARY

Our brains are constantly rewiring themselves. New neuronal connections grow and unused connections wither away throughout our entire lives. What we do repeatedly with our brains grows stronger. In fact, we are always reinforcing some mental pattern. So ask yourself, what mental qualities do you want to experience more: Equanimity or instability? Wisdom or confusion? Contentment or resentment?

If we criticize or worry consistently, then we will get better at that activity. If we react with anger and then fuel the fire with self-righteous ruminating, our lives will be filled with more and more irritation and frustration. If we practice mindlessly letting our attention wander and jumping from one thing to another, or changing our minds, our focus and our intentions, then we strengthen the habits of obsessive, compulsive, distracted, and/or delusional thinking.

On the other hand, if we persistently focus our intention and attention without distraction on qualities we desire, then we will develop these qualities. For example, if we regularly practice empathy or equanimity or if we practice inclining our attention toward kindness and compassion, then we will develop new patterns and new habits. If we bring our attention to our bodies and let go of tension over and over, we will become more relaxed in our everyday lives.

Presence is being fully connected to here and now, just as it is. It is important to actively cultivate presence in daily routine activities such as eating and bathing or in mini-practices of bringing the attention to the breath several times a day. Sitting still in silent meditation for more than ten minutes several times a week helps to further lay the groundwork for being present in our daily lives.

Presence is fundamental to the practice of genuine validation. We learn to be deeply present with our own experience as well as fully attentive to the other person, to their feelings, their words, and their deeds.

Cultivating mindfulness

1. Being mentally present

- Mindfulness is paying attention to what we are doing, while we are doing it, to be present with what is going on around us, and to see clearly our own internal experience.
- We are open-minded and accepting of what is happening in the present.
- Presence can be cultivated. We are present and we sustain our attention on our own experience, what we see, hear, and feel.

Validating with mindfulness

1. Focusing attention on the other

- Listen, listen, listen. We listen with our whole mind and body to the words that the other is saying.
- We give full attention to the tone of voice, facial expressions, body language, behaviors, and personal space.
- We actively seek to understand their inner experience: feelings, desires, thoughts, and needs.
- Listening mindfully is good for our relationships and good for our own health.

2. Attending to our own experience while in dialogue

- We bring our awareness to ourselves.
- We stop insisting, correcting, or giving our opinion or advice, and instead listen, this can change the course of the entire conversation for the better.
- We are aware of our emotions and we do not respond from an emotional state of mind.
- We try to be honest, consistent, and congruent with our thoughts, words, and actions.
- We notice if we are being judgmental or disapproving.
- We are not jumping to conclusions nor trying to think about the "correct" or appropriate response.

3. Responding effectively in emotional crisis

- We are aware of what we want in an interaction and we seek to be effective at achieving our goal instead of proving a point or winning an argument.
- We practice remaining calm and present.
- We act as skillfully as we can.

4. Mindful dialogue

- We listen.
- We do not interrupt.
- We observe the other with our eyes and ears. We speak slowly, clearly, and truthfully without being judgmental.
- We remain mindfully open to our own experience.

The formal practice

- We take 10-25 minutes a day to practice mindfulness (walking or sitting, focused or open attention) in silence, responding with acceptance and kindness toward ourselves each time that the mind wanders from the breath.
- This builds concentration power to help us be more present and centered in our daily lives.

5

ACCEPTANCE

The boundary to what we can accept is the boundary to our freedom.

— TARA BRACH

Bring your attention to your body. Let go of any tension that you notice and relax into your breath. Now imagine the possibility of feeling complete and total acceptance of what is happening at this very moment. Imagine accepting every problem, every situation, and everything that you are experiencing in your life right now. Imagine accepting the entire world, the entire universe even, just as it is. Take two or three minutes to soak in this practice. Afterward, how do you feel?

Most people feel relief when they practice acceptance. Acceptance frees us from fear and suffering. Acceptance is an attitude and a way

91

of thinking that is absolutely necessary for effective validation. It is openness and willingness to experience the present situation with an infinite curiosity—whether such experience is pleasant, unpleasant, or neutral. We let go of our habits of judging and comparing whatever is to how it should be. We begin to see a lot more of the reality that we missed with all of our critical thinking.

Dogen, a thirteenth-century Zen master, once said, "A flower fades and falls even though we love it. A weed grows and spreads even though we do not love it."[1] We may understand our lives in this way. Life includes both joy and pain, and we can't really stop these things from arising and passing. If we are invested in keeping a flower in full bloom or stopping weeds from growing, we will be very frustrated. Thinking that things shouldn't be this way will not change reality. Once we accept the fading flowers and the growing weeds of our lives as part of nature, we begin to find personal freedom.

Acceptance liberates us from the need to chase happiness and avoid pain—a frustrating path that many of us spend a substantial part of our daily lives trying to follow. Accepting whatever is, exactly as it is, leads us to freedom. We might go even further to say that happiness is not the goal. The real goal is liberation from the need to be happy all the time. Acceptance is the path that leads us there.

All this can seem like pretty remote philosophy when we are confronted with emotional pain, intense conflict, or tough problems. Acceptance can seem pretty impossible at the moment that another person is being critical of us, telling us what we should do or how to do it. We may be hooked into anger or fear and with good reason. Metaphors about weeds and flowers may be pretty but can seem pretty irrelevant.

BUILDING TRUST

At work, at school, and at home, trust is fundamental to positive relationships, smooth communication, teamwork, and group effectiveness. If we can't let go of our own judgments and evaluations of another person, we are distancing ourselves from the other person. Judgments and criticism damage relationships. Instead of seeing the other person for who he or she really is, we are seeing an image of our own creation. Maybe we really do find him to fall short of our desires or expectations. Maybe we see how much trouble he has reaching his own goals. Is it possible to stop for a moment, stop pushing for change, change, change, let go of clinging to our own frustration, anxiety, or contempt, and just simply accept—radically accept—exactly what the other is saying and doing, at least for a moment?

When we carry around judgments, we are seeing others through our distorted vision of how we *think they are* and comparing that to how we *think they should be.* It is not a good way to develop a relationship. Imagine having a "friend" who smiles and says polite things to you, but all the while you are getting indirect communication that he is judgmental of your personal choices, critical of what you do, comparing how you respond to how he responds, often evaluating the things you have done. One day, he manages to come up with a few validating words. Is he suddenly going to make your list of trustworthy friends with whom you can share your dreams and frustrations? Of course not! Until he accepts you totally for who you are without judging or criticizing or correcting you, you will never be able to trust him to confirm anything about how you feel. When we feel accepted by another, we are more likely to open ourselves to the other and tell them how we are feeling and what we are experiencing.

Most people think that trust is constructed as a result of making and keeping promises. I propose, however, that total acceptance of another person for who he or she is can be more fundamental to the construction of trust than just keeping promises. I am more likely to trust someone who accepts me exactly as I am, without criticism and without wanting to change me, than I am willing to trust someone who merely follows through on his commitments. Being judgmental and critical of another is invalidating and it is so common. People sometimes get together and seem to enjoy sitting around and criticizing others. It probably does more relationship damage than just about any other behavior.

People who have a very rational approach to life sometimes have difficulty understanding the role and importance of cultivating a genuinely accepting attitude as a means to deepening trust and communication in a relationship. One such rational father described his relationship with his twenty-nine-year-old daughter when he first learned about validation:

"I love my daughter, Angela, even if she is not turning out like I expected. I don't understand why she won't talk to me. She is always angry and I just want what is best for her. . . Last week I validated her anger, even though it was way out of proportion with what had happened. And she wants to become a nun and go live in another country. I tried to validate her desire and I suggested that she might try to contact the convent near where her brother lives—he knows some people there –and she just got mad at me again and hasn't spoke to me since. Every time I try to validate and help, she just gets mad at me and walks off in a huff."

This dad can't stop judging his daughter and telling her what she "should" do or telling her how to run her life. And whether he critiques her directly or not, he is surely communicating to her that she can never make a good decision for herself. Of course his daughter is angry at him all the time. He believes that he knows better than her how to manage her life! His judgmental attitude was apparent to everyone in the room as he described this situation to others.

It can be difficult at home or at work to let go of judging, criticizing, and controlling—that is, to really let go from the bottom of the heart. Part of the job of supervising others or managing the work of others involves evaluating their work and telling them what to do. Radical acceptance can seem contradictory to these roles, and indeed many people find it especially difficult to develop an open and accepting attitude toward others who are different. At work many of us spend enormous amounts of time thinking that things should *not* be as they are, that others should be more one way and less another. Though it may seem counterintuitive, practicing acceptance of things just as they are—even if they are imperfect, inefficient, or mistaken—might reduce our own anxiety or frustration and eventually help us to be more effective at making changes for the better.

Acceptance is not simply keeping our mouths shut and stifling our verbal criticism of others. If the heart has not fully accepted, then the facial expression, tone of voice, and unsaid words communicate judgment or disapproval loud and clear. This does not mean that there is no place for trying to change the behavior of others—such as requesting, negotiating, or rewarding behavioral changes. It is just that acceptance is the first step—prior to effectively creating change. Acceptance is a profound connection with the present moment with a level of interest and curiosity that becomes a silent inquiry into what is really happening. It is a scientist observing the result of an experiment. Everything that is observed in the present moment is fully accepted with curiosity, openness, and even wonder.

Acceptance liberates us from the endless automatic thoughts and emotional reactions that come from believing the *should bes*—for instance, "Life should be fair," or "Things should be different," or "It shouldn't be like this." Well, right now it is like this.

When you hear your internal voice saying such things, ask yourself, why *should* that situation be different? Because it's not fair . . . And why should that be fair? Because it's not right . . . And why should things be right? . . . If you keep asking yourself that question, at the end of the day, all those moralistic *should bes* just boil down to "That's how I want it to be."[2] What you are feeling is a personal desire for things to be different—a desire for the world to be better or a desire to be happier. This incessant desire for things to be different seems simple enough, but it is really at the root of a gnawing restlessness that can grow into something very painful.

Imagine a totally open experience of accepting whatever arises in the present moment. We feel what we feel; it's just like this, nothing more and nothing less. Maybe it's uncomfortable, but that's just the way it is right now. We also accept whatever another person is feeling, exactly as they are feeling it, in the present moment. There is no resisting or fighting with the present reality. There are no internal judgments and comparisons. It is what it is. Thus we accept. We let go of all the *shoulds* and *have tos*, such as "You have to get a job," "You should not yell at me," or "I should not be sad."

Wait a minute, you may be thinking. *Isn't this just giving up? How can I surrender to such hopelessness?* Perhaps the concept of surrender is useful—up to a point. If we surrender to a feeling of fear, we may finally allow ourselves to feel it. We may finally stop trying to calm down, relax, or minimize the fear and instead approach it and experience it. There may be a microsecond in which the experience of surrender and acceptance intersect. But if surrender implies closing our eyes and giving up all hope and expectation of things ever being different, then that is not acceptance. Surrender is passive; acceptance is active. Acceptance is looking at something, being with the experience, actively and curiously approaching it—as a scientist might approach his work. Acceptance investigates what is going on. And acceptance of things as they are will keep us present to these things as they change. Surrender will not support presence.

Eugenia was a receptionist at a law firm. She was generally outgoing and positive, but she was easily distracted, her self-confidence was low, and the approval of others was very important to her. A few administrators and paralegals criticized her attitude and tried to correct her way of completing assignments. These critiques and advice only served to heighten her insecurity. Eugenia became more anxious and defensive about her work. Soon her colleagues were sharing stories of her bad attitude and her mistakes. She began to feel downright paranoid. She arrived at home stressed and resentful of her job. She was no longer the cheerful and positive receptionist who'd been hired for the job. Eventually she quit to avoid the negative, judgmental attitude around her.

Eugenia's colleagues might have practiced more acceptance and patience. Instead of jumping to conclusions about her, they might have asked her if she needed help or just had more patience that comes with acceptance. Eugenia did find a company where she was accepted and treated as a valued person even if she did not get everything correct right away. A little validation of her emotions helped her remain centered and positive. As her confidence grew, so did her competence and skills.

Perhaps the most insidious way to destroy mental well-being is cling to judgmental and critical thoughts - about ourselves as well as others. With little effort, but a lot of repetition, we can begin to see these negative thoughts for what they are and let go of them. We can see how damaging they are to ourselves and others. Others become a reflection of what we believe about them, and we lose the possibility of an authentic relationship.

Victoria, a college professor, and her daughter Cheryl had a long history of conflict. At age seventeen, Cheryl announced that she was dropping out of high school. This was unacceptable to Victoria and she was furious with her daughter.

Cheryl's father stepped in. He tried to understand her world from her point of view. He tried hard not to be judgmental of her even if he did not agree with her decisions. During these conversations, he asked her if she might be interested in taking a couple of classes at the local community college. He offered to go with her to find out more about it. She agreed and eventually enrolled.

Long after Cheryl had struck out on her own, Victoria was still critical of Cheryl—including her weight and her eating choices, how she handled her job, and her relationship with her boyfriend. This functioned to keep her daughter distant from her and did nothing to improve her own well-being, while her daughter was flourishing more and more each year!

Dear Self,
You are not perfect. Nor will you ever be!
And it's OK.
Love,
Me
XXOO

To move toward letting go of judgments, criticisms, and comparisons, we must practice with ourselves. We are often our own worst critics. We expect ourselves to be perfect in so many ways. If we are constantly comparing ourselves to a higher standard of achievement, we will generate disappointment, frustration, and anxiety.

Many people get caught up in a spiral of self-criticism. Whatever they do, it's never enough. They hardly appreciate their own determination and effort when they do reach a goal. They minimize its importance while eyeing an even higher standard of achievement. Every little mistake is played over and over again in their heads. The inner critic is in charge. Peace of mind is impossible to achieve. We destroy our own mental well-being by mentally beating ourselves up day after day.

We need to notice our internal critics. We need to treat ourselves—including our internal critics—with more kindness. As Kristin Neff points out, her internal critic wants the same thing that her whole self wants: to achieve satisfaction, peace of mind, and/or joy. [3]

If we focus only on the fact that we *have to* be the best or that we *should* be better, we are blinding ourselves to reality and bringing suffering upon ourselves. The more we compare ourselves with others who are smarter, happier, more talented, or better at just about anything, we are likely to generate self-despair. As we nurture an attitude of acceptance toward ourselves, acceptance of our feelings and reactions, acceptance of our intentions and where we are in our journeys, we will move toward self-validation and find life to be more satisfying.

Our own emotional responses are important to acknowledge and accept. I may be anxious that my loved one will get angry, so I either avoid saying what I really feel or yield to most of her demands. I may be afraid that my loved one will act impulsively and injure himself, so I do whatever I can to try and keep the peace. It is really important to acknowledge and accept my own emotions and my own deficits in managing my needs and limits. I accept my internal emotional experience *and* I work toward making changes both internally and externally. Balance.

Many of us, at one time or another, find ourselves on an acceptance roller coaster. It gets really complicated when emotional arousal is high. The automatic judgments seem to slip back in despite our best intentions to be accepting. But remember, things are not right or wrong; they are just things that we don't like. And we want them to change them. And our judgments, our *should bes*, in turn, increase our emotional arousal. Before we get ourselves into an extreme emotional state, we must take the opportunity to practice when we are totally calm or only slightly irritated or nervous so we can start changing old habits and patterns of thinking and acting.

STAGES OF ACCEPTANCE

When we *accept* instead of judging, evaluating, or thinking that things should be different, this is a big *change*. And it is an internal change that changes our reactions to situations. This silent, internal change in one's own attitude causes changes in the responses of others. Perhaps they get less defensive or more open to admitting their fears or seeking help with problem solving. Communication and trust improve.

So let us enter the paradox and begin to make profound changes within ourselves by radically accepting all that is, such as it is, in the present moment, in ourselves, in our loved ones, at our jobs, in our communities, our government, and in all those around us. After all, not accepting reality does not change it. And changing reality requires an acceptance of the facts of reality.

The first step toward acceptance is being aware that we have the choice to accept. When we notice ourselves turning away from the path of acceptance, it is possible to turn our minds back. We often find that we must accept over and over. We may have to let go of discouragement, shame, and guilt to accept once again. And we may wake up tomorrow and have to make the decision once again to put in the effort to let go of resisting reality. We need to be willing to respond to each situation wholeheartedly and without reservation or reluctance. We respond to the present moment, ready to do just what is needed. We approach with compassion for ourselves, our loved ones, the current situation, and even the whole universe. Nothing less. We do not try to fix things or to be in control, nor do we sit on our hands when action is needed. Instead we act from our wise mind and our open heart.

How do we accept someone's chaotic, aggressive reactions or the judgments and criticisms that fly out of the mouths of others? How do we accept hurtful comments? These are not effective behaviors that we want to validate! Acceptance is dialectical. We can accept that *this person [he, she, we, or I] is doing the best they can, given all the conditions in a specific situation. And yes, indeed, at the same time it is possible that they could do even better.* These dialectical conditions are at once distinct and also totally integrated. When I am doing the best I can in the moment, there is an inherent and continuous belief that I can do better. What about when I felt I was slacking off? I wasn't doing the best I could. Yet if we really examine all the antecedents and causes for why I was knowingly slacking off, everything from the thoughts I had at that moment to all the events in my whole life that came before, we would have to agree that, given all the things that led up to this moment, slacking off was, in fact, the best I could have done in the moment.

A lot of acceptance is about the past and the present. We cannot change the past and, believe it or not, we cannot change this present moment. In this very second, everything is as it is. Yet it is also obvious that everything is in a constant state of change. Nothing in our universe is permanently stable. We are all just like the flowers that fade and fall. Sometimes we get caught up in emotional reactions, thinking that things will always be a certain way forever. Rest assured, that is patently untrue. The future is uncertain but it will certainly be different from the present.

Acceptance often emerges in fits and starts. It can be episodic—periods of acceptance and periods of denial. Acceptance can occur in stages. Christopher Germer describes these stages clearly:

After an initial bout of aversion, we start the process with curiosity about the problem and, if all goes well, end with a full embrace of whatever is occurring in our lives. The process is usually slow and natural. It makes no sense to advance to the next stage until you're entirely comfortable with where you are at the moment. The stages are:

1. Aversion—resistance, avoidance, rumination

2. Curiosity—turning toward discomfort with interest

3. Tolerance—safely enduring

4. Allowing—letting feelings come and go

5. Friendship—embracing, seeing hidden value

Our first, instinctive reaction to uncomfortable feelings is always aversion. For example, we avert our gaze when we see something unpleasant. Aversion can also take the form of mental entanglement or rumination—trying to figure out how to remove the feeling. After a while, when aversion doesn't work, we enter stage 2: curiosity. "What is that feeling?" "When does it happen?" "What does it mean?" When we know what we're dealing with, and if the pain doesn't go away, we may enter stage 3: tolerance. Tolerance means "enduring" emotional pain, but we're still resisting it and wishing it would go away. As our resistance erodes, we enter the fourth stage—allowing—letting difficult feelings come and go on their own. Finally, as our lives adapt and deepen, we may find ourselves in the friendship stage, where we actually see hidden value in our predicament.[4]

Practice 1: Accepting Hands

Try practicing acceptance. Bring to mind something that you need to accept. It could be a present situation, current behavioral patterns or habits of yourself or someone else, or something that happened in the past. Try not to use something that has to do with the future, especially medium and long-term, since we cannot predict what will happen in the future. Before proceeding with the exercise, decide what stage of acceptance you are at in the present moment regarding this issue (1-5). Once you have decided on one specific thing that you need to accept, check to make sure that is definitely reality based on actual facts. "This line is moving slowly" or "It should not take so long" are both judgments. "It is slower than I expected," or "I am feeling impatient and I want to leave" are better descriptions of reality based on facts without judgments.

Once you decide what you need to practice accepting, put it into words. Mentally repeat it on each exhale, imagining a slow, calm and relaxed tone of voice. While repeating it on each exhale, rest your attention on the sensations of your hands for a few minutes in any of the following postures:

Standing up - Relax your shoulders and bend your elbows to bring your palms face up. Leave your hands unclenched, fingers relaxed and slightly separated.

Seated - Place your hands on your lap or thighs. Leave your hands unclenched, palms up, fingers relaxed and thumbs slightly separated.

Lying down - Place your arms at a 45 degree angle out to your sides, with your palms face up and your fingers relaxed open.

After completing the exercise, notice if your level of acceptance (1-5) changed at all as a result of this exercise.

Observing

Most unsolicited advice and criticism generates a response of defensiveness, anger, disappointment, or sadness. Perhaps our intention is to help someone and we don't mean to be critical or judgmental. Perhaps we are defending ourselves, trying to prove ourselves correct and, hence, the other wrong. As long as we are making comparisons, telling another what they should do or how they should be, we are criticizing their way of doing or being. This can be hurtful and can shut down communication with others. And the more sensitive the other is or the closer the relationship, the more it can hurt.

If you are a parent, a manager, or in any type of leadership position, it has been your job to make comparisons about others and see how they measure up to norms and standards. You have spent years doing your best to guide, teach, advise, correct, and just help others make their way in the world with as little suffering as possible. Of course you are kind and compassionate and that is pure acceptance, right? Well . . . not exactly.

Let's take a step back to understand how we can be totally accepting and at the same time genuine when our friend, colleague, or loved one is not acting in their own best interest, is ineffective at reaching their goals, or is even increasing their own pain and suffering. Perhaps an adult child is living independently but their choices often result in failure. Or an aging parent is critical and irritated at seemingly everything. Or our spouse or a co-worker are often arguing and in conflict. How can we accept such behavior?

One key acceptance strategy is just observing. What we can see, hear, or touch is a fact in the present moment. We let go of trying to deny, ignore, or change the facts or the reality that we cannot change in the present moment. OK, so my kid is smoking pot, drinking beer, throwing things, starving herself, or even disappearing for the weekend. Whatever is reality, we accept as reality. Acceptance doesn't mean we like it or approve of it. We just accept the facts and let go of judging as "good" or "bad." We describe what we see and hear, touch, smell, or taste. If we don't, then in the middle of those events we are so tempted to judge and find unacceptable, we will probably not notice exactly what is going on.

Acceptance does not mean that we give up all hope for change. We can be accepting of the present reality and simultaneously hope for change. We cannot close our eyes to the situation, but we can let go of automatically reacting. We absorb it all. We accept it all so that we can fully understand the situation. Then we can respond in a measured way in which our goal is to be effective. A judgmental and non-accepting response usually is one that is aimed at just removing our own anxiety or discomfort with the situation.

This is not to say that if we saw someone trying to jump out a window, we would not immediately move to stop them. *Of course we would!* We would do everything possible to stop them from doing so. Remember, we validate only what is valid. When someone's life or health is clearly in imminent danger, responding effectively takes priority over everything else. And when the immediate danger passes, or even perhaps after a longer period to allow everyone's emotional states to cool down, then we can ask what happened. We will be far more effective with an attitude of openness and acceptance, listening deeply to what our loved one has to say without injecting automatic responses based on our own fear.

Sam had been able to give up drugs, but he could not give up his angry rages. Every time he would get angry and throw things, his mom, Maria, would start to cry. Maria would automatically think something like, *Not again! He is never going to be able to manage his life. He will never get this right.* She would feel utterly hopeless, powerless, and desperate. Worse, if she thought the neighbors could hear, she would feel deep embarrassment. Meanwhile, when Sam's mother started crying, he would think, *She's trying to make me feel worse. She is useless.* With these thoughts, he would get even more angry—and kick a wall or a door or something else even harder.

Sam's mom, Maria, first had to learn to manage her own fear and sadness so that she could begin to practice acceptance of his emotion without responding passively to his behavior. One day she was able to say "Yes, Sam, it is frustrating as hell. I know you are furious and your situation is tough. Feeling angry makes perfect sense. I get it. I also want you to know that if you keep yelling at me or break something, I will open that door and walk out. I refuse to stay here and watch you further destroy yourself, your things, or me . . . And afterward I will expect you to repair whatever you damaged, including your relationship with me."

If we can begin to observe our judgments and let go of immediate and intense desires to make things different, then we can slow down our automatic reactions and lower the intensity of our emotions. At the same time, we open ourselves up what is happening, to an empirical understanding of a situation or an experience. Remember, we can't make everything all better for anyone else. It's impossible. With acceptance and validation, we can leave the responsibility for solving a problem where it belongs—with the person who owns the problem. This does not mean that we roll over and play dead or that we just say yes!

Marshall Rosenberg offers various tools to distinguish between observations and evaluations as a fundamental basis for his work in nonviolent communication. Rosenberg points out that combining observation with evaluation is likely to cause others to hear criticism and resist what we are saying. Observations are concrete descriptions with a specific time, place, and context. Evaluations may be inferences, analyses, opinions, generalizations, etc. When evaluations become fused with observations, communication can become invalidating.

For example, "You are being stubborn" is not an observation; it is an evaluation. On the other hand, we might be descriptive without being judgmental: "I made three specific suggestions, and you explained to me why you don't want to try any of them. I can't think of any other way to do it." Such an observation opens dialogue and invites the other to respond. Read the following examples of evaluations, followed by observations. Notice how the evaluation has an underlying message of criticism and the description seems to be more accepting of the present reality, without necessarily approving of it.

- Evaluation: "You never listen to me."
- Observation: "I am talking to you and you keep looking down at the newspaper. It gives me the impression that you are not listening to me."

- Evaluation: "She is always asking for money and she can't control her spending."
- Observation: "Yesterday I gave her $100 to buy a pair of sneakers and she bought makeup, hair accessories, and ice cream instead of the sneakers that she told me she needed."

- Evaluation: "You are so unreliable."
- Observation: "You said you would be here at 4:00 and it's 5:15."

- Evaluation: "He is manipulative."
- Observation: "Yesterday when I told him 'no,' he began to plead with me and made promises to clean his room every day if I would say yes. We had a loud discussion for 20 minutes. When I finally said OK, he suddenly smiled and his tone of voice became soft and pleasant."

Practice observing and describing without evaluating, interpreting, or judging. Practice when you are alone with your thoughts. Practice when you are in a conversation at work, at home, or anywhere.

Practice 2. Deepening Acceptance From Within

Choose any moment of a situation in which you are interacting with another person. Mentally describe to yourself everything that you observe the other doing and saying in completely non/judgmental terms. Just the facts.

Then turn your attention inward and observe and describe to yourself all the internal feelings, emotions, and thoughts that you have as a result of what the other does or says. Notice any discomfort and any urges to make the discomfort go away.

Turn your attention back to observing the other person, then turn your attention to observe and describe your own inner experience once again. Go back and forth for a few minutes. If you have the opportunity to write down your observations, thoughts and feelings afterwards you may find it to be an interesting and useful exercise.

Acceptance starts silently from within our hearts. Acceptance is the absence of giving advice, trying to make things different, or anticipating the future. Acceptance is being open to what arises in the present moment just as it is. We try to understand the internal subjective experience of our loved one (emotions, feelings, sensations, opinions, and beliefs) as well as the context in which the experience takes place.

We "shed all preconceived ideas and judgments about the other person. We freely turn the floor over to them while we empty the mind and allow our whole being to become one big ear."[5]

Let's take a step back and start with a simple statement that someone says and then we will see examples of how we can validate this statement with acceptance. This validation with acceptance can be given regardless of whether we agree with a statement.

1. Reflect back without judgment

Someone says *"Tom is a stupid jerk. I can't stand him."* How can we possible validate this statement, especially if we disagree? If we have been practicing acceptance, it should be obvious that we are not going to correct this statement, we are not going to criticize it, and we are not going to try to evaluate it. It is not our job to agree or disagree but to validate what is valid with total acceptance—that is, nonjudgmentally. Without approving or disapproving such a statement, without evaluating whether it is effective, we can reflect back what we understand—to determine whether or not we understand. If not, we can ask for more information.

Possible responses that just reflect or clarify what we understand may include the following:

1. "Ok. So if I get this right, you think Tom is a jerk."
2. "Wow, you really don't like Tom, do you?"

When we reflect back, our tone of voice can express surprise or it may be useful to reflect back just a little of the tone of voice that was used by the other person (a hint of the emotional tone of voice, in this case probably frustration or anger expressed by the speaker).

Reflecting back was a communication strategy first promoted by Carl Rogers, the founder of humanistic psychology. Although effective, the simplicity of reflecting back was probably responsible for some of the criticism that erupted over this therapeutic technique. Rogers put of end to the controversy by saying that his real goal is not to just "reflect back feelings," but to determine if his understanding of the other person's inner world is correct. "Each response...contains that unspoken question, 'Is this the way it is in you? Am I catching just the color and texture and flavor of the personal meaning your are experiencing right now? If not, I wish to bring my perception in line with yours.' " However, Rogers was clear that reflecting back was beneficial for the other person too, noting, "I know that from the client's point of view we are holding up a mirror of his or her current experiencing. The feelings and personal meanings seem sharper when seen through the eyes of another, when they are reflected."[6]

2. Ask what happened with acceptance

We can also communicate acceptance by not correcting, but asking for more information. Remember that with a beginner's mind we are not prejudiced by the past, thinking *not again* or *what now*. We try to explore the facts of the situation from the perspective of an unbiased, outside observer. However, we cannot confuse facts with thoughts, beliefs, opinions, or emotions, and we need to remain clear about their separation. We definitely need to understand and practice separating these things. If beliefs, emotions, and opinions seem to be confusing, consulting chapter 2 can help us disentangle thoughts, feelings, and actions when another is describing a situation.

1. "So how did you arrive at that evaluation of Tom?"
2. "What happened?"
3. "Did he do something that made you angry?"
4. "... Then what happened? ... And what did you do?"

We must remember, at this stage, there are only two reasons to speak —to check that we understand or to ask for clarification, repetition, or more contextual information. We are not trying to change the other person's mind, we are not trying to solve their problem, and we are not trying to teach them anything. We are listening to learn. As we listen, we try to relate to what the other is saying. If the story is complicated, then for each major point, we need to make a sentence to confirm that we are getting what they are trying to put across. We check it out with the other and we let them correct it, if necessary, and add to it if they want to. We take it in and we 'say back' what they have changed or added, until they agree that we have said it just as they feel it.

3. Communicate acceptance of an opinion—as an opinion

We can look for opinions and accept them as opinions, not as a fact. Everyone is entitled to their opinion, right? (It will not help to say that!) We want to communicate interest, curiosity, and acceptance of an opinion.

1. "Sounds like you have a pretty strong opinion about Tom."
2. "Tom must have done something really stupid to give you that opinion of him."

Note: If we are engaged in dialogue with a person who regularly tends to minimize their feelings, we should really stick with steps 1, 2, and 3 until there is clear agreement and confirmation from the other that we "get it." Moving on to the next step too quickly with someone who denies their feelings will sabotage the trust that we are trying to build. For some people, it may be quite a while before we get there.

4. Communicating acceptance of feelings

For many people, especially emotionally sensitive persons, the most effective acceptance strategy may be to identify the emotion that is felt by the other, rather than the actual words. Remember, *the emotional experience is always valid*. We can communicate acceptance by stating what we observe that indicates what emotion the other is experiencing. Responses of this type may include the following:

1. "Yeah, I can imagine Tom being really irritating."
2. "Wow. Tom must have done something to really piss you off!"
3. "It sounds like you are really angry with Tom."

Notice how each of these statements reflect a personal observation. An observation does not tell the other what they should be feeling. They don't begin with the word "you." Instead the subject is I or he or it. "I" am the one who hears or sees evidence of an emotional expression. "He" engaged in an action. "It seems like," or "It seems to me." In all cases, we want to avoid starting acceptance statements with "You" because they can be interpreted as accusations, especially when we are speculating and we are mistaken. "You are angry" can be met by "I am NOT angry!!" or even "No. I am feeling sad, but now that you've accused me of being angry I'm pissed off . . ." We generally want to avoid starting acceptance sentences with "you."

We communicate to other people that emotional responses are understandable and make sense, especially in the current circumstances. When emotions are already aroused, we focus on acceptance. When emotions have cooled, we can discuss strategies for change. While our young friend is boiling with anger at Tom, it would be invalidating and ineffective to try to convince him to forgive and forget. He would most likely defend himself and his anger would probably increase.

Our young friend who is angry at Tom is an example of someone who is in using emotional mind and using few words. On the other hand, some people talk a lot and hardly seem to take a breath. Eugene Gendlin, author of the therapeutic strategy, *Focusing*, describes how we put together this process of listening, reflecting back, and communicating acceptance in a longer and more complex dialogue:

"Suppose a woman has been telling you about some intricate set of events, what some people did to her, and how and when, to "put her down." First, you would say one or more sentences to state in words the crux of what she said as she sees it. Then she corrects some of how you said it, to get it more exactly. You then say back to her corrections: "Oh so it wasn't that they all did that, but all of them *agreed* to do it." Then she might add a few more things, which you again take in and say back more or less as she said them. Then, when you have it just right, you make another sentence for the feeling that the whole thing has, "And what's really bad about it is that it's made you feel put down."[7]

Gendlin goes on to point our that there are three ways to know if we are getting it right. The first is when the other goes deeper into their problems. For example, the person may say, "no it's not like that, it's more like..." While our words may have been wrong, what matters is that the other is engaged in both the dialogue and in moving more deeply into defining and understanding their experience. The second sign of getting it right is if the person sits in silence, satisfied that we understand, or contemplating their own understanding. (I often hear a bell going ding-ding-ding in my head when there is silence because it usually means that something constructive is happening.) The third sign that we are getting it right is that the other person relaxes. Their face may become less tense, they may exhale an audible sigh, or they may sit back in their chair.

Gendlin also indicates two ways that indicate we did it wrong. Either the other person just keeps repeating what they already said or they give up and change the subject. [8] We may just have to let it go for the time being. (Don't worry, the universe delivers endless opportunities to practice acceptance!)

EMOTIONAL ACCEPTANCE - SELF AND OTHER

Acceptance of emotions goes in both directions—outwardly to the other person, and inwardly to ourselves. Amy learned to do this with her husband, Alex, who had a strong temper and would sometimes get to the point of yelling and swearing. Of course she just wanted to run away and leave him when he started screaming. However, she decided to consult a professional to see if there were any strategies that she might use to improve her relationship with her husband, whom she loved in spite of his impulsive temper, and who was kind and generous when he was calm.

After learning about the power of emotional acceptance, she learned to validate his anger when it arose, without her fear taking over and then running away. This was a turning point for her. By fully accepting her fear and fully accepting his suffering in his uncontrolled anger, she found courage. It was courage to open her eyes to the situation and describe it aloud. It was courage to allow her husband to feel what he was feeling and courage take responsibility for her own feelings and needs.

- "It sounds like you're pissed off right now. I'm going to watch television." She would go into another room and watch a movie. Often he would join her, sometimes not.

- "I can see you're angry and I prefer to eat alone." She would leave dinner on the table and carry her plate of food to another room.
- "I feel like you are angry at me and blaming me for your problems. I'll be back in a while." She would get up, collect her things, and go out.

Acceptance is not passively rolling over and accepting rude or even violent behavior without doing anything. On the contrary, acceptance is seeing exactly what is going on, eyes wide open, and responding not out of a desire to avoid or suppress what is happening, but out of a desire to effectively help the other as well as care for oneself. Amy found acceptance, but she had to practice again and again over the next two years. During this period, her husband decided to get some help to manage his anger and it made a huge difference in their relationship.

What if a person's emotion is really *not* acceptable?

Let us not forget that emotions are always valid! Not just emotions, but also moods, temperaments, or whatever internal experience (such as obsessive styles of thinking, difficulty sleeping, worrying, hunger, likes and dislikes) are genuine, authentic, and legitimate internal human experiences and all have underlying causes and antecedents —*even if these feelings are not wholesome or effective.* Emotional validation can be difficult to understand and put into practice for many people, especially when the emotional responses extend into mood, temperaments, and mental disorders. In general, *moods* are more muted and longer-lasting than emotions. For example, one might experience an intense anger for a short period of time, but one could feel irritable all day long. Beyond moods are *temperaments*, the readiness to evoke a given emotion or mood that makes people melancholy, timid, or cheery. And still beyond such emotional dispositions are the outright *disorders*, such as clinical depression, unremitting anxiety, emotional instability or personality disorders.[9]

Whether or not someone meets diagnostic criteria for a disorder at a certain point in their lives, we can be sure that everyone experiences intense emotional suffering sooner or later. When an intense emotion arises, we cannot simply change how we feel. If someone is extremely sensitive, emotionally dramatic, and impulsive, it has serious negative effects on interpersonal relationships. It can be really hard for family, friends, or coworkers to deal with. Others cannot always see mental or emotional "suffering." If this person were unable to walk and confined to a wheelchair, it might be a lot easier to accept their limitations. We might be more inclined to make adjustments to accommodate their suffering. When someone cannot control their emotions or some impulsive behaviors, or when someone habitually avoids contact and over-controls their emotions, it can be hard to understand or accept. If they are angry and their anger is often directed at us, well, that may be the most difficult of all to accept and validate.

Carol's boss was a "screamer." Being in the construction business he often found it effective. When suppliers, architects, or bankers were not getting him what he wanted when he wanted it, he would yell, insult, or threaten them. Often they responded by rushing around to fix the problem so that he would calm down. He received a lot of reinforcement for his bad temper over the years.

Yet Carol's boss never behaved this way with her. She was fully present and patiently listened to him when he described the pressures and priorities he was facing. When he was calm, she was positive, attentive, and helpful. When he was angry, she accepted his anger *without fear* but gave him a lot of space. If his irritation was directed at her, she ignored the sarcasm or subtle attacks and she often took a short break at such moments to give him time to calm down. When she made a mistake, she took full responsibility, without extensively defending herself. Her presence and acceptance had a calming effect on her boss, and he treated her even more respectfully and professionally. Others who tried to tell him to calm down or defended themselves only seemed to inflame his temper.

Carol eventually changed jobs. She learned that her calm demeanor and her nonjudgmental attitude toward others had a powerful effect. She wanted to develop this talent and put it to good use. She eventually moved into corporate mediation, helping individuals and groups to resolve conflict and work together effectively.

What if a person finds their own feelings unacceptable?

Some people are emotionally sensitive, and others are very rational and controlled. (And some people jump back and forth from one extreme to the other.) Emotional validation may not work for a person who regularly denies or minimizes what they are feeling. Think about it. If you are not feeling anything, it would not be useful or validating for me to insist that you really are feeling something, no matter how obvious it might be. It may be more effective to find validity in their thoughts, instead of their feelings. If emotional validation does not work, we can look for how someone's reasoning makes sense, their opinion is interesting, or their desire is important. We all have the right to have our own thoughts, opinions, and desires, and we can communicate acceptance of opinions and desires, even when we disagree with them.

Michael, a college professor had four children. He had always been especially close to his oldest daughter, Paula. She became an all-star athlete in high school with a straight-A average. Her standards were high, but she was low on patience and tolerance for others. As an adult, she took out most of her scorn on her father (who was generally kind and gentle) and stonewalled him for months at a time when he unwittingly said or did something offensive. Paula denied having "feelings about these events." She insisted she wasn't angry, she just did not have anything to say to her father. Michael had learned that validating Paula's emotions was not effective; it tended to deepen her denial and increase her scorn. It was more effective for him to accept her opinions, accept her desire to do things her way, and allow her to follow her own path. He tried his best to listen, asked questions, and communicate interest and acceptance.

Whether a person's emotions are out-of-control or over-controlled, one can look for the emotion to understand and explain at least in some way, their behavior. Yet some people may be disconnected from or in denial of their emotions. Chapter 8 offers validation strategies and approaches that may be useful to improve our relationships with others whom we perceive as emotionally stoic, overly self-controlling, or obsessive and rigid in their style of thinking. Accepting another's thoughts and/or feelings may be the first step toward change--and may be a change in and of itself.

Acceptance involves letting go of judgments and evaluations and allowing reality to be just as it is. When we turn toward our loved ones with acceptance, we build trust and deepen interpersonal relationships. We accept them for who they are and for what they are feeling in the moment. Acceptance is not approval; it is patience and openness to the present moment.

Practicing acceptance is a path to one's own personal freedom. We become observant of our own feelings, sensations, and thoughts and accepting of our own experience just as it is in the moment. We stay with our own experience, our current feelings, even if they are uncomfortable and we want them to go away. For example, we might experience our own anxiety by just being with it and observing it, accepting all its physical sensations fully, without acting on it or trying to make it go away.

Cultivating acceptance

1. Building trust

- We let go of judgments, criticism and comparisons!
- We accept whatever emotional state our loved ones are experiencing.

2. Finding freedom

- We free ourselves from the endless automatic thoughts and emotional reactions that come from believing the *"should bes."*
- We are open to observing, acknowledging and accompanying others' (and our own) emotional experiences.
- We accept that we cannot make everything all better for our loved ones.
- We observe our own emotions in the present moment.

3. Self-acceptance

- We practice accepting our own fear, anger, disappointment, etc. without impulsively acting on them or trying to escape them.
- We observe the high standards that we set for ourselves and we let go of clinging and comparing ourselves to such high standards.

4. Changing the mind toward acceptance

- When we accept things as they are instead of just wanting them to be different, that is a big change.
- Acceptance is a dynamic process that we may have to do over and over again.
- Sometimes we just have to accept how hard it is to fully

accept a situation that we don't like. Sometimes we have to start by accepting our own reaction to the situation.

- Acceptance has stages. It is not exactly a steady and progressive advance. Some days it may feel like it is one step forward and two steps back: **1. Aversion**—resistance, avoidance, rumination. **2. Curiosity**—turning toward discomfort with interest. **3. Tolerance**—safely enduring. **4. Allowing**—letting feelings come and go. **5. Friendship**—embracing, seeing hidden value

Validating with acceptance

1. Observing vs. evaluating

- We do not mix observations with evaluations or judgments. We practice observing and describing the facts of a situation without evaluations or judgments.

2. Verbally communicating acceptance

- We communicate to the other that their responses make sense and are understandable within their current life context or situation.
- We reflect back what we understand without judgment.
- We ask for clarification or context with openness and acceptance.
- We try to identify an opinion with acceptance.
- We try to identify an emotion with acceptance
- We practice accepting whatever feeling, opinion, or desire the other person experiences; it is their human right to feel, think, and want.

3. When emotions are "not acceptable"

- *Even if it is extreme, the emotion is still valid.*

- If the other person denies their own emotional experience, no matter how obvious it may be to others, it is invalidating to insist that they are in an emotional state.
- We can validate opinions and desires as valid and important for the person who experiences them.

We cultivate radical acceptance deep within our own hearts. We may have to choose acceptance over and over again. We also practice observing instead of evaluating. We thoughtfully reflect on an emotional response and we try to see how it makes sense within a given situation. When we practice radical acceptance, our verbal communication is genuinely congruent with what we feel inside, we feel a fuller sense of integrity, and we will be perceived by others as trustworthy.

6

EMPATHY

You can only understand people if you feel them in yourself.

— *J*OHN *S*TEINBECK

Carl Rogers, the founder of humanistic psychology, considered empathy to be a vital component of helping others change their lives for the better. It is one of the fundamental components of nearly all psychological counseling. Rogers defined empathy as:

Perceiving the internal frame of reference of another person with accuracy and with the emotional components and meanings which pertain thereto as if one were the person, but without losing the as-if condition.[1]

This definition aligns with contemporary views of empathy which includes three components:

1. **Emotional recognition** - "*Perceiving. . .with accuracy*" is a largely cognitive component, such as being able to name the emotion or describe the facial expression, gestures, or tone of voice and being able to clearly communicate what is observed. It is not purely cognitive, because if one cannot *feel* an emotion due to faulty neurological functioning for example, one may not recognize this in another person.

2. **Emotional resonance** - "*with the emotional components and meanings which pertain thereto as if one were the person*" is an emotional component in which one actually feels what the other person feels, if only for a brief moment. We need to be able to connect to our internal experience, our own feelings, reactions, beliefs, thoughts, and internal sensations so that we can have empathy for understanding what another is experiencing. Said another way, if we regularly dismiss, deny, or dissociate from our own experience, we are unlikely to relate with empathy to the internal experiences of others. Some people tend to be very rational or are uncomfortable with their own emotions are probably able to validate with *presence* and *acceptance* more easily than with *empathy*. If you tend to be very rational or if you "live in your head" more than in your heart, then read carefully and do the practices in this book. Empathic responses may require extra resonance practice for someone with a very logical personality.

3. **Emotional stability** - "*without losing the as-if condition*" or we will experience either emotional contagion or our own automatic emotional reaction. When we are in an emotionally charged state of mind, our capacity for empathy is diminished. We may look out at the world and see and hear the cries of suffering, sadness, or grief, and find that too much pain wells up within us. Drowning in sadness over the suffering of others is emotional resonance or emotional contagion, not empathy. Empathy occurs if we are firmly grounded so

we don't fall into the emotional pool. Empathic responses may require extra grounding practice for emotionally sensitive persons.

The need for emotional stability may help explain why some of our sensitive friends, colleagues, and loved ones are not able to exercise as much empathy for us as we would sometimes like them to do. They may be too sensitive, vulnerable, or volatile. Meanwhile, to achieve our objectives and desires for the relationship, to improve our communication, or to achieve our shared goals, we may have to go out of our way being empathic toward them to be effective.

Being emotionally stable, separate, and secure requires us to stay in touch with our own feelings. When we have insight into the emotional response of another, we have to tolerate or regulate our own distress that might emerge from such insight. Without connection and self-regulation, empathy cannot be sustained. Without empathy it may be impossible to effectively respond with genuine validation and actually relieve suffering.

There is no doubt that we can cultivate more empathy through focus and practice—or stamp out a lot of empathy through the promotion of social discrimination and aggressive behavior. The practice of mindfulness fosters emotional stability and increases empathy. It is important to practice regularly. In fact, right now as you are reading this page, take a break and try the following exercises.

Practice 1. Cultivating Emotional Stability

A. Bring the attention to the breath for a few minutes. Close the eyes and feel sensations in the face, neck, and shoulders. With each exhale let go of any tension in the face, jaw, and throat. Notice the muscles settling into deeper relaxation.

B. Bring the attention to the breath and feel the abdomen expand and contract. Then put the attention in the sensations in the soles of the feet. Feel the connection between the feet and the ground. With each breath imagine this connection grow stronger.

Practice 2. Cultivating Empathy by Observing Another

Find a friend, colleague, or loved one doing something. Imagine that you have just met this person and know nothing about them. Observe with patience, interest and curiosity being completely open to everything that you see and hear. Be totally present for the other without forming any evaluations or interpretations. What is this person's inner experience at this moment? What feelings do you have as you observe the other from where you are? Now try to imagine, what would it be like to be in their shoes?

It may feel a little strange or unsatisfying at first. It can feel much more satisfying to advise, correct, or evaluate, especially if such commentary is habitual.

THE SCIENCE OF EMPATHY

It seems that empathy is possible thanks to what's known as the "mirror neuron system" in our brains. For example, if I am watching someone experience the feeling of disgust when they are eating something, the very same areas of my brain are activated as if I were actually eating something disgusting and experiencing my own disgust. Watching someone cry activates the same brain sector as actually crying. When we watch a movie, our brains are generating a parallel activity in the same regions that would be active if we were actually living out the experiences of each character! The same viscera-motor centers of the brain that are activated in our own experience are also activated when we observe the experience in another.

The mirror neurons seem to dissolve the barrier between self and others. Called "cells that read minds," the mirror neuron system supports the incredible speed with which children learn. Research has shown that the amount of activity among the mirror neurons is in direct relationship to empathy scores and social competence on assessment scales. Persons with severe autism do not show any activity of the mirror neuron system, further confirming the hypothesis of the strong relationship between mirror neuron activity and empathy/social interaction.

The mirror neuron system supports a direct, experiential sharing of mental states that is pre-analytical. We observe someone eating ice cream and enjoying it. We automatically know something about this person's mental experience, even if we don't start craving ice cream at that moment. We don't even realize that we are empathizing. The mirror neuron system is engaged in some type of automatic parallel mental activity.

Of course we are fully aware that we are not one with the other person and we don't know what the other is thinking. Our interpretations of their inner experiences are hypotheses, and we have to be mentally flexible and open to learning new information if we are to be effective at interpersonal communication. Some attachment theorists use the word "mentalizing" to describe this combination of empathy and the cognitive awareness of mind states of self and other. To be effective at mentalizing, human beings need to have experienced a secure attachment to their primary caretaker during infancy. Bateman and Fonagy put it this way:

Infants are constitutionally primed to expect to find a version
of their internal states mirrored by their caregivers. These
mirroring responses are necessary to help them learn to

represent their internal states both to themselves and other. If a small child does not have access to an adult who is able to recognize and respond to his internal states he will find it very difficult to make his own experience meaningful. Ideally the child needs an adult to reflect his state of mind in a manner that indicates to the child that it is not the caregiver's but the child's mental state that is being expressed. We think of this as "marked mirroring" and consider it analogous to what a good psychotherapist does in reflecting the patient's affect—combining accuracy of mirroring with a sense that she is [supporting the patient to manage his or her mental] experience.[2]

Not having formed a secure attachment with a primary caretaker can create problems with one's ability to mentalize, and these problems may result in unstable relationships and interpersonal conflict throughout life. Up to half of the general population exhibits an insecure attachment pattern as adults, and this can result in *intermittent deficits in empathy*. This does not mean that one cannot mentalize, it means that we can incorrectly interpret the internal experience of another even if we are carefully observing them. This is most likely to occur if we are in emotional mind, for example feeling insecure, embarrassed, angry, or in any other type of emotional mind.

The phenomenon of empathy is observed in all mammals that require care and nurturing for offspring that are unable to fend for themselves from birth. It seems entirely reasonable to hypothesize that all animals who imitate and learn from their mothers have mirror neurons and experience empathy to some degree. Empathy ensures reproductive success in child-rearing. In human beings it further contributes to survival because it assists individuals in prosocial behaviors (considering the needs of others independent of oneself), gathering and hunting for food, detecting predators, and courtship as well as in child-rearing.[3] Mentalization extends our understanding of others feelings and experiences by giving meaning to what we empathically observe and feel.

VALIDATE BY PRACTICING EMOTIONAL RECOGNITION

A basic way to validate is to look for the emotion and name it. Emotional recognition sounds easy, but it can be difficult when someone is giving us ten different reasons for why everything is wrong and telling us what they want us to do immediately to correct the situation. We can get quickly lost in the logic that is being spun out, especially if it is confusing or distorted. We may respond out of fear and/or anger. We start defending ourselves. We try reasoning. We totally forget all of our validation skills and conflict escalates.

Recognizing another person's inner feelings involves "mind reading." We put our mirror neurons to work by carefully observing and listening to the mental state of the other. Obviously we also check for accuracy, and avoid making assumptions. "How are your feeling?" is often useful to try to understand the emotional response that we are seeing. If we feel anger directed at us, we might ask, "Are you mad at me?" or "Did I do something to offend you?"

With empathy we try to understand the behaviors of another with as much direct observation as possible. We have to ask ourselves all the time, *What is the emotion that I am hearing and seeing?* Are we observing a secondary emotion, which is just a by-product of a primary emotion? We want to open our eyes to see if they are experiencing shame or fear underneath their anger or sadness. What is the emotion underlying the words, behavior, tone of voice, and facial expression?

Once we recognize an emotion, we can try to corroborate it with the other person. This is validation. For example, we can propose a hypothesis: "If I understand correctly, you are really annoyed at him." We can ask directly: "Did you feel sad when she said that?" Or we can simply share our observations: "It seems to me that you have been feeling nervous." Such corroboration is tentative and open-ended. A bald statement such as "You're angry" might backfire. For one reason, they might have simply been pensive, but once they're accused of being angry, their anger is triggered. If the other responds with brows furrowed and yelling back, "*No*, I'm *not* angry," it might be prudent to downshift just a little, saying, "OK, so you're not angry," and pausing to allow that response to settle. Empathy is not insistent. We may try asking the other, "So tell me, what's on your mind? Are you worried about something?"

Note: It is very helpful to practice building a vocabulary of words that describe emotions so we can label what we are feeling and also what we are observing in others. "If I understand correctly, you were feeling..." and pick the word most likely to resonate with the other person based upon what you observe—frustrated, irritated, fed up, impatient, stressed out, or furious, for example. (It was tempting to put a sample list in an appendix to this book, but a quick look in an online thesaurus for just the word "irritated" showed forty-four synonyms. Readers should build their own vocabulary lists based on their own needs and contexts.)

Someone who often minimizes their emotional response may disagree with a label that suggests an emotional intensity stronger than they are willing to accept. The use of words that imply less intense emotional responses may be more acceptable to the other person (and therefore be more validating). For example, a young woman might deny that she was *angry*, but agree that she was *frustrated* at the boys for ignoring her and *impatient* because they were late. Or we might know someone who denies being depressed but agrees that he has been *in a funk*. Knowing someone is sensitive to feeling shame and uses many shame escapes, we might comment *how uncomfortable* it must be to have to others looking at them. Other words that may be generally acceptable in the fear family include: *stressed, pressured, worried*; in the anger family: *grouchy, upset, frustrated*; in the shame family: *timid, sheepish, embarrassing*; and in the sadness family: *down, low, blue, or in the dumps.*

I will never forget a moment that I had after boarding an airplane when I was putting my bag in an overhead bin. A young woman jumped up to help me push the bag into the space and then she closed the hatch. As I began to move toward my seat and I heard her say loudly and sarcastically, "Your welcome!" For one second I felt a surge of anger and the impulse to say that I did not ask for her help nor did I need it. In the next second I just froze in order to cut off my reaction. But the best I could do in that moment of frozen anger was to look at the floor in her direction and somehow squeak out the words, "Rough day?" Her shoulders slumped and she instantly looked sad. She quietly responded "Yeah" and nodded her head. My own anger dissolved. We exchanged a knowing glance. At that moment, I somehow landed on words that communicated recognition of the essence of a stranger's internal experience in a simple, understated way. The consequence of that comment was that we had a moment of connection instead of nasty conflict.

To experience resonance with the emotional state of the other, we imagine experiencing the same situation and imagine feeling the same way. At first this may seem impossible. We might think, "I would *never* start shouting or crying or I would *never* feel embarrassed or afraid in such circumstances or he/she is really *insecure*, and I can't relate to that." Our judgments and criticism will just keep growing from there, and it is unlikely that we will arrive at meaningful dialogue.

We might have to look deeply inside of ourselves, checking for resonance, insight, or just to try and understand how their response makes sense. We may believe that we would not react to something in the same way or with the same intensity, but the question is: *Is there a seed of the emotional response that resonates? If I were in your shoes, could I possibly feel the same way?* For example, we can probably understand how someone could react with frustration if their objectives were blocked because we can feel that frustration. We can understand how someone might be disappointed if their expectations were not met because we can connect with that disappointment. And we can also see clearly how someone might feel anxiety from being pushed around in a crowded place or having to speak in front of a group or attending a party, even if we would not experience the same intensity of emotion but we could certainly understand feeling nervous to some degree.

We recognize emotional suffering in another and look for emotional resonance, and we try to respond in open and flexible ways. "I know you are uncomfortable with the situation. That would make me feel really frustrated." Such empathy must be authentic to be effective. We must feel and believe what we are saying in order to communicate empathically. The emotional resonance must be *real* and the response must be *genuine*. If we feel something as a result of resonating with the feelings of the other person, we can communication that as well. "It seems to me that you are sad and I wish there were something that I could do to help." If we actually share the same feeling of the other, we can communicate that clearly. "I know how important this is to you and you are probably worried about it. It makes me nervous too, so let's sit down and talk about it when we both have time."

Cultivating emotional stability for effective validation

Emotional stability is the third core aspect of empathy. It is that part of us that must stay grounded to recognize the "as-if" condition that Carl Rogers describes. It is what prevents us from engaging in emotional contagion and losing control instead of remaining effective and validating.

If we get caught up in the grip of our own automatic emotional responses, we are not attending to our own emotions, nor the emotions of the other person. While we are under the influence of our emotions, our actions are locked into the urges and impulses of these emotions. On the other hand, we may be totally focused on the words and the reasoning that we are hearing, without awareness of the emotional state of ourselves or the other. When we reach this point, we have to take a mental step back. We have to empathically attend to ourselves first! We have to recognize our own distress and relieve our suffering with our own attention and kindness or we cannot feel empathy for another. Once we are centered and grounded, we can take a deep breath and look for the emotion in the other person's experience.

An important part of the development of emotional stability is the reduction of vulnerability to negative emotions. This consists of four basic components: (1) a regimen of self-care, including regular sleep, healthy eating, exercise, abstinence from drugs and alcohol, and proper medical care as needed; (2) a regular mindfulness practice; (3) regularly scheduled pleasant activities; and (4) regular life activities that are meaningful and generate a sense of competence, such as work, school, sports, hobbies, or volunteer activities. If we find that any of these items are missing from our daily lives, we should start to plan how we can begin to incorporate them to reduce our vulnerability to experiencing negative emotions.

Another important part of emotional stability is the cultivation of positive feelings. Positive feelings can be nurtured by inclining our attention towards the positive and paying less attention to the negative. For example, if we find ourselves worrying about our future, we can focus on being grateful for the things we have in the present moment. If we are frustrated or angry with someone, we can remember the times they were helpful. Also, the practice of mindfulness and acceptance of the present moment tends to change that which seems neutral to a positive experience. And a sure-fire way to improve positive feelings is to generously help others in need or to make others feel better. (Just try making the cashier smile the next time you buy something!)

In the moment of heightened emotions or interpersonal conflict, it can be helpful to connect to our own breathing, especially the exhale. We may have to stop grabbing on to our racing thoughts and breathe. Then we pay attention to what we are feeling in our bodies. There are a variety of research studies that show how labeling emotions helps us regulate them.[4, 5] To *label* an emotion, we have to take a step back while we are feeling the emotion, and this subtle shift in awareness helps slow down the emotional response. Interestingly, it is not just effective to label our own emotional responses. In addition, describing the emotional expression of another can help us regulate our own emotions. For example, one study showed that observing and describing the emotion in a photo of an intensely emotional face resulted in a less intense affective reaction than just observing the photo. Labeling the emotion actually diminished brain activity in the amygdala (the "fear center" of the brain) and increased cerebral activity in a part of the brain that is implicated in regulating emotions.[6] Thus, attaching words to the emotional response we are observing in another may not only validate the other and help them regulate their emotions, but it appears that it also helps us stabilize our own emotional reactions to the situation!

Practice 3. Emotional stability in a difficult relationship

Think of a time when you were not at your best. It could be a situation in which you acted in a way that you later regretted what you did or said. Perhaps your response caused pain or suffering in others and you felt remorse afterwards. O perhaps you just did something which you are not very proud of. Think about what triggered your undesirable response, Remember the events around the situation and how you felt before and after. Notice how your feelings and actions urges were evoked by something–everything has a cause.

Now remember a situation in which another person treated you or others badly. Perhaps it is a person who can be "toxic" to be around. Try to put yourself in their shoes and imagine how they feel. Knowing from personal experience how it is possible to be hurtful toward others, let go of judgments and try to see how understandable their response was, exactly as it was, when it happened. Perhaps you can even put yourself in their shoes and imagine how they felt.

Empathic interpretations

We all make interpretations about ourselves, others, and the world around us. It is wise to be aware of our interpretations and consciously try to make them as empathic as possible. Emotional stability is essential. We can check whether our interpretations of other people's behavior are empathic by asking ourselves, would they be likely to agree?

Deficits in interpreting the actions and intentions of others go up when we are in emotional mind. Accuracy in interpreting others behavior improves when we are calm and centered, as well as open hearted and empathic.

CONSEQUENCE ≠ INTENTION

The consequences or the results of an individual's actions do not necessarily reflect intention. For example, "my husband is picking a fight" or "my colleague wants to make me mad." Just because two people have a fight, does not mean that one person was plotting and scheming how to create conflict. Feeling angry does not mean that this was the intention of the other person. It is a lot easier to not get swept up in inaccurate interpretations when we are calm and grounded.

We also sustain empathic interpretations by remembering that an emotional reaction is usually not under a person's control. Someone can't just *get over it*, even if they *just try harder*. These qualities are complex and include biological components such as brain functioning. A little empathy can help us regulate our own automatic emotional response and that of others. So let's put ourselves in the shoes of another to try to understand their view of the world with empathy.

Validating with Empathy by Tentative "Mind Reading"

Empathy "reads minds" (or, rather, reads face and tone of voice). We try to identify the emotional experience of another with our hearts and then put that into words. We name the feelings of the other in a tentative way, open to being corrected. We can validate feelings, desires, discomfort or any type of internal experience by describing how we resonate with their experience.

Let's put our mirrors neurons to work. We tentatively identify what another is feeling and connect it with the event or situation that we think probably triggered the emotion. This identification is a hypothesis and we remain willing to abandon our hypothesis if the other asserts a different experience. Below are some examples of validating responses with all three aspects of empathy: emotional recognition, emotional resonance, and emotional stability.

Ana was on the verge of tears waiting for a call from her boyfriend. Her friend noticed a thought arising *Oh no, not again*. She let that thought pass and opened up her heart to Ana. She tried to empathically connect with her: "You haven't heard from your boyfriend, have you? It must be so disappointing if he can't find five minutes to call. Have you been thinking about him all day?" Ana did not say anything. "When did you last speak to him?" Ana's eyes dried up and she began to talk.

Brianna was agitated as she spoke loudly and rapidly to her mom about a situation at school. Her mom was confused and did not know if Brianna was anxious or angry but she felt an urge to calm Brianna down. She tried to respond by recognizing and resonating with Brianna's anxiousness from a place of grounded centeredness. "Brianna, this seems really important to you aaand…" she said with excitement in her voice, but then took a deep breath and continued speaking a little more slowly, "There is so much energy here that I am having trouble following all the details. Can you start over and explain to me what happened step-by-step?"

Carlos was clearly angry when he told his brother, Jose what his father had said to him. His brother recognized the situation as typical of his father, and he found it annoying. He understood how much it really sent Carlos into a rage. Jose responded with empathy, "He really said that to you? Wow, that would suck! No wonder you are furious!"

Diana's mother was trying to tell her what to do to solve a problem when Diana screamed, "Mom! You never listen to me!" Her mother paused. Inside she was shocked and angry but she knew she did not want to escalate the situation. She took a moment to breathe and to feel her feet on the ground. She gave herself just enough space to listen to her daughter's words and to connect with her frustration. She responded from her heart, saying, "Right. I know it is irritating to feel like your mother is not listening. Sorry to interrupt. Go ahead. Please."

Ellen walked into her boss's office speaking loudly and rapidly about a coworker. Her boss could hardly follow her complaint and he did not have time or interest to hear a litany of complaints. He held up his hand to motion her to stop, however, he decided to relax into the moment and try validation. "I can hear your frustration, and it sounds like it is justified. Can you please slow down and explain what happened one step at a time? I only have a few minutes, and I can't promise anything, but tell me what happened."

Each of these responses illustrates 1) a connection with the other person's feelings and one's own feelings with an open heart, 2) putting into words how the other person's experience makes sense and an invitation to explain further, and 3) an active grounding and centering via feeling the feet on the floor and/or connecting with the breath. These three steps may occur in any order, but all are present in these brief examples of validating with empathy. Practices 1, 2, and 3 in this chapter can be helpful to develop validating with empathy.

Bring to mind someone with whom you have a difficult relationship. It does not have to be your worst enemy, but someone whose responses do not always generate a feeling of warmth. Imagine getting up, taking off your shoes, walking all the way over to this person and stepping into their shoes. Can you see things through their eyes—with their unique history, beliefs, habits, preferences, skills, coping mechanisms, problems and problem-solving abilities, values, and emotional dispositions? Clearly it's not easy being inside someone else's skin for their whole life! Maybe there is emotional discomfort almost all the time. Even when things are looking good, there may be a profound lack of ease.

Is it possible that this person finds that a sense of wellbeing is elusive, and instead feelings of shame, emptiness, not belonging, anxiety, sadness, or anger tend to be common experiences? And in the midst of all this emotional and physical pain, the rest of the world doesn't see, doesn't understand, can't help, and even seems to be blaming this person for their problems.

Now you can take off their shoes, get out of their skin, and put your own shoes back on. And if you really have been able to put yourself inside the skin of the other and tried to understand their internal experience, then you might begin to feel their pain. But you must stay grounded and connected to your own experience to validate with empathy.

Sandra, age sixteen, often got home from school and went straight to her bed and many afternoons stayed there until dinner. Her mother had tried many times to convince her to go out, nagged her to do her homework, and even yelled at her to get out of bed, all of which resulted in insults or tears.

One day her mother changed tactics and went in and said to her, "I know how much you have been through and how tough it is to find the energy and the motivation. It seems like you have been feeling sad and hopeless for a long time now. I probably can see only a small percentage of your suffering. I'm not sure if I could stand it; I think you may be a lot stronger than me. It must be unbearable." Sandra was silent, and after a few minutes Mom squeezed Sandra's hand and left. A half hour later, Sandra came out of her bedroom. She started talking about a memory of doing something fun with her mother years prior. Mom tried hard to be present, to listen, and to reflect back those memories.

Let's see yet another example of empathic emotional validation. Remember to look for emotional recognition, resonance, and stability.

Cleo was working on her degree while her husband, David, worked as a computer programmer. David got home tired one evening, and the house was disorganized and the kitchen was piled with dirty dishes from the night before. Cleo was watching television. David was fed up, and it came through in his voice: "Cleo, can't you pick up around here? You're sitting around here watching TV, and I have to work all day." Cleo exploded. She began yelling, defending herself, describing how horrible her day had been, and finally insulting him and accusing him of having an affair at the office.

David went from irritated to furious. This time, however, he noticed his fury before responding. He took a deep breath and managed to refrain from attacking back. He took another breath. He noticed that he was also confused and even a little afraid of what his wife might do, given her history of emotional crises. He listened to her tone of voice and observed her face. In that moment he was able to connect with her emotional reaction, more than with the logic of her words. Even though he didn't think her anger was justified by the situation, he could see and label her anger.

"Cleo, I know you are angry with me right now, and I see you are in a lot of pain. It must be really horrible to feel this way. I know that I am frustrated too right now." Cleo's anger began to melt.

Days later Cleo explained that she had woken up with a sense of anxiety and was terribly worried about recent fights she had with her husband and exams that she had to study for, and these worries had consumed her day. She had been trying hard not to call David all day, since she often called him up to five or six times a day—a subject of frequent heated discussion. She had been doing her best to manage her anxiety and worries on her own. When he arrived home, she was distracting herself from her negative thoughts and feelings by watching TV. She felt that he hadn't even noticed or appreciated her efforts to not call him. Of course all hell broke loose when he walked in the door and criticized her.

BEYOND EMOTIONS - UNIVERSAL NEEDS AND DESIRES

Underlying every emotional response is a universal need—that is, a legitimate human desire. Wants, desires, and needs all have validity. If this seems hard to accept, let us begin by thinking about the desires and needs that we all have as human beings. Food, water, recreation, and rest are obvious physical needs. But of course we all want more than that.

For example, we all need to somehow feel a sense of belonging or a sense of connection with others. Human beings are extremely social creatures and mutually dependent upon one another, so it is easy to understand that belonging and interpersonal connections are universally needed. A chronic feeling of loneliness or emptiness or sadness may be related to the need for belonging or connection when that need is unfulfilled. Fear of not getting such needs fulfilled in the future may arise. Anger with ourselves or others may emerge when we are blocked from fulfilling our needs. Envy may be triggered when we see others who have their needs met. If we look hard enough, we can find a universal, unmet need underlying any emotional response.

Marshall Rosenberg has written and lectured extensively about nonviolent forms of communication. Rosenberg describes the universal and legitimate needs that help us understand human motivations and emotional responses.[7] Such needs may be grouped into the following areas:

- Physical needs such as food, shelter, and movement
- Caring, appreciation, emotional security, and love
- Recreation and fun
- Relevance, integrity, meaning, and self-worth
- Contribution, mutual support, interdependence, participation, belonging
- Autonomy in choosing one's own goals and values
- Celebrations or rituals to mark achievements, milestones, and losses
- Spiritual communion, inspiration, order, and peace

Notice that the needs listed first are such fundamental human needs that we would die if those needs were not met. An infant will not survive without having needs 1 and 2 met. As a toddler learns to walk, needs 3 and 4 are essential for human development. Needs 5–8 become increasingly relevant throughout childhood and adolescence. Most of us will never stop having any of these needs throughout our lives. Our priorities will change and the relative importance of our needs will change, but these needs will remain fundamental to our physical and emotional wellness. It is worth noting that among all the universal human needs, validation touches upon the needs at level 2, just after food, shelter, and water.

The list above is not an exhaustive list of human needs and desires. It is a starting point of those that are the most universal. For example, someone may have a desire for leadership or economic wealth. These specific desires are indeed legitimate, and we can empathically acknowledge and validate them. We can probably even connect them to more universal desires such as autonomy and self-worth.

Reviewing the situation with Cleo, who was anxious at home all day trying not to call her husband at work, we might see how Cleo's anger arose from her needs for emotional security, belonging, and interdependence. She had been suffering an enormous amount of emotional instability and insecurity throughout the day, and perhaps what she really needed at the moment David arrived home was some soothing or physical nurturing or empathy. David's anger may have been triggered by an unfulfilled need for order and calm upon arriving home from work. We can see how both of their needs are valid. We can also see that neither of them identified and articulated their own need that was underlying their emotional responses; instead they each automatically blamed the other for their anger.

Almost all emotions and desires can be related to unfulfilled needs. We have to practice looking for such needs. We can start with ourselves and then, with empathy, we can try it out on others.

Practice 4. Name the Emotion, the Event, and the Unfulfilled Need

Think of a specific situation that you experienced recently that resulted in emotional arousal. Name the emotion you felt. Try to identify the specific event that triggered the emotion. Now reframe the emotion as a response to an unmet universal need or needs. What were you needing at time?

∾

Practice 5. Look for the Needs, Values, and Desires

Observe and identify the emotional response of another. Let go of all judgments, blame, or criticism. Try to imagine what universal human needs, values, or desires this person is experiencing in the moment that the emotion arose, although the other may not have been conscious of them. Empathically see their emotional response as an indicator of which universal need they may be expressing in the present moment.

Validating emotions and unfulfilled needs and desires

If we come upon someone who is already in an intense emotional state, maybe we can't identify the emotion or the situation. Nevertheless, we can still empathically recognize their emotional pain and reflect their emotion in our tone of voice. It doesn't take much more than just jumping in: "Ohh, what happened?" We listen to their response and accompany them in their suffering. We can further validate the emotional response as understandable given the situation. We can deepen understanding by observing what legitimate need may be unfulfilled.

If we know a little more about the situation, we can try to identify the underlying unmet need or desire. (It is really useful to practice with oneself first!)

Here are some examples of identifying one's own emotion and underlying need:

- I'm feeling really irritated today. (*emotion*) I've had people annoying me all morning and I'm under a lot of pressure and I have to get this document finished today. (*underlying need— integrity and self-worth—specifically, meeting a deadline at work*)
- I feel like I'm living in fear. (*emotion*) I'm nervous and I can't

seem to focus. I'm worried about my son, who was furious this morning when I had to leave for work. Now he isn't answering his cell phone when I call. (*underlying need— interdependence—specifically, wants son to be happy*)

Here are some examples of identifying another person's emotion and underlying need:

- It seems like you're very nervous. (*emotion*) I see you smoking one cigarette after another and pacing around and looking at your telephone. I imagine that you want your boyfriend to call you even though you broke up with him. Of course you want a stable relationship. (*underlying need: emotional security and love—specifically, a stable and loving intimate relationship*)

Jack's mother was eighty-five and she was forced to sell her house where she had lived for the past fifty-five years and move into an assisted living facility. She started to seem irritated and intolerant one minute and then sad and scared the next. She became unusually defiant and oppositional during this phase of her life.

Jack could not keep up with her changing moods, and she would usually deny her feelings anyway. When Jack discovered how to validate her underlying needs, especially her need for autonomy, a sense of contribution and mutual support, and a feeling of relevance and self-worth, he was able to maintain longer conversations and help her remain more balanced during this very difficult transition period. Some the phrases he learned to use tapped into these universal needs:

Autonomy: "Mom, you're in charge" or "You're the boss here" were very effective at helping Jack's mother feel like she had some control over her life as she was worrying over how to manage moving and selling the house.

Contribution/mutual support: Jack validated his mother's need for social interaction even when she was ambivalent about it: "We all need people around to talk to." "Everyone needs regular human interaction." He remembers saying to her, "People can be annoying, but we need someone to talk to every now and then." She found this statement particularly validating to her internal experience and fully agreed with him.

Relevance/self-worth: Jack found it difficult to validate his mother's emotions, especially when she tended to be angry and reject social connection, but he found it effective to validate her need to feel relevant and worthy: "You are a person with integrity, and that means something to other people." He once defused her angry rejection of another person by reminding her of her own values in a way that she could not deny, saying, "I know you value kindness because you taught me to be kind to others."

It can be hard to validate the emotions of people who tend to distance themselves from their emotions. It may be useful to sit at a table with pen and paper and carefully look over the list of universal needs and write down some ways to validate this person based on their needs that seem to be particularly at risk of being unmet. It will require empathy and it may be useful to spend a few quiet minutes to mentally put ourselves into the other person's shoes and wear them for a while to understand what they are really needing in a given situation. (For more tips on what and how to validate when interacting with persons who have less awareness of their emotions, see also chapter 8.)

CHAPTER SUMMARY

Empathy is a biological component of being human. If we communicate with others, if we learn, and if we love, we must be able to understand the internal experience of others. We practice developing empathy by mindfully observing and describing our own emotions. We can also develop much more refined empathy as we become better at carefully listening and observing others and resonating with the thoughts and feelings of others. We have to really try to put ourselves in their shoes.

Empathy consists of emotional recognition and emotional resonance, and it also requires a level of emotional stability. Intense emotions can trump empathy. To respond with empathy, we must be true to our own experiences in the world and not lose ourselves to the internal experience of the other. When we empathize with another, we almost become a participant in their internal world ("perceiving the internal frame of reference with accuracy and with the emotional components and meanings which pertain thereto"), but we remain an observer of that world. We need to develop the *mental flexibility* to adopt the subjective experience of the other ("as if one with the person") and the *capacity to self-regulate* our own mental and emotional processes so as not to lose the "as-if condition."

Among psychology researchers, there is broad agreement that empathy implies at least three different processes. We know how others can feel based on our own personal experience, we have the cognitive capacity to recognize what the other is experiencing by seeing and imagining their experience, and we have emotional regulatory mechanisms that keep track of the origins of self and other feelings.[8]

Once we understand emotions and begin to be mindful and accepting of all emotional experiences in ourselves and others, we can validate others for whatever they are feeling in the moment and see how their emotions makes sense in their particular situations. We can also use empathy to validate someone's experience in terms of unmet needs or desires. Our emotions, needs, and desires are always valid as part of our internal experience of being human.

CULTIVATING EMPATHY:

1. Empathy component 1: Look for the emotion

- See if you can recognize the emotion by observing the face, tone of voice, posture, and movements of the other.
- If it helps, imagine the name of the emotion flashing across the forehead of the other! Imagine that this emotion is doing the talking.

2. Empathy component 2: Emotional resonance

- Listen and connect with empathy.
- Connect to the internal experience of the other. Imagine what it would be like to walk in their shoes, including having their background, their history, and all the contextual and causal events leading up to their particular response in the specific situation.

3. Empathy component 3: Internal stability

- Carefully listen to your own inner experience.
- Pause for one complete breath. Connect with the feeling of the soles of your feet in contact with the ground.

Validating with empathy:

1. Recognize the emotion

- Acknowledge the emotional state of the person just as it is in the present moment.
- Recognize how discomfort, suffering, and an immediate intense desire to escape the experience of an intense emotion may explain seemingly "manipulative," chaotic, or ineffective behavior.

2. Wholeheartedly observe the other and feel your own response to the other.

- What are your feeling?
- What are you observing and feeling that the other person is feeling?
- Validate the emotions as reasonable, understandable, natural, or even expected.

3. Ground yourself if needed

- Connect with your breath.
- Connect with your feet.
- Let go of tension in the body.
- Allow yourself to be corrected by the other person and modify your understanding of the their emotion as needed.

4. Validate needs and wants

- Figure out what universal and legitimate needs the other is experiencing in the present situation and which underlie the emotion, and try to empathically connect with these needs.
- Validate the emotion as legitimate based upon the underlying needs and wants.
- If those needs are not clear, ask what it is that the other person is needing right now and then reflect back what your understanding of their needs are.
- Note: Some people tend to deny their emotional experience. It may be more soothing and effective to validate their needs and wants as universal, understandable, or important.

Empathy is part of human nature, but we can develop it to a much deeper level with a little practice. We find that developing empathy, like practicing validation, enriches all of our interpersonal relationships and often brings more personal satisfaction to our own lives.

7

COMPASSION

When you are deeply touched with an understanding about the suffering of others, you feel a pull to do something.

— *Janice Marturano*

According to archeologists, fossils show that about one million years ago our ancestors evolved into a species that looked after their old and diseased as well as their young. Compassionate caring greatly increased our ancestors' chances for survival and reproduction, and it was imprinted onto our genes. [1]

We are all wired to experience compassion, and we all benefit from the prosocial behavior that compassion evokes. It is as much a part of our genetic makeup as is fear or selfishness. If we set ourselves on a path of compassion by focusing our attention on feelings of compassion and directing our behavior toward acts of compassion each day, then fear begins to diminish and the path of compassion becomes wider and wider—until one day we realize it is so wide that there is no more "path" and all of life is compassionate.

Compassion is not pity, nor indulgence, nor is it feeling sorry for someone. Compassion is the natural urge or desire to reduce suffering upon recognizing that someone is in distress. It builds upon our growing foundation of mindfulness, acceptance, and empathy. We set our intention to be present and accepting, and we are sensitive to the feelings of others. Then compassion goes even further: we are committed to responding in ways that relieve suffering. It is a response to distress with prosocial intentions.

This definition raises the question that Linehan so pointedly asked at a time when *compassion* was just becoming a popular term among social scientists and psychologists: "Is wanting to help sufficient? Or do you need to actually help?"[2]

Clearly compassion must include more than just a desire or spontaneous urge. It must include action. Paul Gilbert, author of *The Compassionate Mind,* defines compassion as a "basic kindness with deep awareness of the suffering of oneself and of other living things, coupled with the wish and the effort to relieve it."[3] Gilbert's definition is important because it not only includes an effort to relieve suffering, but it also recognizes the suffering of *oneself* to be equally as important as the suffering of others. Compassionate effort can be a courageous act born from the caring desire to help another and the wisdom to know how to respond.

Thich Nhat Hahn adds another component to the definition of compassion that we can appreciate in our validation practice. He defines compassion as "the ability to offer relief from suffering."[4] Thus we move toward a concept of acting in a way that is skillful at ameliorating suffering. It seems that compassion consists of the impulse, energy, motivation, and skillfulness to engage in an act of altruism.

So we are not describing just attitude and intention; compassion also includes words and deeds. But there is a lot of suffering in this world. What if there is nothing we can actually say or do to help? "There is still a tremendous amount of power in just wishing someone well in a focused and conscious way," says His Holiness the Dalai Lama. We can sustain the desire and commitment for another to be free of suffering within our hearts until the moment arises when we can be effective. [5] We benefit greatly from developing an attitude of compassion and filling our hearts with the courage to act, even when the opportunity is not present.

"Wishing someone well in a focused and conscious way" is much more than just empathy. Richard Davidson, one of the world's leading experts on contemplative neuroscience, points out that "compassion and empathy each activate some of the same circuits in the brain, but there are important differences. Compassion activates circuits that have been associated with positive emotions and reward, while empathy does not. Also compassion activates areas of the brain that are related to 'pre-motor signals,' or urges, to actively engage in pro-social behavior."[6]

If we choose compassion to be one of the guiding principles of our lives, it begins to organize what we pay attention to and how we think and behave. We open our hearts to the desire to reduce distress, pain, or suffering in ourselves and others; we recognize this suffering; and we validate it with compassion.

Genuine validation is an act of compassion. This is not without benefit for oneself. Compassion is one of the most effective ways to develop happiness, awaken joy, and give one's life meaning and purpose. The happiness that arises from compassion is not based on an attachment to something, a happiness that goes away when that "something" is gone. Like a gift truly given from the heart, genuine happiness and even joy emerge from being compassionate.

BARRIERS TO COMPASSION: THREAT VERSUS SAFETY

If we stop long enough to notice, we will see how all of our experience of being human is referenced around suffering and the end of suffering. *Suffering* can include any threat to our well-being, physical discomfort, or mental dissatisfaction. For example, if we sit or even lie still long enough, it becomes clear that there is no position that our bodies can tolerate indefinitely without having the need to move and relieve discomfort. Our bodies and brains are wired to monitor dissatisfaction, discontent, pain, or threats and then act in some way to stop discomfort and increase satisfaction or safety.

Human beings have been programmed by and for evolutionary survival, and compassion is part of that programming. Specific combinations of neurological circuits, neurochemicals, and hormones act together, and these systems generate mental states, energy, and urges to effectively and immediately move away from suffering and toward comfort, safety, and satisfaction. The experience of being in either a threat mode or a safe mode is fundamental to how we feel and how we respond.

When we are in a dangerous environment or feel threatened, it is difficult to detect safety. We are likely to misinterpret social cues, and our capacity for compassion deteriorates. Worry, anxiety, and stress distract us from our good intentions, interfere with our moral reasoning, and hijack our commitment to being compassionate. Just as we learned in the last chapter that emotional stability is necessary to experience empathy, we cannot respond with compassion if we are focused on avoiding threat. Let's explore how compassion can help us move into safety mode by understanding some of the physiological systems that have helped us survive and thrive.

THE SELF-PROTECTION SYSTEMS

Brain scientists offer an evolutionary perspective to understanding the physiology of feelings (combinations of physiological activity, physical sensations, mental states, energy, and urges to move away from suffering and toward safety). Two recent theories are especially relevant to compassion: Stephen Porges's "polyvagal system," responses that occur when the vagus nerve is activated,[7] and Paul Gilbert's "emotional regulation systems," responses connected to the activation of the limbic region of our brains versus the prefrontal cortex.[8] Further rounding out these researchers is the work of Thomas Lynch, who describes five types of neurological responses that are automatically triggered each by a specific type of cue.[9] Below is a diagram of self-protection systems that integrates their theories about human experiences with regard to threat and safety and reflects the systems proposed by Lynch.[10]

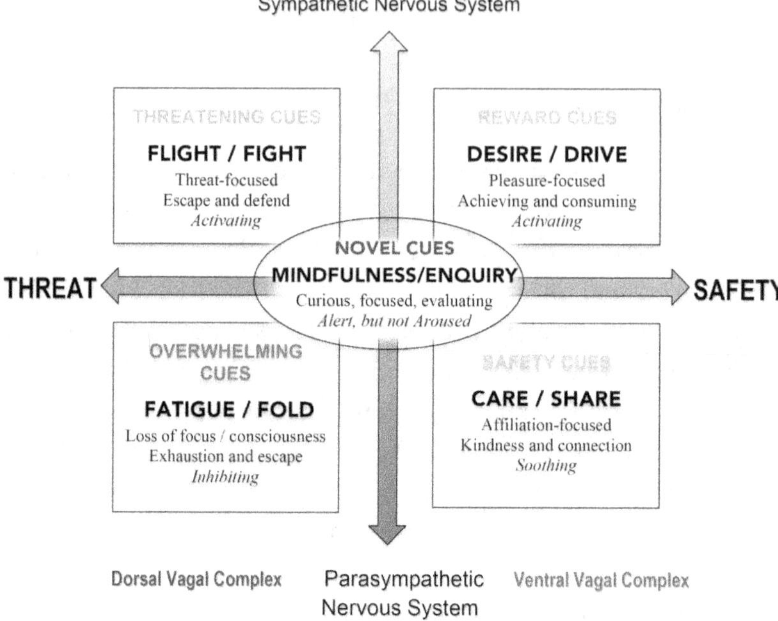

Five Neurological Networks underlying emotions and moods

I like to call these "self-protection systems" because they are necessary and effective for *human survival*. These systems protect us from mortal threats. They help us remain alive from one day to the next. The self-protection desire/drive and flight/fight systems are especially important for the creation and maintenance of that *sense of being a separate and independent self*. In other words, they maintain the "ego" as distinct and separate from the natural interdependent, integrated, and endless flow of sensorial stimuli. They reify the sense of *me* and *mine* with thoughts, feelings, and perceptions of being separate from rest of the universe and in need of protection. Thus the self-protection systems protect our lives and our egos.

· · ·

1. Flight/fight system

Our ancestors lived with the menace of predators and other life-threatening danger. In fact, those who survived to pass along their genes were the alert ones who avoided becoming lunch for some tiger. We are the sons and daughters of the fearful and the courageous whose flight-or-fight systems were in the best condition.

We were born with a type of radar system that is always on, unconsciously scanning for danger. Our attention and memory are biased toward threats and danger. Threat cues activate our *flight-or-fight system* is activated and energy is sent in the form of chemicals (including cortisol and adrenaline) and electricity throughout the body to react. This is an ancient neurological system based in the brain's limbic region (our "reptilian brain") and linked to the body through the sympathetic nervous system.

When the flight/fight system is activated, our ability for empathic, pro-social signaling becomes especially impaired. If this system is activated for a short period of time, it can be extremely effective and useful for surviving to continue a life of safety and comfort. If it is chronically activated, however, through systematic worry or by assigning negative value to our experience or thinking, it can end up stimulating inflammatory mechanisms that lead to chronic illness, accelerated aging, preoccupation with failure, and other measurably destructive effects.

2. Desire/drive system

Our ancestors needed energy and motivation to hunt, collect food, and obtain shelter, mates, clothes, and items of social position, just as we do today. Humans seem to be compelled to create, move toward, or increase that which is gratifying or pleasurable. The *desire/drive system* is the motivational system that anticipates pleasure and pushes us to construct, organize convenience, create beauty, avoid errors and excel. Gratification and pleasure are the positive rewards the drive our cravings, whether we are at work or at play. Desire is sustained by the excitement we feel when we "win" or from the pleasure that we get from positive stimulus that makes us feel good.

Dopamine is one of the many neurochemicals involved in desire and craving. It focuses our attention on pursuing what we want. However, craving that hit of pleasure can be chronically activated and result in bad habits and even addictions. Addictions are not just about drugs, alcohol, or cigarettes, but also can be an intense or compulsive desire for shopping and buying, eating, text messaging, internet surfing, working long hours, or anything that makes us feel excited, powerful, or like a winner, or just gives us that glow of feeling good, if only for a few moments. In the worst cases, eventually the "hit" is not even pleasurable. It just brings temporary relief to the craving. Pleasure and desire are no longer functionally related. In many types of addictions desire may be intense, but it is largely insatiable.

3. Fatigue/fold system

When we are exhausted, trapped, or overwhelmed we may just surrender and pass out. We may experience a feeling of numbness, despair, depression, or exhaustion. This system involves a severe loss of energy, weakness, and perhaps the urge to isolate oneself.

The *fatigue/fold system* that is triggered by overwhelming cues (that may be overwhelming positive excitement as well as negative trauma or stress) may force us to rest and recover from exhaustion or loss when we reach a physiological state of "burnout" or "breakdown" that is physical, mental, and emotional. *Fatigue* is not just feeling tired or sleepy. It can be a distressing and persistent sense of physical, emotional, and cognitive exhaustion, lethargy, depression, or intense shame. *Fold* implies fainting—a total loss of consciousness. These responses are controlled by the pathway of the parasympathetic nervous system known as the dorsal vagal complex which slows heart rate, breathing, and body movements, we lose all facial expression, numb out, and feel less pain.

Why is it useful to understand these self-protection systems when we just want to develop compassion? Compassion can fall away if we perceive a threat, if we get swept up in a need to protect our resources or to consume more, or if we are in the depths of despair. In today's society the pressure of many competing demands keeps our threat and drive systems going. Even worse, many of us actually expect to find happiness by running back and forth between fight/flight and desire/drive. We live alert to and fearful of threat and trying to avoid danger while buying and acquiring more and more. The competitive nature of our jobs and our market-driven society pushes so many people onto that treadmill. Running on fear and desire offers temptations that have been widely embraced in our society today. We may achieve "wealth" based on mortgage and debt. We may realize "beauty" after plastic surgery and cosmetic procedures. We may become "celebrities" with no talent via social media or reality TV. We can reach athletic achievements using performance-enhancing drugs. Any one of us can even immerse ourselves in social networking to surround ourselves with "friends" who "like" us but don't even know us. We can even find "esteemed colleagues" who exchange job recommendations but whom we have never met! These strategies are remarkably ineffective at cultivating true happiness. We need to learn and practice moving into genuine caring and sharing which requires us to stop interacting with hardware and software and instead interact with "wetware" (real sentient beings)!

4. Care/share system

After escaping predators, hunting, building, or recovering from disaster, we needed "cave time" or protection and security within our "tribe." Safety cues include sharing food, caring for wounds, telling stories, and resting under the watchful eyes and ears of others. Our *caring and sharing system* is associated with feeling connected, cared for, and accepted. The parasympathetic nervous system is in safe mode for the body to experience kindness and connection as well as to undergo rest and digest. Bonding is soothing and calming and involves the release of chemicals such as oxytocin and endorphins.

When we feel safe, calm, and nurtured, we tend to be exploratory, prosocial, and altruistic. When we are engaged in the other systems, especially the threat system, we are not able to be compassionate, prosocial, or altruistic.

The world is not perfect within the caring and sharing system, however. The human need for belonging and recognition can result in a tribal "us against them" mentality—an attitude that has led to prejudice, racism, war, dispossession, and torture for thousands of years and has no end in sight. The potential for cruelty is deep within the brains and genes of each one of us. Compassion is not just sharing, generosity, and kindness among our family, our group, or the citizens of our country. Gilbert warns us that "we may have to be courageous in the face of anger, potential shame, personal uncertainty, and fear [of rejection] in order to stand against the crowd and listen to the voice of compassion."[11] Indeed, seen from this perspective, interesting new compassion-based solutions may emerge in response to rising tides of discrimination, prejudice, or nationalism.

5. Novelty/Inquiry System

Upon perceiving something unusual or novel we may focus our attention on it, perhaps trying to decide if it is safe or threatening or simply trying to understand more about it. It may be a new sound or an unusual silence. Novelty puts us into beginner's mind in which we are simultaneously still and alert. If it continues to last, we may feel wonder or awe. We focus our full attention with curiosity. This automatic evaluation process is often thought of as unconscious, but it can indeed be a moment in which we are fully aware of the fact that we are trying to figure out if something is safe or threatening or just appreciating that which is amazing.

Each system is useful and necessary to survival. There is no bad system! But our health and happiness is dependent upon having the five systems in balance. It is the affiliation-focused system that calms and soothes us, and all too often it is the weakest of the four systems and in need of personal development. The systems that focus on threat and resources are often overactivated, creating drama, tension, and stress that is not always healthy. The reward system is over-activated in workaholics, perfectionists, and compulsive personality styles. Too much time in fight/flight or desire/drive and we fall into fatigue/fold. So instead of avoiding threat or gaining reward, we can nurture our affiliation-focused system through empathic social connection, such as genuine validation. In this chapter on compassion, we find ways to move out of flight/fight, desire/drive, or fatigue/fold and move into the care/share quadrant. Don't forget—we saw in earlier chapters how to develop the novelty/inquiry system through mindfulness, presence, and acceptance.

An 80-year (and counting) research project on happiness and longevity is the Harvard Study of Adult Development, begun at Harvard University in 1938. Results continue to emerge from this study, but it has already shown that an active affiliation system with meaningful personal relationships results in better health, longer and more meaningful lives, and greater happiness. In fact, one of the greatest predictors of longevity is the combination of close personal relationship(s) and daily brief interactions with multiple persons.[12]

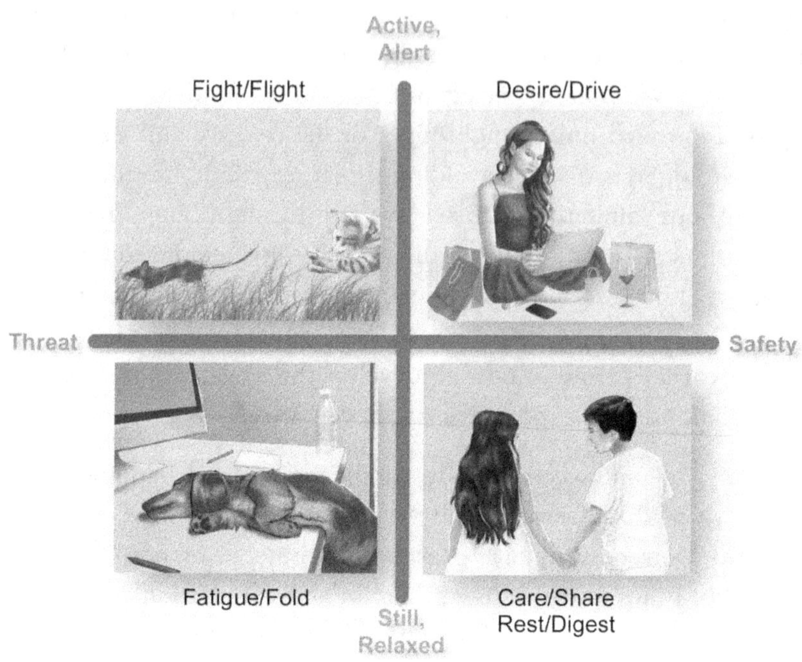

OK, one might say, so I do want to live longer and be happier. But how might compassion help us in our daily lives . . . and especially in a highly competitive work environment? The example below illustrates how Matthew, who was quickly losing an important negotiation, had to get out of both the "hunting" and the "being hunted" modes and activate his caring/sharing mode in order to succeed.

Matthew wanted to sell his half of a software company that he had founded with a close friend, Bill. They had reached a written agreement for the price that Bill would pay him. A whole year passed and his partner had one excuse after another for not closing the sale. Throughout the year, Bill became more defensive and mean-spirited, saying things like, "You haven't really done anything to earn this money" or "You are just leaving me with all the problems" or, even worse, "I am never going to be able to pay you because the company is not making anything."

As frustrated as Matthew felt, he knew that if he responded with anger, they could end up in court for years, with all his money going to legal fees. I suggested to Matthew that he develop more compassion for Bill. He had to wholeheartedly focus on reducing Bill's suffering with his words and deeds and validate his feelings. In response to one of Bill's attacks, he responded by saying, *"Bill, I know that you are very worried about the future of the company. I also know how honest and hardworking you are, and that will probably be one of the keys to your future success. This company will continue to grow because of you. I will always be available if anything comes up. You know where to find me."*

Matthew had to hit the pause button on his own automatic defensive reaction and deeply enter into Bill's experience. He had to soften and relax around his partner and open his eyes and ears. He saw that Bill was not just angry, he was also afraid. Validation helped soothe Bill's anger and fear about the future of the company (the threat-focused system) and reassure him that the company would indeed grow as a result of his hard work (the reward-focused system). Validation increased his sense of safeness and connection (the affiliation system), so he was more inclined to meet his commitments to Matthew. At every meeting Matthew connected with Bill in an authentic and compassionate way and genuinely validated his fears, his worries, his hard work, and his strengths and internal resources. Within a few months Bill did pay Matthew—without any lawyers.

Cultivating compassion

Our fight-or-flight system is easily activated by real and perceived threats that trigger fear and anger, such as making ends meet and paying the bills, demands at work, or grades in school. Our desire/drive system can get pressed into overdrive in a consumption-oriented economy and we find ourselves filling our homes with stuff they we hardly appreciate. Our caring and sharing system can get relegated to last place with all these pressures. It can be further deactivated and challenged by fewer and fewer personal and face-to-face connections, a lack of intimacy, and an addiction to electronic communications. We can jump between fight/flight and desire/drive only for so long. Eventually we reach unhealthy levels of fatigue and we fold.

Perhaps the best starting point for developing compassion is beginning with compassion for oneself. Each of us is equally deserving of compassion. We can all suffer from a sense of shame or feelings of low self-esteem or self-worth. Nobody passes through life without being criticized, doing things we later regret, or having habits that we would rather not have. A sense of shame can arise when others think we are inadequate, when we think that others think we are inadequate, or when we think that we are inadequate. As we saw in chapter 2, a sense of shame can be accompanied by self-criticism and even self-attacking, and these seriously undermine our sense of well-being.

Rather than feeling support, kindness, and enthusiasm for ourselves when something goes wrong, many of us feel anger, disappointment, frustration, or even contempt for ourselves. We have all these emotional responses as if there were a real threat, but the source of the threat usually arises from within and the target is ourselves! We need to cultivate an attitude of self-compassion to render powerless the self-critical thoughts that generate shame or are generated by shame. This is a practice that can last a lifetime and can continually expand and deepen our sense of satisfaction, joy, and meaning in life.

Developing a more compassionate self can involve practices that include contemplations of mental images and mental words, recitations of compassionate phrases, compassionate gestures, writing about compassion, conversing about compassion, and engaging in altruistic action. Practice 1 below begins this journey with thoughts and gestures to develop more self-compassion.

Practice 1. Self-compassion

Close your eyes and bring to mind a mistake that you made and felt bad about, an activity that you struggled to do, a situation in which you were angry or disappointed with yourself, or a difficult skill that you are learning. Notice whether there is a tendency to criticize yourself, devalue your efforts, or focus only what you have *not* accomplished instead what you *have* accomplished. Imagine receiving and holding critical thoughts within pure awareness that is kind and friendly.

Now put one hand over your heart and focus on feelings of kindness and gentleness toward yourself (and that inner critic of yours that also just wants to protect you!). Mentally focus your attention on your heart and connect to your breath. Bring both hands to your heart and imagine that the love that your heart generates is being reflected back to you by your hands and expanding to your whole body. Be your most compassionate for yourself and accept whatever feelings arise with loving compassion.

THIS EXERCISE MAY HELP US TO RECOGNIZE THE DISTRESS THAT WE experience when we are being self-critical. Perhaps we will gain insights into the tendency to set high expectations for ourselves. Remember, this inner critic just wants to protect us. We might check which self-protection system is in charge. Is there a threat? Something to push away, escape, or fight? Is there a desire or drive to achieve, to earn, or to do? Are we jumping between the two? Remember that our self-protection systems don't want us to suffer, but maybe they are not so effective when we are neither hunting nor being hunted.

There is actually an established step-by-step path to developing compassion. It begins with developing compassion for ourselves, then for our loved ones, next for acquaintances and strangers, and, yes, ultimately even for people who do not treat us well or try to hurt us, and finally for all sentient beings. It is necessary to develop and practice self-compassion, especially if we are worn out and angry at our loved ones, our colleagues, or others. To that end, we can continue to be mindful and accepting of our own internal experience as well as others'. Compassion is developed through direct and patient observation of our own emotional experience, especially including all the unpleasant feelings we would rather avoid.

Practice 2. Classical compassion training

Self-compassion—Repeat this phrase over and over for 10 minutes:

May I be safe and protected, free from inner and outer suffering. May I be healthy and happy. May I have an ease of well-being.

Compassion for another, a loved one, an acquaintance, or a person who is disliked—With a specific person in mind, repeat this phrase over and over for 10 minutes:

May you be safe and protected, free from inner and outer suffering. May you be healthy and happy. May you have an ease of well-being.

Compassion for all—Repeat these sentences over and over for at least 10 minutes, oriented toward all human beings or all sentient beings:

May we all be safe and protected, free from inner and outer suffering. May we all be healthy and happy. May we have an ease of well-being.

ANOTHER EXERCISE FOR DEVELOPING COMPASSION IS DERIVED FROM THE Tibetans, who have practiced the cultivation of compassion for thousands of years. One method of compassion training is called *tonglen*. In this practice we imagine that we *breathe in the undesirable* and *breathe out the desirable*. This is in direct opposition to what we are normally inclined to do! Our common approach to life is that if something is unpleasant, we push it away, and if it is pleasant, we hold on to it. Without a connection to a vast, open heart and an accepting mind, the tonglen practice is not possible to realize.[13] The concept that we can inhale unpleasant suffering and exhale compassion and acceptance is a form of alchemy within our hearts that requires courage, love, and acceptance.

Practice 3. Inhale suffering. Exhale compassion.

Tonglen training is an ancient Tibetan practice that is more complex than we can make space for here. Try each of these simple exercises based on this practice a few times a day for several days. Identify a specific time to practice and mark your calendar so you don't forget!

A. Whenever you notice an unpleasant emotion, an uncomfortable feeling, stress, tension, or even physical pain, observe this real and tangible discomfort and breathe it in. Then breathe out whatever would be comforting, soothing, or helpful. For example, perhaps you're at work and you notice feeling some stress, tension, and discomfort in the pit of your stomach. Breathe in all this unpleasant stuff. Perhaps you might imagine it to be a dark, black smoke. Bring it closer. Get to know it. Bring it right into your heart. Imagine that your heart contains a white light of pure, loving compassion. The black smoke of suffering may dissolve into the white light. Then exhale the radiant light from your heart, or exhale a feeling of compassion, acceptance, or love, or just a spacious and relaxed feeling. Let it go. On the in-breath enter into the discomfort once again. On the exhale, let a compassionate response flow out. Continue inhaling suffering and exhaling loving compassion for a few minutes.

B. Do the same exercise, but observing the suffering of another; imagine inhaling their suffering and exhaling a compassionate response. It could be a homeless person, a sick person, a frustrated friend, or a distressed colleague. Everyone experiences suffering, so the opportunities are endless.

C. Sitting quietly, observe the breath for five minutes. On each inhale, think "suffering." On each exhale, think "compassion." Imagine the alchemy that your heart performs as suffering is transformed to compassion.

This practice may help us when we are facing someone in pain, suffering, and/or emotional mind (including a moment of anger directed at us). We can allow our bodies to soften, and we open our eyes, ears, and mind to silently enter into their experience and extend them compassion directly from our hearts.

Compassion training has the effect of improving relationships with our loved ones and increasing our own personal sense of happiness. To develop true compassion, first we practice being kind rather than harshly critical toward ourselves, we perceive our experiences as part of the larger human experience, and we practice holding painful feelings in mindful awareness. Then, when we turn our compassion toward our loved ones and others, we focus on caring, concern, tenderness, and an orientation toward supporting, helping, and understanding, particularly when we perceive them to be suffering or in need.[14]

The cultivation of a loving concern for other people's well-being has a surprising and unique benefit: the brain's circuitry for happiness is activated, along with compassion. Loving-kindness and compassion practices also boost the connections between the brain's circuits for joy and happiness and the prefrontal cortex, a zone critical for guiding behavior. And the greater the increase in the connection between these regions, the more altruistic a person becomes following compassion meditation training.[15]

Compassion benefits the person practicing compassion very quickly; as few as seven total hours of practice over the course of two weeks leads to increased connectivity in circuits important for empathy and positive feelings, strong enough to show up outside the meditation state per se. This is the first sign of a temporary change becoming an enduring trait, though these effects likely will not last without daily practice. But the fact that they appear outside the formal meditation state itself may reflect our innate wiring for basic goodness.[16]

Validating universal traits: Intention and happiness

Validating with compassion recognizes our common humanity, and we usually do not have to search very hard for this sense of human experience if we are already practiced in compassion and heartfelt intention to relieve suffering. Compassionate validation digs deep to validate in order to relieve suffering. We all have inherent intuition, good intention, effort, knowledge, or inner wisdom and we can look for evidence of that in others and validate any or all of those capacities.

Mark owned a computer service company with his brother Sam, who had an "anger problem" that had lost them clients in the past. Mark was beginning to resent his brother's behavior. It seemed like Sam had gotten even more rigid and easily irritated over the years. Mark was worried about losing another client and then having to meet the next payroll. Mark decided to try a more compassionate approach with his brother.

Both were present in a meeting with a corporate client who was blaming Sam and his team for service problems. Mark could see Sam's anger heating up. He reached out to Sam, gently touching his arm and saying to him softly and calmly right in front of the client, *"I know it's frustrating, Sam. You put a lot of work into this project. I also believe that you are the expert here with the experience and knowledge who can find the right solution. Can we listen to these guys and make sure we understand what they would like us to do for them?"* Mark recognized that Sam needed some validation for his hard work and also some support in order to get through the meeting without becoming aggressive. Those words were enough to help Sam contain his reaction in the moment.

Mark clearly had to be grounded in his own safety and affiliation mode to help his brother move out of fight/flight and into care/share. If Mark were anxious, he would be far less effective at validating Sam. Anxiety may send the message "I want you to feel better so I'll feel better." Mark calmly and effectively validated his brother's feelings and his hard work, enabling the two to work toward resolving the problem together.

In today's world, many of us find ourselves self-critical. It is not uncommon to do things that result in more pain and suffering. Some people even talk about how they punish themselves or how they must like to suffer. But compassion does not accept this interpretation. Instead, it holds that nobody wants to suffer, that it is a human desire to be free of suffering. Everyone just wants to be happy. We all seek to be content or satisfied with our lives.

Many people live or work in abusive environments that they cannot easily leave. Many have a history of being in abusive situations or have gone through other types of traumatic experiences. Some people are not very skillful at managing their lives or reaching their goals even if they live in supportive environments. Many people have difficulty focusing their attention, letting go of obsessive thoughts, regulating their moods or emotions; they may have addictions, impulsive behaviors, or any number of other limitations and challenges. These are a few examples of situations that some people may interpret as indicating a desire to suffer. Compassion does not validate invalid beliefs.

Among people with lots of problems and suffering, validating the desire for happiness may begin as an invitation to look together for the possibility of wanting to be free from pain and suffering or the valid desire to feel peaceful.

Doris, a very successful graphic designer, confided in a close friend, saying that her bulimia and tattoos were proof that she liked pain and suffering and that she needed to punish herself. Her friend responded, "Doris, in my heart I don't believe that any human being really wants to suffer. I believe that deep inside we all really want to be peaceful and happy. Maybe . . . is it possible that the bulimia and tattoos are an attempt to escape suffering, not born of a desire to cause it?" Doris paused to reflect on what her friend had said. It was as if a light bulb went off in her head. "You know, you are right. I feel relief right after I purge . . . and I am happy right after each new tattoo."

FUNCTIONAL VALIDATION: SIMPLE ACTS OF COMPASSION CAN SPEAK LOUDER THAN WORDS

A colleague once pointed out that validation should not be reduced to "acting like a doctor who just puts on a sad face when someone is bleeding to death." This is not validation. If we want to communicate how important a person is and how much their pain matters to us, we will take the shirts off our backs if necessary to stop the bleeding! That is known as "functional validation."

A clear, simple, and direct form of compassionate communication is to just help. We see someone struggling or in need, and we may ask whether they need any assistance, support, or backup and we give it to them. There are times when we all need help. Functional validation asks what we can do to relieve suffering and then follows through.

Dennis had worked for an international energy corporation for 40 years, and his final assignment was working abroad to facilitate a joint venture. Dennis felt like he was doing nothing but unnecessary paperwork and he was being constantly criticized by local staff (who were also former competitors). Halfway into the assignment, which was supposed to be the pinnacle of his career, he had begun to feel bitter and resentful.

Dennis was talking to Maria, the HR director of the foreign affiliate, and he described the situation. Maria listened, and at first she felt that her team was being attacked unfairly. Although her first impulse was to defend the others, she made a renewed effort to be fully present. She softened her body and relaxed into it. She reminded herself of what it would be like to have to live in a foreign country. She knew that Dennis had worked hard and had a very distinguished career. She listened to his tone of voice and she noticed how his fists clenched slightly and his face turned red.

Maria responded spontaneously, *"Dennis, how can I help? Really. This should not be happening. I want to help make this right. Let's see what we can do to fix this."* He was disarmed. His anger instantly melted. Upon hearing her response, possibilities seemed to expand and the world seemed less threatening. He was so relieved that for a second he almost felt like crying. They began to talk about concrete ways that she could intervene to reduce prejudicial attitudes and facilitate more effective conferences. Then she picked up the phone to schedule meetings with members both teams.

Examples of simple, validating acts of compassion someone might include the following:

- If a someone is distressed, offer something beyond words

that is comforting for that person—for example, a cup of tea
or a cookie, flowers, or a pillow.

- If someone starts to cry, offer a tissue.
- If a loved one has their feelings hurt, step forward and give a
  big hug (asking permission if needed).
- If someone wants to talk, pull up a chair and give your
  undivided and caring attention.
- If a person is sad, wordlessly reach out and put your hand on
  their hand or on their shoulder.
- If someone on the street asks you for change, give some
  change without judging how they are going to use it or if
  they deserve it. (Just assume that if they ask, then they
  need it.)

Try these until they become natural responses. You'll be amazed
because you will probably feel good doing it after practicing a few
times. With friends and family this may be easier than with acquaintances or strangers. Think of gestures and actions that communicate
kindness, care, and concern and that are appropriate to the social and
cultural norms of the environment.

The technical term for these compassionate acts of validation, as
opposed to words, is *functional validation*. This kind of validation is
implicit and unspoken. Our deeds respond to the needs of the other.
If someone says "Leave me alone," the validating deed would be to
walk away. If someone says "I don't feel like talking about that," then
we change the subject. If someone says "I'm afraid," we offer protection. If someone says "You never listen to me," we give them our undivided attention with no defense or excuses. Of course, we may have
to read between the lines of what someone is saying, but nonjudgmental validation can teach others to ask for what they want.

I explained functional validation once to a family of three kids and
their mom. The youngest (age 8), who clearly understood the
concept, turned to me at one point with her eyes wide open and said,
"What about those times when you say 'leave me alone' but you

really want the other person to come closer?" I gave her a big smile and leaned forward and softly said to her, "Well we have to learn to ask for what we really want in order to be effective at getting it! Nobody can read our minds. Asking for what we want is a very important skill to practice. If you want someone to come closer, you might have to say something very direct, like *I need a hug. Will you please give me one?*" From the corner of my eye I saw her mom with a big smile and a nod of support.

Practice 4. Random acts of kindness

Do something kind for someone else. Pay the toll for the person in the car behind you. Allow someone to go ahead of you in line at the supermarket. Offer to pick up or carry something for an elderly person. Stop and ask an acquaintance or a shopkeeper how their day is going and listen deeply with openness to really understand. Tell a stressed-out-looking person how much you like their clothes/hair/bag/etc. (of course, only if such a comment is genuine!) Don't avert your gaze when someone asks for money and let go of any judgmental thoughts that may arise. Carry change in your pocket and wish someone good luck and a good day with a smile. Find a simple act of kindness and do it deliberately and fully. Of course, don't forget to do acts of loving kindness for loved ones as well!

COMPASSION MAY INCLUDE ACCURATE *INVALIDATION* (OF THAT WHICH IS NOT VALID)

Acts of unwavering love and compassion can include saying "no" to a loved one who wants money for drugs, spanking the child who ran into the street without looking for the third time, and taking away the car keys from a friend who has had too much to drink. We can validate the feelings *and* say no: "I understand that the drug would relieve your distress and craving right now, *and* am not going to give you money." "You were having fun *and* it is very dangerous to run into the street." "You may not be happy about it, but I love you *and* am not going to let you drive home in your condition."

Compassion can mean saying no to others out of responsibility for one's own self-care. Such genuine compassion can be a major healing process for turbulent minds and relationships. With razor-like focus, we can validate that which is valid and not reinforce or validate that which is not valid.

Maryann's tall, handsome, and athletic husband was a veteran who had served in Afghanistan. While he could be charming, warm, and good-humored, he suffered from post traumatic stress symptoms in which he often experienced panic, depression, or raging anger. Love and validation came naturally to Maryann, but seven years into the marriage, she was exhausted and on the verge of leaving him.

She knew that his pain and emotional suffering was real. And it was also true that, as much as she might love him, she could not *make* him happy, nor was it her responsibility to do so. She learned to validate the needs and emotions of both her husband and herself, even if it meant saying "no" to him. She began to practice validation and communicating her limits to helping him:

- *When he complained that she wasn't doing enough for him:* "That must be very painful, to have a wife who does not support you enough. It sounds like you feel you are alone or powerless or worse. I also have to tend to my own needs sometimes or I will have nothing left for me *or* you.
- *When he was calm and they had time to talk:* "I know there are moments when you are haunted by the war. I have seen you suffer for years. You are so strong; I don't think that I could endure what you have gone through. I can listen, but I can't make it all better.

She practiced validation and self-validation:

- *Once he yelled at her and she was taken aback:* "That's got to be infuriating for you, but it scares me when you yell at me like that. I don't like to be yelled at." She went into another room and closed the door.
- *Another time he yelled at her and she was instantly angry:* "I know you are frustrated, *and* when you yell it makes me angry, too. I'm taking a timeout."

When Maryann began to validate her husband's experience *and* care for her own needs, he did not like it at first. In fact, she was modeling the very behavior that she wanted from him. She was patient and persistent about the need for her own self-care. Probably as a result of her distancing herself to care for herself better, he eventually sought out effective, evidence-based treatment for trauma.

True compassion does not reward or validate invalid behavior. Validating invalid behavior often enables the other person to continue engaging in the unacceptable or destructive behavior. It contributes to making the other person even more ineffective and less capable of change. Over time they may feel incompetent or ashamed. They become an "invalid" in the true sense of the word. Validation includes accurate invalidation as an act of genuine compassion.

Drew was 21 and his parents were separated. Drew had dropped out of high school and spent almost of his waking hours on his computer. One day his dad stopped in to visit him, and the two got into a heated discussion. At one point Drew exploded in a rage and punched his father. Dad left the house furious and called Drew's mom from his car to tell her was calling the police. His mother managed to communicate just enough emotional empathy for his father's anger that he agreed to postpone the call for a few hours. They also agreed that there had to be immediate and serious consequences for Drew's behavior. Mom wanted to respond out of compassion, not out of anger. She called Drew and validated his frustration, anger, and fear and said she was on her way to see him.

Instead of the police, Mom called an ambulance. The paramedics arrived and she briefed them before they went into the house. They checked his blood pressure several times over the course of their conversation, showing obvious concern that it was dangerously high with a wink toward his mother. They told Drew that he had go to the hospital overnight for observation, and Drew nervously agreed. That night his father obtained a court order for psychiatric treatment to contain his son's violence. Drew wasn't happy about the legal mandate for treatment, but he had little choice.

This is a good example of validating that which is valid (anger) and also accurately invalidating—through action—that which is ineffective or unacceptable (physical violence). Drew's mother was a validation pro! She had been studying and practicing validation for a full year before this event and had already built a lot of trust and acceptance that had been missing in their relationship through most of his difficult adolescence. The presence of the police would have increased Drew's aggression and, at the very least, seemed be an exaggerated response to a situation that the father had some responsibility for escalating. The accurate invalidation of Drew's violent response toward his father was a dramatic turning point in his personal development, which was probably only successful because of the mom's genuine validation of his suffering over the course of the prior year.

Compassion is an ethical and prosocial response to human suffering. It entails a loving response to others, the urge to act effectively, *and* the skillful means to do so. Validation is a skill of compassionate communication.

Compassion is misused if it is limited to one's own family and friends, one's own race or religion, one's own socioeconomic class, and so on. We begin the practice of compassion with ourselves and our loved ones, and we must extend this practice to all human beings (or even all sentient beings). Being kind to others when it is against social norms is not easy. It is not easy to stand up against adolescent bullying at school; workplace mobbing; sexual, racial, or religious discrimination; or prejudice against others for their age, weight, or political party. These all occur when compassion does not extend beyond others "like us."

Try validating a stranger, especially someone of a different race, religion, or political party. It may not be easy, but it just may be the most personally rewarding type of validation of all.

When we are open to seeing the suffering of others as part of our common and shared humanity and we name that suffering, we are validating with compassion. When we move out of our threat-focused form of reacting and engage our affiliation system with helping or connecting with validation, that is compassion.

We saw four biological, neurochemical systems that form the basis of emotions: fight/flight, desire/drive, fatigue/fold, and care/share. Ideally these are in balanced in ways that maximize wholesome living and a meaningful life. Today too many people jump between threat avoidance (fight/flight) and reward (desire/drive) in a fruitless effort to find satisfaction without developing their system for affiliation and nurturing. When we validate with compassion, we are nurturing both our own and others' care/share system and engaging the system that truly awakens joy and a profound satisfaction with life. Compassion can be cultivated through specific mind training techniques that go back at least 2,500 years

As we develop validation skills, we gain more clarity and effectiveness to help others become freer from stress and suffering and more connected to their own sense of wellness. This can have a far-reaching impact on how we relate to ourselves and others. Our world begins to expand. We become a little less focused on ourselves and the desire to achieve more, have more, and hold on tightly to what we already have. As we become more compassionate (toward ourselves and others), we also have less anxiety and fear. We feel safer and more secure in the world. Relationships and communication improve. Our health may even improve. Compassion is powerful.

Understanding and cultivating compassion

1. Compassion defined

- Compassion involves kindness, awareness of suffering, a caring connection with other humans or sentient beings, the desire to relieve suffering, and effort or skillful action toward this end.
- Compassionate caring is a product of human evolution that creates emotional balance and prosocial behavior that is fundamental for human adaptation and survival.
- Compassion is effective for regulating emotions and soothing emotional distress.

2. Self-protection systems

- Compassion may be blocked by our threat-focused system, our resource-focused system, and our fatigue/fold system and may also be nourished to counterbalance these other self-protections systems.

3. Cultivating compassion

- The roots of compassion can be strengthened through mental and behavioral training until it becomes an ever-present habit.

- We regularly practice compassion contemplations with words, images, or both. These include self-compassion training, classical training, and tonglen. (Try any one of them for 2 minutes a day and work up to 20. Your brain will be changed for the happier after 7 weeks, according to the science!)
- We look for opportunities to practice mindfulness and kindness with loved ones, friends, acquaintances, and strangers.

Validating with compassion

1. Validating universal traits

- We look for and validate good intentions, knowledge, intuition, or inner wisdom.
- We validate the desire for happiness and for freedom from suffering that every human shares.

2. Offering functional validation through deeds and actions

- We engage in acts of compassion in response to another's needs or problems, not just with words, but also with action.
- We do what is needed to relieve the stress or suffering of the other (or ourselves as an act of self-compassion).
- We might look directly into the eyes of the other and ask, "How can I help?"
- We get up and lend a hand when it is needed and effective.
- We reach out with a hug when it is helpful.

3. Saying "no" out of compassion

- We follow through in a way that is *truly effective* at reducing suffering (not simply saying yes to whatever request is made).

- Immediate relief of suffering does not justify acts that result in long-term prolongation of suffering. For example, out of compassion we can say no to the drug addict who wants another fix or to the child who wants more candy.

4. It's not just for my tribe

- We treat ourselves as being equally as deserving of love and kindness as any other person.
- We treat others outside of our family, community, or group, with compassion even if they are very different from ourselves. Every human being is equally deserving of compassion without prejudice.

8

WISDOM

I have been practicing meditation for over ten years and now I can sit still on a cushion for an hour. And I can be the same contemptuous idiot that I always was! But now when I screw up, I know that I am like every other human. Those embarrassing mistakes are my greatest learning opportunities, and the people who trigger my frustration and anger are my greatest teachers.

S ome people say that our brains are like biological "machines" that generate a constant stream of energy in the form of movement of chemicals and electricity. This brain machine is programmed before birth and continues to be wired and rewired as we grow. Our minds receive messages from our brain machine, and many of these messages are actually quite deceptive and confusing and lead to a wildly inaccurate perception of reality.

According to this model, it is the mind that is responsible for making choices and decisions about the information that the brain is delivering, often in the form of incessant chatter and infinite amounts of information via our senses. The mind actively guides us with an inner wisdom—wisdom that can be nourished when we attend to our direct experience as it unfolds, noting causes and discriminating between wholesome and unwholesome consequences.

Mary, a successful lawyer and public defender, was at the end of her rope with her son, Mark. His life, like those of his friends and peers, revolved around video games and electronic social networks. When he was not avoiding his mother, he was irritated with her. Mary, frustrated and burned out from arguing with him, told him he had to move in with his father, who lived in conditions that she considered filthy and unsanitary. He left the house that day.

Mary was expecting an apology from her son, and she had been planning out all the conditions that she would put in front of him when he decided to move back in with her. Two weeks passed, and her son had not once called. Sometimes she felt like crying. She could not accept her son's behavior, and she could not find anything to validate in either her son or herself. She had lost touch with her wise inner guide. She was believing the thoughts that her brain machine generated without really discriminating between the wholesome and unwholesome consequences. How had this happened?

CULTIVATING WISDOM: INTEGRATED BRAIN, INTEGRATED MIND

When we are under stress or in emotional mind, our capacity for working memory is reduced, our problem-solving abilities decline, and our cognitive capacity is diminished. Our minds become agitated by our emotions, and our thinking can be hijacked. We can become caught up in a vicious cycle of negativity.

Back in the chapter on emotions, we saw how we can get caught up in these feedback loops that become vicious cycles. When we are sad, we tend to think sad thoughts, see things from a melancholic perspective, and then maybe even criticize ourselves for being such losers. Or when we are angry we can think only angry thoughts, we can see only how unfair life is or how others should or should not act, and we tend to blame them (or ourselves) for doing something wrong. In anxious mind, we think only anxious thoughts. We may be highly focused—on planning our attack or our escape, for example—but we do not mentally process the big picture.

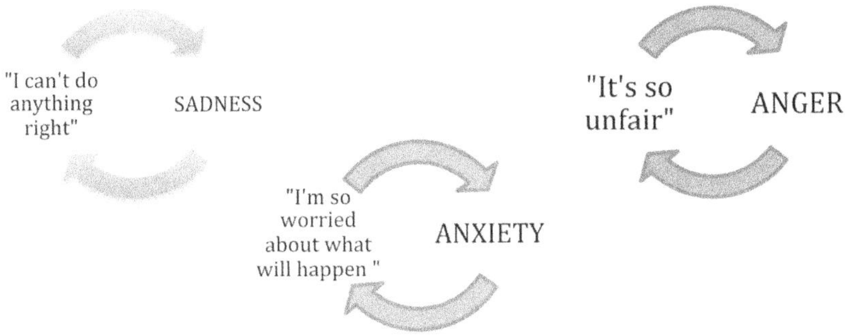

How do we get out of this vicious cycle? The first step is to recognize that we are experiencing an emotion, or perhaps in "emotional mind." Without the ability to notice our inner experience right here and right now, it will be very hard to respond from wise mind.

If the emotion arises from a problem or situation that we can fix, well, then we should fix it! But maybe it is not resolvable right now. Or maybe our emotions are too intense for the situation, or perhaps not even justified by the situation, or simply not effective. We might just have to distract ourselves if the emotion is extreme. But if we can observe, accept, and even welcome the emotion that is already present (even if it was not invited), then that will be the path of wisdom.

As we know from the practice of mindfulness, recognizing that we are in emotional mind is the first step. Then, by bringing our attention to the breath and letting go of tension with each exhale, letting go of negative thoughts, and attending to the act of breathing over time, little by little this helps move us away from emotional hijacking and toward a more integrated wise mind.

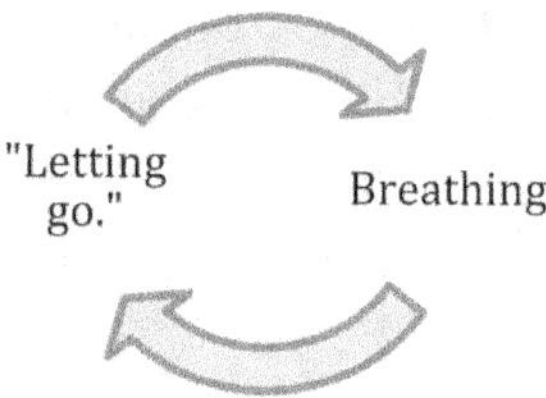

Bringing our attention to the breath over and over again leads us out of emotional mind and into wise mind. It can free us from emotional hijacking or the vicious cycle of suffering. Remember, we are not trying to cut off emotional experiences; we want to integrate them with reasoning. Becoming centered in wise mind by listening to all our senses connects us to reality through our bodies—what we see, hear, touch, smell, taste, or feel physically—instead of experiencing our thoughts as reality. Wisdom arises naturally out of mindfulness practice.

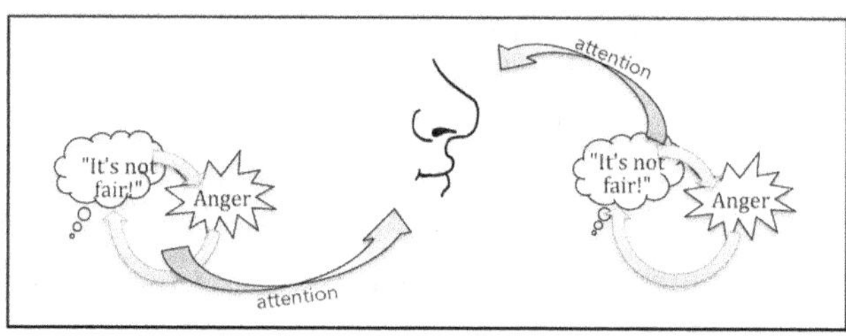

If we get into the vicious cycle of negative emotions and negative thoughts, there are only two options: (1) Cut off thoughts or (2) Let them pass. Either way, during or after the thought arises, one must recognize that it is a thought and put one's attention somewhere else . . . such as the breath.

The brain is integrated when functional regions are internally synchronized and also in sync with other regions. Wise mind arises from this brain state. As we saw in chapter 3, wise mind is the synthesis of rational mind and emotional mind. Our rational mind is logical and calculating. Our emotional mind is empathic and energizing. The holistic integration of reason and emotion is wise mind, the basis for effective decision-making.

Aristotle also links the integrated mind with "practical wisdom." Practical wisdom arises when reason, desire, feeling, and behavior are interwoven together into the "golden mean." It is not necessarily a quiet, centered response; the golden mean refers to the most appropriate and effective combination in a given set of circumstances. Extreme outrage or joy, soft compassion, or even physical violence may be the right and wise response in a particular situation.

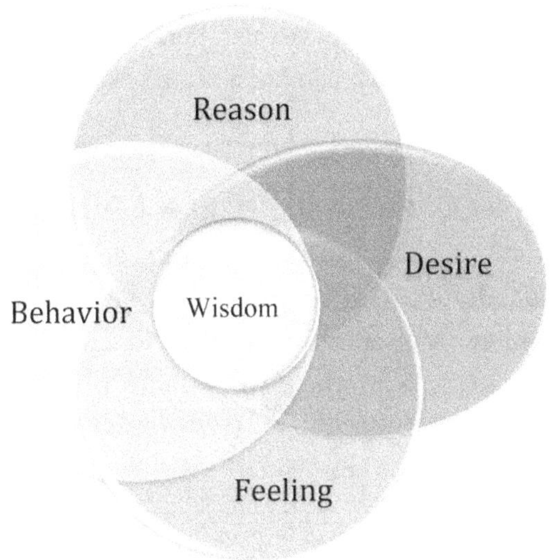

Practice 1. The golden pause

What is going on right here, right now? Take a moment to focus on your breath and then bring your attention to the following four questions, one by one:

1. What am I doing? Notice exactly what you are doing and what is going on around you.

2. What am I feeling? What are you feeling in your torso, in your neck and shoulders, in your face? What other physical sensations arise? What emotional feelings are present?

3. What am I thinking? Notice what thoughts arise—or what you were just thinking about.

4. What do I want or need? Step back and look at the big picture. What are your needs and aspirations? What do you really want to get out of this situation, this hour, or this day?

Close with a conscious breath.

If you feel the need to extend the pause for a few minutes, go right ahead. You have just connected with yourself, centered yourself a bit, and practiced a wise pause.

Let's check in with Mary again. Despite her career success, Mary often gets home and leaves her wise mind at the door. She is tired and becomes irritated with her son, Mark, as soon as she sees him on the computer. Mentally she begins to criticize him and feel underappreciated as a mother; worse, she might be ashamed or guilty of her mothering without even being aware of it. She can't validate anything. The best she can do in this state is avoid Mark. It should be no surprise that they experience a lot of conflict in their relationship.

Imagine that Mary takes her time going home. She lets go of problems at work and mentally shifts gears to appreciate the present moment and soften her internal experience. Perhaps she pauses before going into the house. She notices the tension in her body and relaxes a little. Before entering she loosens her grip on her expectations and connects with her intention to be present, patient, and effective in her interactions with her son. Their conversation unfolds very differently. Perhaps she even asks herself, "What am I needing right now?" and tends to herself first.

DIALECTICS AND PARADOX

The wise sage understands that there is no ultimate truth. All truth is relative and dialectical. Wisdom comfortably enters into this paradox; wisdom becomes this paradox. Dialectics says that things that appear opposite and incompatible may also be integrated and inseparable.[1] There is more than one truth, more than one perspective from which we can understand reality. For example, things appear stable and permanent and yet they change from moment to moment. What can be more stable and permanent than a mountain, for example? Yet if we observe it carefully, we can see that it changes in color, sound, temperature, water content, etc.—biological activity and geological changes occur continuously. A mountain changes from year to year, from season to season, from day to night, even from moment to moment. Stability and change occur at the same time. The world is in constant flux and nothing is absolute, as it may appear. Wisdom is the full appreciation of the dialectical view that everything is relative.

Examples of the wisdom of dialectics are everywhere. A mother wants to protect her child. She also wants her child to become independent and unafraid of taking risks. A manager is doing the very best he can in the face of complaints from his supervisees. It is also true that he can do better in the future as he continues to do the best he can. These examples help us to get out of rigid thinking or emotional mind and find creative and wise solutions.

"All activities should be done with one intention" is an ancient paradox. How could this be possible? Everything done with one intention? Let's take a step back and connect with our wise minds. What would be one intention that we bring to everything we do? It would have to be something universal: love . . . compassion . . . maybe kindness. What would happen if we took the attitude of wanting all our actions to directly or indirectly benefit others? Is it possible to want all our actions to increase our kinship with our fellow human beings?

For some people this leads to yet another paradox. Why would I wish my actions to benefit people who treat me badly, who criticize me, or who are abusive? Frankly there are some people out there who are not kind, and they do not deserve my kinship.

Okay, so let's imagine Frank, a person who is, according to all those around him, a downright mean and spiteful person. Now imagine that the whole world began to treat Frank kindly. Imagine that Frank had all his needs met and all his desires fulfilled. If Frank were happy and content, he would not be mean or spiteful. Of course, if Frank has done something to deliberately cause you pain and suffering, it may not be easy to wish him happiness. Doing so may even be the opposite of what every cell in your body wants. But if you and Frank cross paths regularly, eventually you will see that his suffering is your suffering and his freedom from suffering is your freedom from suffering.

Seeing situations from a dialectical perspective supports validation. We can see how something may be valid and invalid at the same time. Perhaps we just look for only what is valid and let the rest go, or we describe both sides of the picture. We can also see how two people can have two different truths at the same time and both can be valid.

John was complaining to his neighbor about his 18-year-old son. "I don't understand him at all. I think he just smokes pot. He doesn't know what he wants to do with his life and he actually embarrasses me." The neighbor softly responded, "You know your son a lot better than I do. It is definitely possible. It must be really hard to see him without the kind of direction and communication that you think he should have."

John's frustration and anxiety went down a little. "Yes, it is, and I don't really know what to do. He doesn't ask me for advice, and I can't help him if he doesn't ask. So it's really frustrating." His neighbor tilted his head to one side and raised his eyebrows, saying, "I spoke to him yesterday and he seemed pretty clear about what he wanted. He is not a bad kid. He needs his father—even if you feel he is pushing you away."

John's neighbor could validate John's feelings and also the desires and behaviors of John's son. He could identify the validity of both points of view. Below is another example in which a young man named Justin found a way to validate both the feelings of his friend Susana and the behavior of her mother.

Susana, 17, was at school talking to her friend Justin. "I hate my mother and she hates me. She told my brother she didn't even care if I ran away from home. I don't have anybody and I can't stand it anymore."

Justin actually thought that Susana's mom was a reasonable person. However, he put himself into Susana's shoes. "I bet you felt totally betrayed when your brother told you that! That must have hurt. Your mother must have been really pissed off to say that because I have never heard her say anything bad about you."

Intellectual humility and radical openness

When we get right down to it, there is so much that we don't know.

Intellectual humility, a major subject within the philosophy of wisdom, is the patient recognition of what we don't know. It is a level of acceptance and comfort with not knowing.

Sometimes we are absolutely sure that we are "correct," even when we are just assuming or guessing. (I have probably come across as being a little smug myself sometimes, even as I have tried to validate or teach validation skills to others. I might have to get down off my pedestal to explain humility!) Instead of making assumptions and interpretations and acting as if they are true, we are wiser to embrace humility and be open to new information.

Toni Packer taught of form of meditative inquiry that fully embraces intellectual humility:

"We have a real urge to be 'in the know.' Knowing things is highly valued—we are well rewarded for having all kinds of information stored in our brains and being able to pass it on to others. We take it for granted that asking questions means having to get or to give answers—the sooner, the better. Drawing a blank or saying, 'I don't know' is considered weak or embarrassing...

"Instead of automatically seeking the relief that a superficial answer provides, can we start with not knowing and ask the question into not knowing? . . . Not knowing means putting aside what I already know and being cautious to observe freely, openly, what is actually taking place right now in the light of the question. Not knowing means putting up with the discomfort of no immediate answer."[2]

This type of not-knowing is consistent with Thomas Lynch's concept of "radical openness." Practicing radical openness, we are open to "disconfirming information" about what we believe. We are curious, interested, and comfortable with learning new things, seeing different sides to a situation, and understanding others' perspectives.[3] Radical openness is an important component of genuine validation. It involves being open to learning and trying to deeply understand what another is communicating without any defensiveness or fear of being wrong. In fact, it is being radically open to the possibility that the world might prove me wrong—which would be just another opportunity to learn something new.

Humility and radical openness ask questions and listen to the answers with a beginner's mind, instead of thinking that we already know how the other will respond. It includes a healthy self-doubt, in which we do not take ourselves too seriously and have a sense of humor. (As opposed to unhealthy self-doubt, in which we appear willing to question ourselves, but underneath we are convinced that we are right or we feel unfairly accused and harbor resentment.) Asking questions with humility can be faked. Faking it is annoying and can even be a form of passive aggression. That is the opposite of humility and openness. Fully embracing intellectual humility and radical openness can result in feelings of joy and awe.

Validation with humility and openness takes us beyond the golden rule, "Do unto others as you would have others do unto you." If we stop here, we are assuming that our own experience is the litmus test for how to treat others. Is that true? People of different backgrounds and abilities may have completely different needs. Being open to being wrong and learning from our mistakes about what we know, or believe that we know, goes a long way toward interacting with others in a way that is validating and grounded in wisdom. We do *not* believe that "I" am smarter than "you," nor that "I" am able to solve "your" problems. We communicate, for example, *I know less about you than you do. I want to understand your experience. Tell me what it is like to be you. I am here to learn!*

Practice 2. How intellectually humble and open are you?

1. If someone asks you for advice about a problem, are you comfortable with saying that you don't have an answer, or do you love to give answers, sometimes believing that any answer seems much better than not knowing what to say?

2. When confronted with a different point of view, do you pause and patiently listen with curiosity, or do you tend to think of counterarguments while the other is speaking?

3. If you already believe that you know everything about something, do you tend to remain open to being wrong by asking thoughtful questions, or do you hammer arguments and counterarguments to convince the other that you are right?

4. Are you secure in your convictions and self-constructs, or are you willing to sacrifice them in order to experience greater flexibility, happiness, or meaning in your life?

5. Can you see the dialectics of the first option in each of the above questions and consider concrete ways to move toward them?

GESTURES OF WARMTH AND HUMILITY

Social signaling really matters in interpersonal communication. A combination of humility, warmth, interest, and openness can be communicated with facial expressions and body language.

Some people may not experience our attempts at emotional validation as validating. There are specific gestures and expressions that can be validating by communicating warmth, connection, humility, openness, interest, etc.

Deference or humility: Moving the head forward and lowering it are ancient ways of communicating deference. Sitting down can also communicate this, especially if the other person is standing.

Concern: Lifting the eyebrows and bringing them slightly together while moving the head forward.

Joy and wonder: Lifting both eyebrows with a broad and genuine smile.

Interest, openness, and curiosity: Lifting both eyebrows and tilting the head to one side.

Acceptance and welcome: Holding one or both palms up with the arms extended forward, head slightly tilted, smiling, and body relaxed.

Practice 3. Combine gestures, facial expression, and words for compassionate communication

When we use words and phrases that are consistent with our gestures and facial expressions, our communication is clear and coherent. Try reading out loud the responses below to imaginary situations as if you were reading a movie script. Follow the instructions for the facial expression and gestures. You may feel ridiculous, exaggerated, or totally false. It doesn't matter. Just try to be the best actor that you can be.

1. Imagine listening to a friend complaining about a problem:

With your head loaning forward, eyebrows slightly turrowed, respond, "Gee, I have no idea what I would do in your shoes." Then, pausing and lifting the head and the eyebrows, ask, "What are you thinking of doing?"

2. Imagine being a parent whose teenager is asking for advice. In spite of the temptation to tell him what you think, you speak slowly and softly, saying, "I don't know, but that's

a really good question." Hold your head slightly tilted, stroking the chin and looking thoughtfully interested, remain in silence.

3. Imagine responding to an anxious and very rational spouse who mishandled a problem at work. With your head leaning forward, eyebrows slightly furrowed, respond, "Honey, that sounds hard. I hate it when I drop the ball. . . It can happen to anyone." Pause and then lift the eyebrows, saying, "What are you thinking of doing?"

4. Imagine trying to validate a relative with health problems who tends to minimize or ignore them: "It sounds like you are taking it all in stride. Are you worried about this a little?" Sit down, lower your head, lift your eyebrows, and listen fully to their response. You could try to speak gently and ask: "Is anything that I can do to help?"

DECENTERING

Responding from a self-immersed, egocentric perspective (imagining that events are unfolding before your own eyes) has a different effect on how information is processed than adopting a distanced perspective (from the point of view of a distant observer such as a security camera or a fly on the wall).[4] Some very interesting scientific research on this issue has shown that people who learn to adopt a distanced perspective are more likely to recognize the limits of their knowledge and the *unknowableness* of the future. Decentering helps us take things less personally, and insecurity is replaced by wisdom.

Practice 4. Decentering—self-immersion versus self-distancing

Think of an event in which you felt anxious or afraid, angry, or sad—a small reaction, not too intense or dramatic. Or bring to mind an event in which you could not decide what to do or in which you reacted in a way that you later regretted, at least a little.

When you recall the event, you probably do so from a "self-immersed" perspective. You may actually remember what happened as if you were seeing it from behind your own eyes.

Now imagine that you are a fly on the wall and try to see yourself and your interaction with others from this perspective. Describe what is happening. How did you respond to others and how did others respond to you? *Be the witness.*

Stepping back or stepping aside creates space. In this space lies greater wisdom. You may analyze what you felt and what evoked that feeling and what led to your response as events unfolded.

How to reason wisely over daily life? Get some distance.

Dora, a doctor working in a public hospital at age 68, often felt resentful that others were not as respectful of her as she believed they should be. One day she was at a diner across the street from the hospital when another doctor approached her about a problem. As he spoke, Dora couldn't believe how insensitive he was, interrupting her coffee break that she was taking outside of the hospital. She felt that people had taken advantage of her kindness for years and she couldn't tolerate it anymore. Her response was curt. Her irritation with her colleague was evident in her tone of voice and her facial expression.

Dora had been trying mindfulness and relaxation techniques that just seemed to make her even more aware of her irritation and less able to control it. What finally made the difference for Dora was stepping back and seeing the big picture. She recognized that she believed that others should know when she wanted to be alone and not be disturbed. She was resentful that she had to say no to others when they interrupted her free time. And from the distanced perspective she also could see that others had no intention of "bothering her" or "taking advantage of her." They were just wrapped up in their own problems.

Dora learned to respond with validation—"That's a really good question" or "I know it is important for you"—and then add, "I can meet you in a half hour in my office to talk about it." Decentering allows us to effectively step back and identify what is valid in others and in ourselves.

ALL THINGS ARISE AND PASS WITH EQUANIMITY

Equanimity is a fundamental skill on the path of wisdom. It is sometimes confused with indifference, stoicism, or apathy. Equanimity is an internal state of balance that goes much deeper than acceptance and leads us toward an inner silence and peace. Equanimity is the practice of not clinging to thoughts and feelings, not identifying with likes or dislikes. Equanimity is integrated into an awareness of the impermanence of all experiences. We remain centered and grounded without grasping and without rejecting anything that arises within our experience.

Shinzen Young teaches us to cultivate equanimity in the body—maintaining a relaxed state even as various sensorial experiences arise, including negative emotions—and equanimity of the mind—developing an attitude of acceptance and appreciation for all thoughts and emotions.[5] He suggests regular "micro-hits" throughout the day. We can regularly check in to our body - breathing in and out a few times, noting what we feel with acceptance, and noting what we are thinking with kindness toward ourselves.

Being aware of and present for the continuous flow of causes and consequences is another classic way to cultivate equanimity, which really is a powerful form of wisdom. How is it that? Through seeing, knowing, and experiencing that everything is caused, then acceptance and understanding arise.

Practice 5. Cultivating the wisdom of equanimity

Sitting still, with your back straight and your shoulders relaxed, take a few breaths. Now, reflecting over your life, think about a time when you felt like you were offering the world your best. Take a few minutes to reflect on those times when you were acting with love, generosity, patience, empathy, kindness, or any other of your valued ideals. Stop reading here to close your eyes and fully remember these moments.

Next bring to mind an event or a period of your life in which you were at your worst, when you behaved in an unkind or disagreeable manner. You are not going to remember these moments with pride, and reflecting on them may even trigger remorse or guilt or shame. These were probably moments when you were under stress or had problems or when your mind was distorted by negative emotions from disappointment, fear, or frustration. At this moment you were not consciously seeking peace and contentment. Close your eyes and take a minute to fully remember this situation.

Next take a step back mentally and see if it is possible to feel a genuine kindness, empathy, or compassion for this person (yourself) in this particular situation when you were not at your best. Take a few minutes to extend a heartfelt desire to be free of suffering with each breath.

Next bring to mind someone whom you don't really get along with, who irritates you, or for whom your heart is closed. Think of someone whose behavior is negative or who is threatening to you or others, who has their own insecurities, frustrations, disappointments, or other mental afflictions. (We know from our own experience that this type of disagreeable behavior can really happen.)

Now take a few minutes to attend to your thoughts and memories of this person. Like a doctor who attends to everyone regardless of their illness, mentally attend to this person with their afflicted mind. Imagine extending a heartfelt desire to this person to be free from suffering, or at least to let go of clinging to or fighting against their pain.

Seeing this person in your mind, think to yourself, "May you be free of suffering." Then take a few minutes and, with each inhale, imagine inhaling the black smoke of their suffering and with each exhale imagine exhaling a white light of heartfelt loving kindness.

If we learn to approach the suffering of our own experience as an opportunity to practice compassion for oneself and for others, we will better succeed at experiencing it with equanimity.

We have a natural, innate wisdom that expands with time, with life experience, and through living mindfully. We learn to differentiate between healthy consequences and detrimental consequences. We learn to be less distracted and less impulsive. We can choose to direct our attention and our intention to wholesome actions. These are choices that we make when we are in wise, equanimous, and compassionate mind.

VALIDATING WITH THE WISDOM OF CAUSES AND CONSEQUENCES

Paying close attention, moment by moment, we can see that everything has causes and consequences: Something does not arise out of nothing. Suffering often arises out of resistance to pain. Sadness turns to anger. Fear is contagious. Thoughts generate feelings. Feelings can give rise to thoughts.

We can effectively validate experiences, feelings, and behaviors based on antecedents (or causes) and consequences. If we know what set off an emotion, we can validate it. *"Of course you are feeling that way, because situation* x *caused it!"* Past consequences condition us to repeat behaviors. If we know how someone has been conditioned by these consequences, we can validate the behavior. *"Of course you get angry and yell at them; the employees usually rush around to solve the problem when you do that."* Note that we can communicate that a behavior is understandable AND that it has negative consequences. *"However, now I have three of your subordinates asking for a transfer. Yelling at people damages relationships."*

If we listen to the other's story and we step back and see this story within the context of the emotions, feelings, and reactions, then we can validate an emotion or desire based upon what preceded it. Every emotion has something that evoked it, and if we can find that, we can validate the emotion by connecting it with what set it off. We can validate an emotion, desire, or need based on that which triggered it or that which happens as a result of it. We can ask questions to understand what triggered the response, and just asking these questions can be validating. Inquiring into the antecedents, causes, or consequences, or making sense of someone's internal experience based on its causes or consequences, are both ways to validate that experience. For example:

- We see a person emotionally activated. Something caused the emotion. What was it? If we don't know, we can simply ask the most basic question, *"What happened?"*
- This person feels this way because of his personal history. What happened in their past that would affect them now like this?
- This person interpreted an event in a way that triggered the

emotion. *"What were you thinking when that happened?"* or *"What was your understanding of that?"* or *"What do you think he meant when he said that to you?"*
- They feel this way because they want or need something and this emotion may help them get it. *"What are you needing right now?"* or *"What were you expecting or hoping for when that happened?"*

Just the assumption that there is an explicable set of circumstances that makes sense behind any thought, feeling, or behavior can be validating (and self-validating, too). This assumption helps us experience or tolerate a painful experience more easily without getting swept up into secondary emotions. It does not mean that all behaviors are effective. But almost of them are understandable in some way.

Wisdom finds the grain of truth that is valid

Validation can be insight into a grain of truth. It can be the realization of that which is factual or effective vs. that which is confused or distorted. Validating something that is inherently ineffective or untrue generates confusion and emotional dysregulation, and it is quite invalidating in the long term. The following are examples of a comment, followed by a response that "validates the *in*valid." Then a validating response follows that validates only the element that is already valid.

1. *"I was dying of embarrassment at the time, and I just couldn't admit the truth."*

Validating the invalid: *It's OK that you lied. You were feeling so ashamed.*

Finding the grain of truth: *That must have been a very painful moment for you.*

2. *"I hate studying. It's boring."*

Validating the invalid: *I can see how hard this homework for you, so let me do it.*

Finding the grain of truth: *It's true, studying can be boring sometimes.*

3. "I'm so fat and ugly."

Validating the invalid: *Well, you could lose some weight, and maybe if you try some makeup you'll be prettier.*

Finding the grain of truth: *Feeling fat and ugly is really uncomfortable. It feels really bad.*

In spite of the best intentions, many people find themselves overwhelmed with their loved ones and validate notions that are not valid.

Wisdom can validate feelings and question the consequences of the behavior

There is another useful and dialectical way to avoid validating the invalid, especially the distorted thoughts and beliefs that tend to arise from emotional mind. First, make sense of the emotions by identifying vulnerabilities, antecedents, or triggers. Then, validate the desires or beliefs—as desires and beliefs associated with the emotion. But there is more than just validation here. We might gently question the consequences of clinging to such desires and beliefs.

1. "Nobody can do anything right around here. I have to do everything myself."

Validate the emotion and question the consequences of the belief: *It has got to be really frustrating that the job did not get done correctly. However, if you don't delegate some of your work, will you get more stressed or less stressed?*

2. "I get back from vacation and I have to start yelling to get people to do things around here."

Validate the emotion and question the consequences of the belief: *I imagine that it is infuriating that this did not get fixed while you were away. I can see yelling gets immediate results. But what does it do to your focus and concentration for your work?*

3. "I am a real people pleaser because I can't stand it if people don't like me."

Validate the emotion and question the consequences of the belief: *We all need to be liked, and nobody wants to be rejected by others. I know I hate to be rejected. However, what are the consequences of trying to please all the people all the time? Is that even possible?*

Wisdom naturally arises with the practice of everyday mindfulness. At its essence, this entails quietly observing antecedents and consequences of actions and events without jumping to automatic conclusions. When we are fully present and paying attention, we observe the unfolding of events clearly and we see how every action lies within a sequence of events. With such practice, we cultivate wisdom and can effectively validate experiences and behaviors as having both observable antecedents (or causes) and consequences.

Wisdom is getting out of that tense focus on me, me, me. Wisdom is stepping back and seeing the good in another, especially if there has been difficulty or conflict with that person.

Wisdom is seeing that there may be two truths at the same time. We may have to simply validate the other's truth, the other's perspective, and accept that their truth is different from our own.

Wisdom is in the dialectical balance of the middle path. We make sense of the emotions by identifying triggers, and we validate the desires or beliefs, but only as desires and beliefs associated with the emotion. We can go one step further, beyond just validation—we might gently question the consequences of clinging to such desires and beliefs.

Developing our own internal wisdom requires practicing the skills learned in prior chapters, especially mindfulness and emotional awareness, to get into integrated mind, or wise mind. Sometimes we have to remember that every one of us, including oneself, has suffered and has caused suffering in others. In emotional mind, we can get swept up in small thinking, tension, or impulsive behavior—just as others do when they are in emotional mind. For example, if we can see that the other person is acting out of anger or fear, instead of thinking that the other is mean and spiteful and just wants to hurt us, we understand the power of seeing the causes underlying everything and the response is equanimity.

A wise and equanimous mind is extremely adept at validating. This is the mind that sees the world from a perspective that is decentered and dialectical instead of dichotomous. It is calm, centered, and grounded because it understands deeply that everything that arises and passes is caused and has consequences.

Understanding wisdom

1. Mental integration

- Wisdom for Aristotle was the "golden mean," the integration of reason, desire, feeling, and behavior.
- We can actively pause and integrate all of these at once and connect with our inner wisdom.

2. Mental inquiry

- Can I see this situation from all perspectives? Am I being open to disconfirming information?

Cultivating wisdom

1. Dialectics and paradox

- Observe the situation from the perspective of another (which is possible even if one is in disagreement with this perspective).
- Look for a dialectical synthesis of a problem or a question. Look for various simultaneous truths. "Of course you are sad and happy at the same time." Search for a synthesis of elements that seem incompatible. "I want my staff to meet increasing productivity goals, and I want them to have a happy family life."
- Inquire into the paradox with patience. "May I do all things with one intention."

2. Accept and question

- Accept the emotion and question the consequences of clinging to a distorted belief. "I know how nervous you are about this exam. Does repeating 'I am going to fail' make you feel less nervous?"

Validating with wisdom

1. Intellectual humility and radical openness

- Develop comfort in not-knowing, become curious, and regularly question assumptions.
- Remain open to disconfirming information that can prove us wrong, without being defensive. Let go of the need to have the answers or to be right.
- Inquire deeply into our own experience and the experience of others.
- Use gestures, facial expressions, and tone of voice that communicate interest, warmth, openness, and nondominance.

2. Decentering

- Take a step back to see the big picture (as if we were a fly on the wall or a security camera in the corner) and all sides of a situation.
- Honestly validate the truth from different perspectives.

3. Equanimity

- Notice how suffering has causes and can in turn cause negative behavior, which then causes more suffering.

4. Validating with the wisdom of causes and consequences

- Identifying what triggered an emotion, thought, or behavior can be a form of validating it. "Of course you were angry—he insulted you."
- Identifying the consequence may be a form of validation. "It makes perfect sense that you told him to leave, because you finally got a little peace."

5. The wisdom to not validate the invalid

- Find a grain of truth to validate.
- Validate the valid and question the consequences of invalid behavior.

9

RESPECT

"In order to have compassionate relationships and compassionate communication, there has to be a fundamental change of attitude. The notion 'I am the helper and you are the one who needs help' might work in a temporary way, but fundamentally nothing changes because there's still one who has it and one who doesn't."

— PEMA CHÖDRÖN

Bring to mind a person who is "below" you in a particular social hierarchy, or someone whom you consider less talented, less experienced, less honest, less capable, or less wholesome in some way. It might be a younger person, a child, or a frail elderly person. It might be someone whom you observe to have difficulty maintaining a job or doing well in school. It could be someone who just tends to evoke your irritation or critical thoughts. Maybe this person did something that had negative consequences for you.

It is possible that you think, "I treat everyone equally." If so, it is really important to deeply question this belief. Inquire deeply into your perspective on others, looking to see whether you experience any thoughts such as that this person "should" try harder, be nicer, or do something different from how they habitually behave.

Keep this person in mind as you read this chapter. Find ways to look into your own beliefs and feelings about this person. Look to see if there are any prejudices and assumptions about status, hierarchy, or different levels of respect that arise in your mind, and question them deeply.

CONNECTION AMONG EQUALS

Respect is a bridge that connects us to others when we treat them, just like us, as competent and capable *and* vulnerable and human. Authentic respect is not treating others as fragile, weak, or inferior, nor as superior, putting them on a pedestal and bowing in homage. We are all equal as human beings and we recognize that it is only grace and providence that create the circumstances we are born with. At our essence, we have a thousand times more in common with our fellow human beings than we do differences. These differences are actually random and miniscule variations, even if they often seem big and important.

When we treat another person with respect, we are treating ourselves with respect. When we criticize others directly, when we complain about them to others, or when we are just gossiping, we should pause and see how engaging in this action is damaging our own dignity, our own sense of inner peace and satisfaction with life. Gossip and criticism seem harmless and may feel like a way to defuse frustration or stress, but when we look very closely at our own experience, we may find that we are really clinging, sometimes obsessively, to our negative or judgmental thoughts and, hence, our internal suffering. We are looking *from* our thoughts instead of *at* our thoughts, which just gets us in trouble in ways that maintain our mental distress and may even shorten our lives!

Respect for others can be intentionally developed. We can start by describing clearly the specific strengths, skills, and talents that we observe in the other. We practice recognizing that others are the best equipped to resolve their own problems and overcome their difficulties. We can respectfully and empathically question ideas or actions with which we disagree, without denigrating others. We trust that other people are strong enough to resolve their daily problems—and we don't expect them to do it our way. So we let go of trying to solve problems for others and instead let others solve their own problems . . . and make their own mistakes. Of course we can accompany others, be supportive of others in many ways, and help others evaluate their decisions, but respect does not solve problems for others. Such authentic respect fosters self-reliance, independence, and freedom (first for ourselves and second for others!). Respect also means seeing a better future for others, just as we do for ourselves.

If respect for another person does not come easily, we can reflect on the other's ability rather than inability. We can focus on their strengths, not just their weaknesses. We can remember the moments when the other was at their best—grounded, effective, and skillful. We can also consider the mental or physical suffering or the difficult conditions that this person is experiencing or has experienced, in some cases for a long time. We can imagine a future when the other will be wiser, more secure, and even more capable. We can connect with and validate the idea that this person can do hard things—hard for them, not necessarily for us! We can practice empathy and compassion to see this person as an equal, a person who just wants to be happy and not suffer, but with problems and limitations different from our own.

It may be difficult, but we can practice respecting the opinions and values of the other person without trying to impose our own values and opinions. If someone has other political views, other religious views, or different opinions, interests, likes, or dislikes, we can still find a way to be respectful, cordial, and interested in their unique life circumstances. Perhaps it is possible to find points of agreement and focus on these. For example, a meeting was organized between black liberal Democrats from Los Angeles and white conservative Republicans from Appalachia to talk about how their neighbors and loved ones were dying from drug overdoses of opioids. Their shared experiences quickly dissolved differences of race, politics, and geography. We are all equal because we are all human and we all want to avoid suffering and be happy. Consistently cultivating this kind of respect for others cultivates respect for oneself.

DIGNITY

Dignity is the full embodiment of respect. It is a respect that flows in all directions, including toward oneself. Dignity implies a harmony between strength and softness. Our behavior, our tone of voice, the words we choose to speak, and even our posture are balanced and composed when we convey dignity. Imagine sitting, standing, walking, and talking with dignity. How do you imagine yourself and what do you see yourself doing? Is there someone who comes to mind when you think of the word "dignity"? What is it about this person that conveys dignity?

Practice 2. Embodying respect

Almost all meditation traditions have something to say about the correct posture of the body. Technically, our posture has nothing to do with achieving spiritual or mystical experiences. One may have a deeply insightful and spiritually transformative experience by tripping and falling into a mud puddle! So why all the focus on the posture? Blaise Pascal wrote in 1669, "All of humanity's problems stem from man's inability to sit quietly in a room alone." Could the right posture help make that possible?

Try this: Sit up or stand with the back straight, the head lifted, the shoulders relaxed and slightly back, and an open heart. Let go of tension. Feel the soles of the feet grounded, in contact with the floor, and the sit bones firmly in contact with the chair. The posture is both soft and strong.

This is a posture that communicates dignity and self-respect to the brain. This posture is perhaps a simple, subtle step toward building self-respect in the face of shame, vulnerability, timidity, or disappointment.

Continue to settle into this posture and feel the body physically balanced, composed, and still. Breathe. Let go of any tension with each exhale. Imagine your head floating upward. Allow the corners of your lips to rise up slightly and your cheeks to rise up. See if you can sit still like this, relaxed and awake, attending to your posture, for 5 or 10 minutes.

When your attention is on body sensations, there is a pause in the default brain network and the uncontrolled chatter of the mind. You just created a moment of peace and sent a positive message of dignity and self-respect to your brain!

At the first major public presentation that Carrie had to give, her head was spinning all morning until it was her turn to speak. Standing at the podium before she began her presentation, facing over 200 people in the audience, it seemed to her as if she stood there for hours, breathing silently while feeling totally paralyzed and helpless. But she didn't disappear or faint or die. She was "still standing and still breathing," as she later described. She was also poised, smiling, and looking around directly at the audience. It seemed that the silence was absolute. She finally broke this endless silence and began to make her points one at a time as best she could.

Later, during lunch, the keynote speaker and his wife came up to her smiling broadly and telling her how "dignified" she was during the talk. Inside she was shocked, but outwardly she accepted the compliment graciously. That is the power of dignity. Even in the depths of shame and anxiety, we can be present, patient, and as composed as possible. Dignity just may shine forth. In fact, holding one's own experience of shame with kindness, curiosity, and dignity is sometimes the antidote for the suffering that shame generates.

Beginner's Mind

We easily treat someone with respect when we don't know anything about them. We don't have any preconceived notions. We see and hear them as they are, not as we have already decided they are, and thus what they are going to do and why. Already "knowing" what the other will say or do is a habit that can arise with colleagues, friends, and loved ones. On the other hand, we usually treat strangers with a respectful "beginner's mind." Perhaps we could practice seeing our colleagues, friends, and family as if it were the very first time that we are meeting them—instead of what our thoughts are telling us about them. What might that be like?

Here are some examples:

- With the respect that we might have for a new neighbor, we express our desire to help or to relieve the suffering of another, and we ask how can we help without thinking that we already have the answers. *"You look tired; can I do something to help?"* or *"That must be stressful. Do you need any support?"*
- Using a cheerful, beginner's mind—even if we believe it is likely that our loved one is depressed or insecure or irritated —we might speak to this person with the freshness and respect of speaking to someone we just met. *"Hi! How are you? What are you up to today?"*

- We assume capacity instead of incapacity when we don't know for sure. *"That's got to be tough. How are you dealing with that?"*
- We open our attention with curiosity, instead of closing our attention with negative thinking or preconceived ideas. *"How interesting!"* with a tone of voice that communicates we really mean it and would love to know more.

EQUALITY IN AN UNEQUAL RELATIONSHIP

If two people are in unequal relationships (for example, parent-adolescent or employer-employee), validation with respect as an equal may be more difficult—and it is even more useful! In any type of domestic partnership, mutual respect is a fundamental aspect of a long-term, healthy relationship. We can communicate equality by acknowledging reciprocal or matched vulnerability through self-disclosure. One might remark, "I would feel the same way if I were in your shoes." Note that it does not have to be hypothetical. One might say, "The same thing happened to me once and I was scared too." Either one can be effective for corroborating the experience of the other (but we don't want to turn the conversation into long stories about ourselves).

Maria was in her last year of high school. She was extremely shy and had trouble making friends and sustaining friendships. She suffered epilepsy, although it had been largely under control for years, thanks to medication. She was very close to her mom, Esther. Maria expected her mother to be chauffer, cook, housekeeper, appointment secretary, and tutor—something that she should have outgrown years earlier. Esther knew that she had been an overprotective mother and she had a lot of good reasons to worry about Maria, but she needed to take a step back. Esther had to let go of taking care of Maria and challenge her become more independent. Below are two examples Esther used to validate Maria's feelings and expectations and also validated her own needs in a way that communicated mutual respect—for Maria and for herself.

Validating with respect and also saying no to picking her up from school:

"I know you don't like going by bus. It can be uncomfortable, especially when the bus is crowded. The bus drivers can be rude, they can drive erratically, and all kinds of people are there. I can get uncomfortable sometimes too . . . I can't take you there because I have other things to attend to, but I will be here waiting for you when you get home. It's hard, but I know you can do it because you can do hard things. I have seen you do it before."

Validating with respect and also respecting oneself:

"I hated washing dishes when I was your age and I still don't like it! And of course I know you have more important things to do. However, please wash the dishes after you use them. When I get home from work and see your dirty dishes, I can get so irritated that I don't feel like talking to you for the rest of the night."

"You Are Just Like Me" vs. "I Am Just Like You"

Alice was impatient, easily irritated, and frequently angry. Alice's own parents were very strict and she had experienced more than her fair share of scolding and corrections in her childhood. Understandably, Alice was highly critical and self-critical. Well-meaning suggestions or advice from others triggered resentment. This was especially true about suggestions from her 50-year-old daughter Candy, from whom she expected an extra dose of respect.

Candy had a very difficult relationship with her mother. As a young adult she moved far away. She always hoped that things would be different between them and was disappointed over and over. Finally Candy practiced just listening to her mom's complaints. She tried hard to say nothing when the impulse to offer advice arose. She also learned a very subtle way of communicating respect when she was listening to her mom talk about her problems and challenges. She discovered that saying, *"I think that I am like you in that way . . ."* had a fairly calming effect for her *and* her mother.

Notice that she did not say, "You are like me." It was "I am like you." This is a very important distinction. "I am like you" sounds more like *my* insight about *myself*. "You are like me" may sound like I am telling you what your experience is or, worse, it may sound like I already know more about your experience than you.

I am like you is self insight and this message is enhanced by a tone of voice that communicates surprise or genuine interest. It is a delightful self-realization, instead of a teaching for the other person, which the speaker already learned. In Candy's case, her message also implies, "I take after you, Mom," which respectfully corroborates Alice's experience. It may be very subtle, but it also follows another rule of validation, which is that we want to avoid starting sentences with "you" because that can be perceived as invalidating, and instead start with "I." (For more discussion on this point, see page .) If I am talking about my own experience, it is hard for the other to disagree with me, it is unlikely to offend the other person, and it is often the basis for honest and respectful communication among equals.

Authentic respect may also communicate that it is not *just* that my experience is like your experience, but that *everyone* has experiences like that. Validating with respect can normalize a response by reflecting on it as a universal response. If what we are suffering is a normal or universal response to a situation, we are not alone and isolated. We are all worthy of respect and we share a common humanity. Like all validation strategies, this may not make things all better, but a feeling of connection to others may help relieve our suffering just a little. Seeing our own painful experience as part of a common humanity that we all share may be grounding and help us connect with our own inner wisdom.

If we have a very difficult time with one particular person, we may tend to evaluate their experience as an emotional outlier, not something universal. Again, we look for the part of their experience that we can validate as a universal human experience.

Vicky often felt insecure and fearful and had an obsessive style of thinking. It interfered with her making decisions and resolving problems. She expected others to listen to her discuss her worries. She needed attention and contention from her family, friends, and colleagues, and sometimes they ran out of time, patience, and empathy. She was hurt and angry when others indicated that they had more important things to do than to listen to her worries and fears.

Her family had to validate her desire for conversation without reinforcing her habit of ruminating. It was a real challenge for them to treat her with respect and validate her equal status as a family member in spite of the fact that she had great difficulty doing things for herself.

"Of course you need someone to listen to you. We all need that. Tell you what . . . I am busy now, but I can be your sounding board for one hour after dinner."

"I know this is important to you. It is normal to want to examine all sides and all possibilities. I have about 10 or 15 minutes to help you think through the pros and cons of one possibility right now. And maybe it would be helpful to think of one option at a time. I can also talk more tomorrow about other possibilities."

"This problem could make anyone nervous. If you can figure out a way to manage your stress a few days without having this resolved, I can sit down this weekend to talk. That would also give you more time to come up with a solution—or at least a couple of options."

"I know this is hard and you're feeling alone. I can't help you decide, but after you decide what you want to do, when you are ready to take action I am more than happy to accompany you."

"Count on me to help after you decide and you are ready to take action. I will be at your side to accompany you as you implement your ideas. I am getting a little worn down with examining the alternatives. I can see it is very hard for you to decide. Sometimes it can be hard to even know what we want, and I don't think I can help you with that."

RESPECT DOES NOT "FRAGILIZE"

We do not treat the other as fragile or incompetent, and we act out of respect. We don't avoid or omit information. We assume that others are capable of being a witness to the truth. We do not hide the truth, nor exaggerate, nor state our value judgments as if they were truth. We allow reality to be as it is and we describe this reality to others, even if it is not what the other was hoping for.

Working in a small law firm, a young associate muttered a complaint about having to do his own administrative work. A senior lawyer gently responded, "Yup, that's right. Unfortunately, life is 90 percent administrative."

The founder of a design company was approached by his partner, who was yelling, "I'll sell my interest and shut this place down if we don't do it my way!" The founder responded, "OK, Rick, if that's what you want to do, you have every right to do it." Rick responded, a bit less loudly, "You're damn right I do." Then Rick remained silent for a while and calmed down even more. After a few minutes later he said, "OK, you know I don't agree with you, so how can we make this work?" He was willing to enter into a dialogue instead of threatening ultimatums.

Respect assumes that, like oneself, others are the authority on their own needs and desires. It is true that we can all have moments of uncertainty, but let's assume that others are perfectly capable of knowing what is best for them—even if they have made mistakes in the past.

Maria had an aunt in a nursing home who suffered from mild dementia and depression. Maria visited her a couple of times a month. It was a responsibility that she shared with her siblings, but they disliked going and their visits usually ended with her aunt crying. Maria usually closed her visits by taking a *selfie* of her and her aunt smiling. What was the difference? Maria treated her aunt with complete and total respect.

For example, one day her aunt said that she was going to get a job so she could move out of the nursing home. "Really?" responded Maria with a big smile and curiosity in her voice. "What kind of job are you thinking about getting?" "I don't know," her aunt said sadly. "Well, maybe I can help you come up with ideas." Maria opened her purse and pulled out a pencil and a pad of paper. "So what are some of the things that you could do?" Her aunt thought a minute and responded, "I can vacuum and dust . . . I can take care of cats. I love cats . . . I can sweep . . ." And they went back and forth, with Maria asking questions and taking notes and her aunt talking about herself. When Maria had to leave, her aunt said, "Well, I'm too tired to look for a job now, but maybe another day. Maria gave her aunt a big hug and left her smiling.

Validating an elderly person with respect is one of the kindest gifts you can give to yourself. What goes around comes around. "Validation therapy" has been developed to work with persons with dementia and memory problems because it is so effective at giving people respect at a point in life when they most need it.

Confrontation and "prevalidation"

We want to do our best to respond to another with respect as an equal. But maybe the other person is often emotionally sensitive.

How can we be truthful, knowing it might trigger painful emotions in the other person and probably generate conflict in our relationship?

First of all, we are honest and tell the truth in a way that is respectful of the other. This can be a form of confrontation with honesty. This may be respectfully telling someone that you disagree. It may be saying no to a request or giving your opinion when asked. Sometimes respect says, "I think that you may not want to hear this information, but I believe you are strong enough to hear this."

However, sometimes it may be smoother if we do what I describe as "prevalidation." This is really handy if I expect a negative interpretation of or an emotional reaction to what I am about to say to the other. "Prevalidation" involves predicting what the emotional response of the other will be before they actually experience it. Like validating an actual emotion, prevalidation is presented as a hypothesis or a possibility.

"I have something to say and I am worried that you will get mad at me."

"You asked me for my opinion and I will tell you, although it may make you angry when you hear what I have to say. I understand you have a different perspective."

"I want to understand step by step what happened, but you might feel that I am blaming you or you might get angry at me for my questions. Can you tell me what you said immediately before she insulted you?"

You will probably feel that it is totally unfair, but we are going to have to rewrite the proposal because we just got some new information.

"Prevalidation" often prepares the other for "the worst" and paves the way to share information, opinions, or advice respectfully. The response is sometimes relief that the interaction was not as painful as expected. Sometimes prevalidation can be effective at preventing an emotional reaction. It should not be overused, however, or it can feel like one is trying to control things before they happen.

INTEGRATING VALIDATION AND ENCOURAGEMENT

We all have personal problems, some people more than others. Everyone also has strengths in spite of their weaknesses and limitations, no matter how profound they might be. We may want to help others see their strengths, see the glass as half-full instead of half empty. Encouragement may be a tempting way to do it. It may be effective, too. Technically, though, encouragement is quite different from validation. "You can do it" will not be validating if the other believes otherwise or if the other really can't just do it.

We can integrate encouragement and validation by providing the evidence, whether based on past experience, based on similar situations, or based on universal human characteristics such as intelligence, wisdom, empathy, kindness, etc. We can note the strengths in another in ways that point to the specific, concrete evidence of that strength.

"I know you feel overwhelmed right now, and I also know you can be strong and resilient. You got through last year, and you were facing a lot more than this."

"It sounds like a tough situation. I have seen you be really strong when the going gets tough. What are you thinking of doing now?"

"You want my opinion? I really don't know. I think you are the best judge of the situation. You know a lot more about this situation than I do."

LEADING WITH RESPECT

In the workplace environment, validation is critical to our teamwork and our success. Treating everyone as a human being with human needs will lead to greater satisfaction for oneself, more effective communication, and deeper interpersonal relationships—whether with the head of the company or with the young student who makes photocopies. What we send out to the world is what we receive.

Peter was a residential building manager. The employees he had to supervise included housekeepers, janitors, doormen, mechanics, and security guards—persons with little formal education and few financial resources. On the other hand, his "customers" were very wealthy persons who lived in apartments worth millions of dollars. The building residents were not always respectful to everyone on the building staff. The building staff felt that many residents treated them like servants.

Peter worked hard—not just to offset this situation, but because he truly bonded with his staff as if they were his own family. He treated his staff with kindness, compassion, and respect. He helped employees with their personal problems. He visited them when they were sick, he loaned them money if they needed it, and he knew most of their families. He had the reputation of being a tough guy with a big heart. After 35 years in the business, he quietly retired without any party, yet he received dozens of notes, letters, and gifts from former employees who had long since moved on to other jobs. A former employee was also responsible for filing the paperwork for his retirement—paperwork that ultimately got him a final bonus that was three times greater than the industry standard.

What is NOT treating others with equality

We respect others as equals, but we must avoid fall into the trap of being rigid or demanding or teasing just because they are "strong."

Gloria, a single mother of three adopted girls, does a heroic job of raising her kids. The two younger girls have some behavioral problems at school, but the oldest, Amy, 18, has always been more mature, more emotionally balanced, and more successful in school than her sisters. One day, when I was with Gloria and her daughter, she told me that she had just discovered that Amy had gotten a tattoo since her last birthday. She turned to Amy, angrily saying, "Just because you are 18 doesn't mean you can get a tattoo. You live in my house. You have to listen to me and do what I say. I'm the mother here. You did not buy that with your money. All your money comes from me." Amy looked away and remained silent. Then Gloria looked at me, a little embarrassed but still angry, and said, "She's not fragile like the others. I can treat her like an equal."

Clearly Gloria was not treating Amy like an equal! She was ordering her what to do as if she lived under an authoritarian regime! Gloria jumped from one extreme of being patient, flexible, and radically accepting of questionable behaviors with her younger daughters, to being rigid and demanding with her oldest daughter, and thinking that was respectfully treating her as an equal.

Respect for another presumes that the other is capable of bearing witness to reality. But respect does not attack or judge or criticize others. We don't discard presence, listening, or empathy. If Gloria did not want her daughter to continue to get more tattoos, she would be much more effective by (1) validating her daughter as someone capable of making her own decisions and living with the consequences, and (2) maintaining a respectful dialogue with her about tattoos and the short- and long-term consequences of her decisions.

Sometimes people misinterpret respecting another as an equal as meaning being able to "take a joke." The belief goes: I can take a joke, so I treat you as if you can take a joke too. Some families habitually engage in mutual mockery and everyone laughs. Sometimes we "roast" a dignitary whom we really respect or we "tease" a loved one whom we really adore. Perhaps there are very special contexts where these behaviors communicate respect through actively "disrespecting" the other, although even in these situations, things can get uncomfortable or even ugly. Probably the teasing between the groom and the groomsmen at a wedding communicates respect, but in most situations joking about others is disrespectful. At work, within families, and among friends, respect is *not* a test of shame or fear. Genuine respect is wholesome for a relationship. It generates trust. When we act out of respect, we care for ourselves and we care for others with dignity—a strong back and an open heart.

Sally and Sarah were sisters, and at ages 8 and 6 they were adorably cute, especially in their father's eyes. Sometimes he would tease them and Sally, the older sister, would roll her eyes and walk away or just ignore him. However, Sarah would become worried or hurt and then angry. But she was so young that her hurt and anger were not at all threatening. In fact, it delighted her father to see her cute angry face and his teasing continued, but Sarah suffered more and more. These interactions came to a grinding halt when Sarah ran to her room crying and Mom appeared, angry and frustrated with her husband's behavior. Dad had no explanation for why he continued to do it and couldn't seem to stop himself.

Sarah's dad was missing empathy in these interactions, but this was also an enormous breach of respect. In these moments, Dad was not in emotional mind; he was in a good mood, calm and relaxed. There was no reason to think that Dad would be hurtful to Sarah. He did not relate to Sarah as an equal in these moments. She was just a cute little child. It was not his intention, but he really was communicating to Sarah that she was not worthy of respect. In fact, this is a behavior that sometimes occurs between husbands and wives. One spouse (often the husband) gets some pleasure from seeing their loved one (often the attractive wife) activated with anger or pouting with sadness and says things or does things intentionally to frustrate the other. For one spouse it is cute or a funny joke, while the other feels real pain.

Truly respectful dialogue is a generous exchange that flows back and forth. There is spontaneity in the interaction because respect makes the interaction safe. We do not judge or criticize or teach the other, and we do not put them on a pedestal, bowing and praising in homage to the other. The older daughter, Sally, responded to her father's teasing by shaking her head and walking away. Her father did not find this quite so entertaining. However, when her father spoke about science or world politics, his two passions, she listened respectfully. She asked questions. He began to speak to her more like an equal in these conversations. The seeds of mutual respect were actually planted by Sally in these interactions when she validated her father's interests.

~

Respect is treating another human being as an equal: competent/capable and vulnerable/human. It sounds easy, but when we are dealing with others who are different—different religions, races, genders, cultures, ages, rank, political parties, or physical abilities—well, being respectful and treating the other as an equal is not always so easy. It may even be difficult to treat a dearly loved, close relative as an equal. It may require intentional practice.

Comparing and differentiating oneself from others or focusing on inequalities creates an "us" and a "them." Seeing others as "them" sets us apart. We not only lose respect for "them," we lose empathy and compassion for "them" and eventually for everyone (including ourselves).

Rick Hanson sums this up beautifully: "So, as a matter of pure personal well-being (as well as a matter of morality), see what happens when you deliberately keep your heart wide open to those who are 'them' to you. Walking down the street or on the evening news, look for the 'them-est' people you can find. The 'them-er' they are, the more your heart will be stretched . . . and remarkably and paradoxically, the more loved you will feel yourself."[1] That is the ultimate respect.

CULTIVATING RESPECT

1. Dignity

- We can embody respect by entering into the experience of mind and body self-respect.
- Dignity is a posture and an attitude of deep respect for oneself and others.

2. Beginner's mind

- When we meet another person, we do not have preconceived notions of how they will respond or what they will be like.
- Validating with beginner's mind is the practice of seeing another person with new eyes, just as they are, instead of seeing them as a reflection of our own thoughts and expectations.
- Ability rather than disability is presumed.

Validating with respect

1. Validating the other as an equal

- We treat the other person as an equal, not as fragile or incompetent, and we act out of balance in the relationship.
- We normalize the response by reflecting on it as a universal response.

2. Recognition that all emotions are universal human experiences

- We respect the opinions and values of the other person without trying to impose our opinions and values on the other.

3. Respect does not "fragilize"

- Excessive helping or resolving the problems of others can be a form of treating the other as fragile or incapable.

4. Nonjudgmental confrontation

- Speaking the truth communicates that the other is strong enough to hear it and to experience frustration or whatever other emotional response may arise.
- It is important to describe without be judgmental.

5. Integrating validation and encouragement

- We encourage another, not through empty cheerleading, but by reminding them of their past achievements. *"Yes, it's hard, and I have seen you do hard things."*
- We acknowledge the inherent intuitive, experiential, and spiritual knowing that is already within the other person.
- The capacity for future validity is presumed. ("I know you can do hard things because I have seen you do hard things before.")

6. Leading with compassionate respect

- We act out of respect for subordinates, employees, and others.
- We recognize that their health and happiness are our priority, just as with our own loved ones.

7. What is NOT treating others as equals

- Scolding, joking, and teasing rarely evoke respect and are almost always invalidating.

10

DEEPENING SELF-VALIDATION

"It's not your job to love me. It's mine."

— *Byron Katie*

If genuine validation is sharing a path of mindful compassion, then one must know that path from first-hand experience in order to share it. The way is presence, acceptance, empathic awareness of one's experience, self-compassion, wisdom, and self-respect. Self-validation puts all of these into thoughts, words, and action.

How can we direct empathy and compassion toward ourselves when we have so much work to manage, when loved ones or others seem to need so much support, and when others can seem to be so invalidating of us? This chapter addresses everyone, but pay special attention if you are a "caretaker," whether professionally, personally, sporadically, or just by nature.

Caretakers may have to practice being even more mindful of their own feelings and needs. It helps to validate another person's internal experience if we recognize exactly what we are feeling. Self-compassion, self-care, and self-validation begin with taking the time to be present and still in order to listen deeply to one's own feelings, thoughts, and impulses. Self-validation is acceptance of one's own feelings, noting or naming them without value judgments. This can include seeing how our feelings, sensations, and thoughts are understandable within our life context. At first glance it may seem paradoxical, but accepting responsibility for one's own feelings and needs is liberating and empowering. It can bring about a sense of peace and enable one to be even more present and more effective in caring for others.

Isabella had found herself arguing with her 8-year-old son about wearing a coat when he went out. He would insist that it wasn't cold and he did not need a coat. This turned into a mother-son fight, which she "won" but with her son stomping around hot and angry with his mother. Isabella finally realized that what was cold for her was not necessarily cold for her son. She paused to validate herself by reflecting, "What am I feeling and thinking in this moment? What am I really needing right now?"

Then she sat down and gently explained to him that she was actually afraid he would catch a cold and she was worried that she would have to take time of from work to be responsible for staying home and taking care of him. For those reasons, she really needed to know that he was paying attention to his body sensations. They came to an agreement that he would put a coat on and leave it open and that he would zip it up if he felt cold and he would also tell her if he got too hot and wanted to take it off.

Accepting the present moment

When we begin to simply observe the act of being conscious and silently listening-seeing-feeling whatever arises within the field of consciousness, we might find that it seems simple, but in fact it is not so easy. It can take a bit of practice to appreciate the experience of remembering to be present continuously.

Thoughts are a type of filter that have been developed and shaped from the context and conditions that we have experienced. Sometimes we confuse thoughts with something else, such as the essence of our being and who we are, or perhaps we confuse thoughts with facts. When we begin to practice self-validation, it can be easy to end up validating invalid thoughts or seeing storylines and interpretations as facts. It is useful to return again and again to the act of just listening-seeing-feeling. Believing our thoughts can get us into a lot of trouble and cause a lot of misery. Accepting the present moment changes our relationship with our thoughts. We observe how they frequently arise and pass and return to listening-seeing-feeling in the present moment. We learn that we do not have to cling to or evaluate the content of every thought—and in fact this can actually increase our suffering.

Accepting the present moment includes "awaring"[1] our internal experience and what is going on around us. If we are in emotional mind, we observe what we are feeling and we might even identify words that describe the feeling—instead of denying, ignoring, blaming, problem-solving, ruminating, or worrying. We can notice and describe how things arise, pass, or morph into something else within the field of awareness.

Practice 1. Acceptance of outer experience—listen, see, feel

Take a moment to listen to whatever sounds arise. Just listen fully, accepting every sound that enters the ears. Count 10 breaths while listening.

Then shift the attention to what you are seeing. Notice colors and textures. Observe what you are seeing as if it were a photo (or a video if there is movement) on display in an art gallery. Count 10 breaths while you are just looking.

Finally shift the attention to physical sensations of the skin. Sensations of pressure, texture, temperature, humidity, tension, and even pulses, vibrations, or effervescence are all sensations that can be felt with the skin. Count 10 breaths while observing what feelings arise from your the skin.

STOP AND LISTEN IN

Emotional self-validation may require us to stop what we are doing and just pay attention to this inner experience. "Pushing the pause button" increases clarity and equanimity as we attend to what we are feeling. How is that? First we just note what is happening. We may close our eyes and ask ourselves, "What am I feeling?" or "What is that?" and "What else is there?" We might notice things like the following:

- *"What exactly is that feeling of pain in my stomach? Tension and heat, the size and shape of a flattened golf ball in my solar plexus."*
- *"I feel like I am trying to hold myself together. What is that telling me?"*
- *"My chest has this heavy black weight. What is under that? What else is there?"*

This is not a one-second exercise. It is important to really take a few minutes to listen to our bodies deeply. We can observe the size and intensity of the sensations. We can ask ourselves what else we notice, what lies under this feeling or behind that sensation, what wisdom our bodies are telling us, or we can just keep asking ourselves, "What else?"

In spite of years of practice doing mindfulness and validation, Carol found herself in a screaming match with her 90-year-old mother. It ended with her mother stomping out of the room, yelling as loud as possible how much she hated being alive and that she just wanted to "blow her brains out."

Carol sat there in disbelief. She noticed the urge to just become numb, to tune out everything and go back to watching TV. She closed her eyes and made the effort to inquire more deeply into her experience.

Carol was not ruminating or replaying events nor justifying her actions in her mind. She did not go running after her mother and try to soothe her. She just sat still, focusing on physical sensations and validating every emotion that came up—especially the guilt, shame, and anger that arose. She let thoughts arise and pass without clinging to them. She was deeply inquiring into her feelings, emotions, and urges, trying to fully experience every subtle aspect of them without turning away—instead of creating a mental story about what had happened or acting out more emotionally impulsive behavior.

We have to practice pausing and listening in before we explode, not after. As soon as we notice frustration or anxiety, we just pause and breathe. When we are aware of losing control of our behavior, we stop, step away, and turn inward to listen in.

Practice 2. Observing inner feelings and thoughts—feel-in, see-in, and hear-in

First bring your attention inside your body. Start with the whole body. Close your eyes if it is more comfortable. Feel the entire body. . . the posture and position of the whole body. Notice if you are experiencing any emotions or inner feelings in your body, particularly in your torso. Spend a few minutes observing physical sensations with a lot of interest and curiosity.

After a few minutes let go of the body and put your attention on your thoughts. Some thoughts are images that you can "see." Some are sounds or voices or dialogue that you can "hear." Some may be experiential thoughts that it seems like you can "see," "hear," and "feel." Whatever thoughts arise, just allow them to arise and pass and wait for the next thought to arise.

If you find yourself swept up in thinking instead of observing thoughts, just notice as if you were *seeing* the thought or *hearing* the thought. Say to yourself "see" if it is a predominantly a mental image or "hear" if it is predominantly a verbal thought. Labeling thoughts as "see" or "hear" helps us see thoughts as thoughts and not get engaged, or, if we are engaged, then just label and let them go.

EMPATHY AND INNER COMPASSION

For some of us, practices such as mindfulness and acceptance are life-changing. As we practice being present, over time we experience greater mental clarity, concentration, and equanimity. The more we practice, the more present, centered, and focused we become. Such practice can improve the quality of our relationships and deepen the experience of work and play. With a deep practice of mindfulness and acceptance, life truly becomes awesome.

For many of us, however, even years of practice of mindfulness and acceptance alone may not give us a complete sense of safety, reassurance, and inner peace. If the emotional system that enables people to feel cared for and receive affection is not accessible, they may rationally self-validate their internal experience and may learn to slow down and even pause the endless stream of worry thoughts. They may see their suffering clearly and even the source of their suffering, but they may not feel a lot of relief. It may help to become centered and grounded, but it is not enough. One can practice mindfulness or meditate for years with great discipline and still continue to struggle being kind to oneself.

There may be a dark hole that presence and acceptance alone cannot fill. There may be an unspecified sense of shame, anxiety, insecurity, or any other "demon" that seems to lurk in the shadows in spite of a practice of mindfulness. Some of us may need to completely reconstruct our ability to fully experience nurturing, love, and compassion. Let's face it: our friends, families, or colleagues are not likely to be giving us all the validation that we need (and deserve!). If our validation and compassion does not include ourselves, it is incomplete.

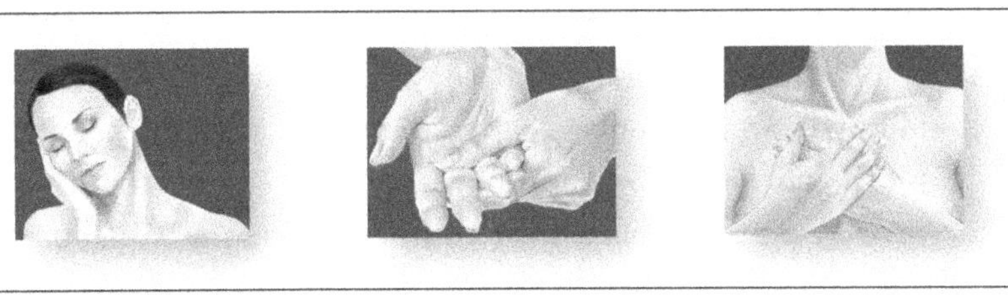

Practice 3. Self-compassion basics

Kristen Neff describes compassion as having three components: (1) recognizing suffering, (2) recognizing that suffering is a shared human experience, and (3) responding with thoughts, words, and gestures of compassion.

This practice includes fully engaging in a gesture of self compassion such as those pictured above: resting the cheek on the hand, one hand giving another hand a massage, and both hands over the heart. Bring to mind a difficult situation currently or recently in your life and then practice a self compassionate gesture while repeating the phrases below. Repeat for all three gestures (or try one of your own).

1. Observe and describe: "This is difficult."

2. Connect with others or universally: "Anyone could have this problem" or "This is part of life."

3. Accompany: "I'm here for you, [say your name]," "I am here to accompany me [or 'you' referring to yourself] wherever I ['you'] go for the rest of my life," or "We are in this together . . . both hands, both feet . . . All these cells in this body are all accompanying me," or simply "I love me."

At the end of one of my family classes, Gabriela, a middle-aged woman, came to see me, saying, "I feel horribly guilty. Just after my granddaughter was born, my daughter refused to see me and talk to me. She told me not to call her, not to write her, and not to go see her. She will not answer my emails or my phone calls. I don't know what to do. I just want her to be happy, but the more I learn about validation, the more I realize I have been invalidating her my whole life."

Once I got to know Gabriela, I realized that she was not entirely exaggerating. She had a lifelong habit of giving her daughter advice, minimizing her daughter's feelings, and being dogmatically judgmental. Her daughter had cut off the relationship because the invalidation was intolerable. Although she understood she had a long pattern of invalidating her daughter's internal experience, it actually took her two years to reconstruct a relationship with her daughter. She left confused and frustrated after each class and she couldn't seem to "get it" even with one-on-one training. Why not?

Gabriela lived in a state of anxiety and insecurity, although she was largely unaware of it. Gabriela tried to suppress her insecurities by creating a world filled with rules. She was certain how a mother should act, how a family should be, and what a daughter should do, and she held on to her rigid beliefs as if they were facts. She only wanted her daughter to be happy, and she claimed to not care at all about herself. She did all the things she believed a good mother should do, *even if it was not what her daughter wanted*. She was in agreement with a therapist who had told her many years ago that she was an "overprotective mother," but that knowledge did not help her mend her relationship with her daughter or get time with her granddaughter.

Self-acceptance and self-compassion helped Gabriela connect to a more dynamic inner world. Observing and naming her own inner experience helped her understand how her emotions moved around and how her thoughts came and went. Very slowly she became better able to manage her own fears and insecurities without plastering her rational and rigid thoughts over them. Self-compassion helped her respond to her daughter with greater flexibility and build a new and less controlling relationship. Self-validation gave her the tools to see her daughter from a dialectical perspective and accept that both of them can have their own truths at the same time.

The first step of self-validation is noticing and accepting. We continue by responding with kindness, love, and respect towards ourselves in the face of pain, frustration, or anxiety. We can generate words, facial expressions, gestures, and actions of self-compassion that actively cultivate new patterns of thinking and acting. We respond appropriately to the question "What am I *needing* right now?"

To build the "muscle" of self-compassion, we need to pay attention to our needs and exercise self-kindness on a daily basis. Three ways to be kind to oneself include proactively caring for one's health, engaging in activities that are enjoyable, and focusing attention on things that are calming, soothing, or relaxing. Some people may have one or two of these "muscles" well developed, while another is weak.

1. Make self-care a daily habit:

Practice taking responsibility for one's physical and mental health and practice doing it from a place of love and kindness for oneself, not out of fear or anger. There are five ingredients to practicing self-care: selecting healthy and nutritious food to eat, exercising or engaging in physical activity every day, avoiding food and drugs that have negative impacts on one's physical and mental health, getting plenty of sleep, and getting medical checkups and visiting doctors as needed.

Self-care is not all or nothing. One may decide to smoke less or to give up sugar-laden soft drinks. One may walk up the stairs instead of taking the elevator. One might take a nap on a Sunday afternoon as an act of self-care. We can increase self-care in small ways that add up over time.

2. Engage in enjoyable activities:

All work and no play is not good for our state of mind. Joy and vitality develop and grow when we regularly make time for ourselves. Doing things that we enjoy increases our resilience to stress and suffering.

It is so important to engage in pleasurable activities every day and fully absorb these experiences by being in the moment. Don't just take them for granted. Really pay attention to what you are doing when you are doing it, especially when it is pleasurable. You will find more and more things are fun and you will cultivate more and more joy.

These activities can include anything that you find enjoyable (walking at the beach, going to a movie, singing, etc.). They can also occur within obligations that we have—as long as we find them enjoyable (cooking, driving, fixing things), but it is also important that we regularly do fun things during times of leisure (hobbies, sports, or recreational activities).

Think of three enjoyable activities that you would like to do but have not done in a while. When you have three activities in mind, open up your calendar and schedule a time to do them.

3. Don't forget actions that calm-soothe-relax:

Learn and practice self-soothing by connecting with any of the five senses. Anyone can self-soothe; it is just a question of trying things out and identifying what has a calming effect and then doing it. Let go of prejudging and criticizing these practices. Just try them with beginner's mind—that is, without any preconceived notions of what the experience will be before actually trying it. Try being openly curious about what enters through any of the five senses. Here are some examples:

<u>Touch and body sensations</u>: Petting animals, taking hot baths, splashing cold water on the face, mindful walking, self-massaging, lying down in bed with freshly washed sheets

<u>Hearing</u>: Soft music, nature sounds, even the humming and whirring of motors

<u>Smells and tastes</u>: Perfumes, savoring special foods, teas

<u>Vision</u>: Art books, photographs, magazines, landscapes, bird watching, going for a drive in the country or a walk in the park and just soaking everything in through the eyes

Consciously self-soothing all five senses, regularly engaging in pleasurable activities, and taking care of one's physical and mental health are acts of self-compassion. Regular practice can prevent caretaker burnout, restore patience and balance, and result in greater levels of happiness and life satisfaction.

Embracing our inner critic

How do you talk to yourself after you've made an error or forgot something? What thoughts arise when you were not as efficient and productive as you expected or when you did not have enough time to do everything that "had to" be done? When something goes wrong, do you tend to focus on resolving the problem without pausing to attend to your own discomfort? Do you find yourself easily irritated? Perhaps you are judging yourself for being too self-critical?

Many of the most self-centered and invalidating persons are just trying to survive the endless scolding of their own internal critics. Often people have difficulty managing their anger, and they are often angry with themselves. If someone else criticized us as much as we criticize ourselves, we might want to punch them in the face. If someone else set standards for us as high as we set them for ourselves, we might want to give up and walk away. If someone else called us a quitter or a loser, we would probably be tempted to go back and defend our honor in a fight. Our own unchecked inner critics can leave us feeling angry, helpless and sad—sometimes all at the same time.

Notice the inner self-critic when it arises. Observe those annoying critical thoughts about your work, your looks, your "bad" habits, your parenting skills, your level of motivation or self-discipline or any negative evaluation about yourself. Respond with kindness toward your inner critic. Your inner critic may not be very effective, but it just wants the very same thing you do: for you to be safe and happy and for you to reach your goals. *In fact, our inner critics often move us away from getting what we really want and need, in spite of just wanting us to be effective, safe, and at peace with others and ourselves.*

Notice the thoughts that arise from the inner critic. Sometimes we might notice a pattern—as if we carried a deep, dark secret and this inner critic were reminding us of our fatal flaw.

"Ugh. I'm such an idiot."

"I can't do anything right."

"Nobody loves me" or "I'll never be loved" or "I'll be alone for the rest of my life."

"I am too _____." or "I am not _____ enough."

"I'll never make it (find a job, get married, get promoted, earn enough money, etc.)"

When these kinds of thoughts arise, welcome and embrace your inner critic. Treat your critic with kindness and see what it really wants in the situation. Direct your attention to feelings, emotions, and physical sensations. Validate these experiences as they arise within yourself.

What emotion am I feeling? What are my feelings telling me?

"There is some frustration. I am a little tense all over. If I take the time to pause and listen deeply, I think this tension really just wants things to be more efficient."

"I am feeling nervous. My stomach is tight. Hmm. . . My stomach wants me to be accepted and liked when I go to this interview."

Our feelings and emotions give us information about our needs. Noticing urges to respond or act in a particular way can tell us a lot about what we might be needing.[2] Sometimes we are not even aware of our own needs and it may be necessary to pause and listen deeply to get clear on this.

Karen was invited to a meeting with a small group of entrepreneurs, some of whom were her direct competitors, who had the idea of creating some type of trade association. She did her best to be cooperative and tried to think of suggestions for ways to be mutually supportive. But she left the meeting with a knot in her stomach, ruminating over some of the comments that others had made. Her irritation and critical thoughts seemed to grow over the next two days. Finally, she sat down to silently listen to what her inner critic had to say about her and tried to validate herself with self-compassion.

At first she could hear only her internal critical thoughts about the others—the thoughts that had been repeating themselves and growing stronger. Then she tried to go back to the meeting in her mind and remember what she had been feeling at the time.

What was she feeling?

I was feeling a little wary, distrustful, of the others. I noticed that I was a little nervous, but I kept trying to let go of tension, relax my face and body, and just be fully present.

What did she think her feelings were telling her?

"I was afraid that I would just say something stupid . . . or they wouldn't like my ideas . . . or that they would steal my ideas."

What was she needing?

I really just wanted to be accepted and respected for being calm and wise.

When Karen took enough time to inquire into her feelings and understand what she really wanted, it became clear that all the negative thoughts and the impulses to criticize others would never lead to her feeling accepted and respected. However, the act of pausing and listening to herself was an act of wisdom and it gave her the insight to act in ways that made her feel *that she could respect herself* for being calm and wise; as a result, the opinions of others became far less important.

Looking squarely at our inner critics and validating our feelings and desires often gives us the focus and energy to fill our own needs. Through this practice of inquiry and self-validation, we can become not only our own best friend but our own guiding light.

. . .

It is a mistake to think that one can be of service to others as much as humanly possible and then just add on extra time for self-care. Cultivating self-care requires some time that actually must be taken away from helping others. Effectively caring for others must be balanced with deep and loving self-care. We need the wisdom to be able to maintain this healthy balance.

Practice 4: Letting go

Letting go can be one of the most difficult practices, but it is the only way to allow us to receive what we want. Balance the things that you have to do with the things that you want to do. You may find that you have too many things that you have to do and have no time for doing things that you want to do. If that is the case, do the following:

Find one responsibility that you have and let it go. Organize whatever might be necessary in order to let it go. Delegate. Ask for help. Resign. Or just drop it. Take one thing out of your schedule. Do not fill that time in with some other responsibility. Keep that space for you and use it in a way that gives you peace or joy or rest or just mental space . . . whatever *you* are needing or wanting . . . Write down a plan to let it go and do it this week!

Self-validation with wisdom steps back to see the big picture, specifically in three ways: (1) expanding our sense of being a separate individual, to include an awareness of our shared humanity; (2) moving away from seeing things in black and white, right and wrong, good and bad, and instead opening up to the dialectical integrated and relational complexities of life; and (3) seeing behaviors and actions through a wider lens of transactional events, each with interacting antecedents and consequences.

1. Shared humanity

Self-validation recognizes that whatever our experience, no matter how odd, unusual or frightening, we are not alone. Our experiences are not as unique as we might believe. We all have the same set of human emotions, desires, thoughts, and needs. Self-validation "normalizes" the situation. It is part of our universal human experience.

- "This is part of life."
- "Everyone has this kind of experience."
- "I am only human!"

2. Dialectics

How do you describe yourself? Extroverted or introverted? Funny or serious? Emotional or rational? The truth is, we are all a little of each, and with different combinations at different times. When we see the world as dichotomous—good or evil, help or hurt, strong or weak, etc.—we are oversimplifying reality. This immature view of the world can make us become more rigid when we are in an emotional frame of mind. The dialectical view of the world sees things in a dynamic and interdependent flow, with seemingly contradictory things happening simultaneously. We don't get stuck seeing the world in only black and white; we see it in full 3-D color.

- "I love the thrill and adventure of taking risks, and I also need to feel safe and protected."
- "This was a total failure. We lost our entire investment. It was also the most valuable learning experience that we could have possibly had. It was worth every penny."
- "Every day the universe offers me another opportunity to practice patience."

Self-validation may include the choice to do things that are not fun, that may even be very difficult or challenging, such as caring for one's physical and mental health.

We can see mistakes as learning experiences and also fully experience disappointment.

3. Transactional antecedents and consequences

Self-validation might look at what caused the emotional suffering and what the result was.

- "Of course I am sad and disappointed; my boyfriend canceled our plans last night. So I Skyped a couple of girlfriends I haven't spoken to in ages, and it was the best evening ever."

Cheryl worked for a bank for 20 years, slowly increasing her responsibilities despite being passed over for several promotions because she had not finished college. Her boss was inconsistent, praising her work and assigning her complex problems that others could not solve, but then giving her smaller raises than her male counterparts received, justifying the smaller raises with a reference to her lack of a university degree. She came close to quitting in those moments, but then her boss would give her some kind of pep talk, an interesting assignment, and a couple of days off to convince her to stay.

"One day I was transferred to another department in an older building and had to report to someone who reported to my boss. I almost quit because it felt like such a demotion and I had to work in such an ugly space. I hated my job more than ever. However, I validated all of my feelings and then realized that the new assignment was interesting and the people seemed nice. A few months later my new boss made me an offer to pay for my college degree if I wanted to go back to school and finish—with a guaranteed raise when I graduate! I just heard that my old boss was transferred out of corporate headquarters to a small office in the South."

When Cheryl could step back and see the whole sequence of events, the moment that seemed to be the worst and the most painful resulted in a blessing. And her ex-boss eventually got his "just desserts" as well.

Unfortunately the world is not always fair. However, it is also true that the seeds we sow will be the harvest that we reap. Wisdom sees this and knows this. Wisdom is patient. Self-care, self-compassion, and self-validation make us better persons who have a greater capacity for helping others be happier.

To be genuinely helpful and supportive to others, we need to be sturdy and self-reliant. A lack of attention to our own personal limits may create a disequilibrium that can lead to exhaustion, burnout, or a state of emotional anesthesia in which we fall further and further away from being mindful of the present moment in our lives. We probably end up pushing others away in this state. Self-validation is useful to help us recognize our own personal limits to how much we can give without becoming worn out, exhausted, or resentful.

How can we remain firm, yet flexible with regard to the urgent needs of our loved ones or others? How can we know when to say no to others before we reach our limits and get burned out?

Victor had a demanding and well-paid job that had very flexible work hours. He often worked from home, where there was a bit of competition for his time and attention. His wife, Natali, worked as a nurse, and her shifts included nights and weekends. The days that she was at home, it was all too easy for Victor to take half a day off and head out to a park with her and the two dogs. On those days, he never really got settled in to his office or was able to concentrate fully on his work. It was also convenient for Natali, who began to depend on Victor's availability to help her when she was at home or to look after the dogs or run an important errand when she had to be at work.

Victor's style was to try to be agreeable and ignore his discomfort with a situation as long as possible—until he exploded. An intense argument would ensue, often leaving Natali in tears. As a consequence, Victor would just want to distance himself from her and throw himself into his work. He would end up stonewalling Natali, but eventually his fear over his job and his anger at his wife would pass and he'd be flooded with sadness and guilt. He realized how much he valued their relationship. Meanwhile, Natali bounced around between feeling desperate, hurt, and angry as his stonewalling grew from hours to days to weeks. This pattern occurred enough times that they were both becoming worn out with their relationship.

We have to pay attention and validate our feelings, thoughts, needs, and desires. We have to have our own priorities for ourselves very clear. The earlier we say no and calmly and patiently stick to it, the easier it is. We don't necessarily have to give a reason. Saying no because "I am who I am" may be the healthiest response, even if others don't like it. We become a *broken record*—enforcing limits as many times as necessary but always with kindness and patience. We may have to let go of internal and external distractions and express needs, desires, and opinions about the personal limits again and again with lots of validation.

Victor was very rational and logical. He sometimes had trouble connecting with emotions, but he could be understanding about cognitive issues such as desires, priorities, and reasoning. How could Victor validate his personal limits long before fury exploded and, at the same time, validate Natali's needs?

To validate *his* personal limits, he had to attend to his priorities. He also had to practice validating Natali *and* say no to her. Victor had to connect with his wise mind and decide when and where he wanted to work. This became a daily practice of spending a few quiet minutes alone at the very beginning of each day. The discipline to set priorities each morning began to expand into the discipline to concentrate for longer periods of time later in the day with an attitude of self-kindness and self-care.

When Natali would ask him for help around the house, he would respond, "Honey I understand you need this done and you want my help. It might take only a few minutes, but I cannot afford to be distracted from my work today. I have a lot of pressure and I really have to put all of my attention and energy on being as focused and productive as possible."

The first time he tried this, Natali responded by rolling her eyes and sighing. She reminded him that he had promised to help. Guilt began to arise, and this was hard for Victor. Remembering the phrase *broken record*, he repeated himself kindly, gently, and firmly: "Honey, I'm sorry. Not today." He was committed to not giving in out of guilt nor getting angry with her for pressuring him. He developed some additional ways to validate his needs and also hers:

- "I understand that this adds to your stress if I can't help right now. This is hard for me too."
- "I cannot be responsible for the dogs this week, but I am available all day on Sunday."
- "Your time at your job is important to you. My time and my work are very important to me."
- At one point Victor hung a "Please do not disturb" sign on the doorknob of his office, and he added a "thank you" in his own handwriting and drew a red heart on the sign.

As Victor got better at gently and firmly saying no to distractions on the days that he worked at home, Natali became more and more supportive of his privacy during his work. They both became more grounded and self-reliant, and they also began to have more fun when they spent time together.

We all have personal limits. The challenge is to recognize and care for them. We often don't realize our limits have been exceeded until we are resentful or burned out. It may be that we let others cross our limits so many times that it seems impossible to establish them clearly. The concept of personal limits says that we cannot blame another person for asking. Instead we take full responsibility for saying no. Compassionate communication that validates our own needs and desires as well as others' can be a very effective way for us to start.

Chapter summary

Self-validation might begin with the following questions: How does that make you feel? What types of thoughts arise? What are you needing in this situation? What would you attempt to do if you knew you could not fail?

Components of self-validation

1. Presence

- Self-validation is taking the time to be present and still in order to listen deeply to one's own feelings, thoughts, and impulses.

2. Acceptance

- It is acceptance of one's own feelings, noting or naming them without value judgments.
- We can see how our feelings, sensations, and thoughts are understandable within our life context.

3. Empathy

- Self-validation directs empathy toward ourselves. We
  experience our suffering fully while remaining grounded.
  We mindfully listen to every nuance of our feelings.

4. Compassion

- Self-validation is the kind and loving response to discomfort,
  distress, or pain. It can mean taking appropriate action in
  response to the question "What am I needing right now?"
- It is a practice of replacing self-criticism and perfectionism
  with kindness and love toward ourselves. We can do this by
  embracing our inner critics with kindness and generating
  thoughts, expressions, gestures, and deeds of self-
  compassion.

5. Wisdom

- Let go.
- Our experiences are not as unique as we might believe.
- See things from a dialectical perspective.
- Recognize how antecedents and consequences are
  transactional. In a relationship, nothing is "all my fault" (nor
  is it all the fault of the other).

6. Self-respect

- Self-validation recognizes our own personal limits to how
  much we can give without becoming worn out, exhausted, or
  resentful and how much we need from others in exchange.
- We can validate our limits and also validate others' desires or
  feelings when we say no to them.
- Self-validation connects us to dignity, self-respect, and
  self-love.

Self-validation is essential when we need to recover from invalidation. It can protect us from feeling destroyed by the anger of others, frightened by the fear of others, or saddened by the depression of others. Carl Rogers described how it is necessary to monitor one's own needs and be aware of how much time, energy, attention, and personal possessions can be given to others without losing oneself in the process.[3] Self-validation gives us the freedom to be centered and compassionate toward ourselves. Once we have established self-compassion, we are more capable than ever of helping to reduce the suffering of others.

AFTERWORD

A NOTE ABOUT PROFESSIONAL SUPPORT

This book is not to replace professional psychotherapy or psychiatry for yourself or a friend or loved one. While we refer to various levels of mental distress and emotional reactivity, from modest to extremely serious, this book in no way represents a replacement to therapy or medication if recommended by a professional. If you believe that you suffer from severe emotional dysregulation, chronic depression, anxiety, or a mental health disorder, you are urged to seek qualified and professional support. It is possible to overcome the suffering that accompanies these illnesses with proper health care. Mental health professionals vary widely in their approaches to treatment. You are advised to carefully choose a licensed and experienced health professional who is trained in evidence-based treatment—that is, specific treatment for your needs that is backed up by controlled scientific studies that have been published in peer-reviewed academic journals.

ENDNOTES

Preface

1. Between 2005 and 2015, the number of people suffering from depression worldwide increased by eighteen percent and the number of people living with anxiety increased by nearly fifteen percent. Source: World Health Organization, (2017) *Depression and Other Common Mental Health Disorders, Global Health Estimates* Geneva, Switzerland: WHO, License CC BY-NC-SA 3.0 IGO.
2. Harvard Study of Adult Development, a longitudinal study of 268 students at Harvard that began in 1938 and continues to the present and now includes the Second Generation Study. http://www.adultdevelopmentstudy.org

2. What Is Genuine Validation?

1. *Emotions and needs are physiological experiences and shared by all human beings, thus they are always valid. Desires, opinions and beliefs are also normal and valid -- when these thoughts are recognized as subjective experiences and not as facts.*
2. *Behaviors and actions may be valid when they are effective and not valid when they are not effective or not based on good judgment or sound principles. Note: These are general rules. The world is not black and white and things may not be just valid or just invalid -- they may be both at the same time!*

3. Understanding Emotions

1. Marsha M. Linehan, M.M., *Cognitive-Behavioral Treatment of Borderline Personality Disorder* (New York: Guilford Press, 2003), p. 150.
2. Paul Ekman, *Emotions Revealed: Recognizing Faces and Feelings to Improve Communication and Emotional Life,* (New York: St. Martin's Griffin, 2003), pp. 233–234.sq
3. Daniel Goleman, *Emotional Intelligence: Why It Can Matter More than IQ* (New York: Bantam Books, 2005).
4. Ekman, *Emotions Revealed.*
5. Marsha M. Linehan, Emotional Regulation Skills training, New England Institute, Wellfleet, MA, August 2009.
6. Brij V. Lal, "Veil of Dishonour: Sexual Jealousy and Suicide on Fiji Plantations," *Journal of Pacific History* 20 (1985): 135-155.
7. Christopher Germer interviewed by Tami Simon, *Self Love: Overcoming Shame, Vimeo* video, 51:27, Sept. 18, 2017, https://vimeo.com/234366949.

4. Presence

1. Palmo, Jetsunma Tenzin, Lecture Buenos Aires, Argentina, April, 2018.
2. This is a basic practice developed by Shinzen Young, as part of the "Unified Mindfulness System."
3. Robyn Walter and Darrah Westrup, *The Mindful Couple*, (Oakland: New Harbinger Publications, 2009), 99.
4. Rebecca Shafir, "Mindful Listening for Better Outcomes," in *Mindfulness and the Therapeutic Relationship*, ed. Steven F. Hick and Thomas Bien (New York: Guilford Press, 2008).

5. Acceptance

1. Shunryu Suzuki, *Zen Mind, Beginner's Mind* (Boulder, CO: Shambhala Publications, 2006), 120.
2. Marsha Linehan, *Mindfulness and Acceptance* (professional training), New England Institute, Eastham, MA, July 2009.
3. Kristin Neff, *Self-Compassion: The Proven Power of Being Kind to Yourself* (New York: Harper Collins Publishers, 2015).
4. Christopher Germer, *The Mindful Path to Self-Compassion: Freeing Yourself from Destructive Thoughts and Emotions* (New York: Guilford Press, 2009), 28.
5. Marshall B. Rosenberg, *Nonviolent Communication: A Language of Life* (Encinitas, CA: Puddle Dancer Press, 2003).
6. Carl R. Rogers, "Reflection of Feelings," *Person-Centered Review* 1, no. 4 (1986): 375-77.
7. Eugene T. Gendlin, *Focusing*, (New York: Bantam New Age Books, 1978), 119-120.
8. Eugene T. Gendlin, Ibid.
9. Daniel Goleman, *Emotional Intelligence: Why It Can Matter More than IQ* (New York: Bantam Books, 2005), 290.

6. Empathy

1. Carl R. Rogers, "A Theory of Therapy and Interpersonal Relationships as Developed in the Client-Centered Framework," in *Psychology: A Study of Science*, Vol. 3, *Evaluations of the persona in the social context*, ed. Sigmund Koch (New York: McGraw-Hill, 1959), 184–256.
2. Anthony Bateman and Peter Fonagy, *Mentalization-Based Treatment for Borderline Personality Disorder: A Practical Guide* (Oxford: Oxford University Press, 2006), 15.
3. Wolfgang Prinz, "Perception and Action Planning," *European Journal of Cognitive Psychology* 9, no. 2 (1997): 129–54.
4. Kevin N. Ochsner, Silvia A. Bunge, James J. Gross, and John D. E. Gabriel, "Rethinking Feelings: An fMRI Study of the Cognitive Regulation of Emotion," *Journal of Cognitive Neuroscience* 14 (2002): 1215–29.

5. Daniel J. Siegel, *The Mindful Brain: Reflection and Attunement in the Cultivation of Well-Being* (New York: W. W. Norton and Company, 2007), 224–25.

6. Ahmad R. Hariri, Susan Y. Bookheimer, and John C. Maziotta, "Modulating Emotional Responses: Effects of a Neocortical Network on the Limbic System," *Neuroreport: For Rapid Communications of Neuroscience Research* 11, no. 1 (2000): 43–48.

7. Rosenberg, *Nonviolent Communication: A Language of Life*, 54–55. (Note: Rosenberg groups the basic needs into seven areas. I modified the groupings into eight areas, separating the needs for contribution, etc., from the needs for caring and appreciation, etc.)

8. Jean Decety and Philip L. Jackson, "The Functional Architecture of Human Empathy," *Behavioral and Cognitive Neuroscience Reviews* 3 (2004): 73.

7. Compassion

1. Penny A. Spikins, Holly E. Rutherford, and Andy P. Needham, "From Homininity to Humanity: Compassion from the Earliest Archaics to Modern Humans," *Journal of Archeology, Consciousness and Culture* 3 (2010): 303–332.

2. Marsha Linehan, class lecture at Advanced Intensive DBT Training, Seattle, Washington, August 16–20, 2010.

3. Paul Gilbert, *The Compassionate Mind* (Oakland, CA: New Harbinger Publications, 2009), xiii.

4. Thich Nhat Han, *The Heart of Buddha's Teachings: Transforming Suffering into Peace, Joy, and Liberation* (Harmony Books: New York, 1998), 157–163.

5. Timothy Desmond, *Self-Compassion in Psychotherapy: Mindfulness-Based Practices for Healing and Transformation* (New York: W. W. Norton, 2016), 9.

6. Richard Davidson, foreword to Timothy Desmond, *Self-Compassion in Psychotherapy: Mindfulness-Based Practices for Healing and Transformation* (New York: W. W. Norton, 2016), xii.

7. Stephen W. Porges, Jane A. Doussard-Roosevelt, and Ajit K. Maiti, "Vagal Tone and the Physiological Regulation of Emotion," in *Emotion Regulation: Behavioral and Biological Considerations*, ed. Nathan A. Fox (Ann Arbor, MI: Society for Research in Child Development, 1994), 167–186.

8. Paul Gilbert, *The Compassionate Mind* (London: Constable and Robinson, 2009), 139–152.

9. Thomas R. Lynch, *Radically Open Dialectical Behavior Therapy: Theory and practice for treating disorders of overcontrol* (Oakland, CA: New Harbinger Publication. 2018), 33–45.

10. Diagram and integration of theories developed by Stephen Porges, Paul Gilbert, and Thomas Lynch with layout inspired by the work of David Peters; see Peters, "The Neurobiology of Resilience," *InnovAIT* 9, no. 6 (2016): 333–341.

11. Paul Gilbert, *The Compassionate Mind* (Oakland, CA: New Harbinger Publications, 2009).

12. The Harvard Adult Development Study is an ongoing study of 268 Harvard

graduates from 1939 to 1944 and 456 men who grew up in Boston's inner city. http://www.adultdevelopmentstudy.org/grantandglueckstudy

13. Pema Chödrön, *Start Where You Are: A Guide to Compassionate Living* (Boston: Shambhala Publications, 1994), 58–70.

14. Susan Sprecher and Beverly Fehr, "Compassionate Love for Close Others and for Humanity," *Journal of Social and Personal Relationships* 22, no. 5 (2005): 629.

15. Daniel Goleman and Richard J. Davidson, *Altered Traits: Science Reveals How Meditation Changes Your Mind, Brain, and Body* (New York: Penguin Publishing Group, 2017), 112–113.

16. Ibid, 250–251.

8. Wisdom

1. Marsha M. Linehan, *Cognitive-Behavioral Treatment of Borderline Personality Disorder* (New York: Guilford Press, 1993).

2. Toni Packer, *The Wonder of Presence and the Way of Meditative Inquiry* (Boston: Shambhala Publications, 2002), 11–12.

3. Thomas R. Lynch, *Radically Open Dialectical Behavior Therapy: Theory and Practice for Treating Disorders of Overcontrol* (Oakland, CA: New Harbinger Press, 2018).

4. Ethan Kross, Patricia Deldin, David Gard, Jessica Clifton, and Ozlem Ayduk, "Asking 'Why' from a Distance: Its Cognitive and Emotional Consequences for People with Major Depressive Disorder," *Journal of Abnormal Psychology* 121, no. 3 (2012): 559–569. See also: Aaron T. Beck, "Cognitive Therapy: Nature and Relation to Behavior Therapy," *Behavior Therapy* 1 (1970): 184–200.

5. Shinzen Young, *Five Ways to Know Yourself: An Introduction to Basic Mindfulness,* 2011, https://www.shinzen.org/wp-content/uploads/2016/08/FiveWaystoKnow-Yourself_ver1.6.pdf.

9. Respect

1. Rick Hanson, "Rick's Reflection: Brothers and Sisters," The Foundations of Well-Being, December 2017, http://beingwellinc.cmail20.com/t/ViewEmail/d/6E78008020C3BA54/8588B67B0A75880B62AF25ACF5E3F0AC.

10. Deepening Self-Validation

1. A word used by Toni Packer to create an active sense of being alert, awake, and paying attention very closely.

2. For more on this, review the universal needs and desires in chapter 5, "Empathy."

3. Carl Rogers, *On Becoming a Person: A Therapist's View of Psychotherapy* (New York: Houghton Mifflin Company, 1961).

BIBLIOGRAPHY

Beck, Aaron T. "Cognitive Therapy: Nature and Relation to Behavior Therapy." *Behavior Therapy* 1 (1970): 184–200.

Chödrön, Pema. *Start Where You Are: A Guide to Compassionate Living.* Boston: Shambhala Publications, 1994.

Damasio, Antonio. *Descartes' Error: Emotion, Reason and the Human Brain.* New York: Penguin Book, 1994.

Davidson, Richard. Foreword to Timothy Desmond, *Self-Compassion in Psychotherapy: Mindfulness-Based Practices for Healing and Transformation, xi-xii* . New York: W. W. Norton, 2016.

Decety, Jean, and Phillip L. Jackson. "The Functional Architecture of Human Empathy." *Behavioral and Cognitive Neuroscience Reviews* 3 (2004): 71–100.

Desmond, Timothy. *Self-Compassion in Psychotherapy: Mindfulness-Based Practices for Healing and Transformation.* New York: W. W. Norton, 2016.

Dimeff, Linda A., and Kelly Koerner. *Dialectical Behavior Therapy in*

Clinical Practice: Applications across Disorders and Settings. New York: Guilford Press, 2007.

Ekman, Paul. *Emotional Awareness: Overcoming the Obstacles to Psychological Balance and Compassion: A Conversation between Dalai Lama and Paul Ekman*. New York: Holt Paperback, 2008.

Ekman, Paul. *Emotions Revealed: Recognizing Faces and Feelings to Improve Communication and Emotional Life*. New York: St. Martin's Griffin, 2003.

Fruzzetti, Alan E. *High-Conflict Couple: A Dialectical Behavior Therapy Guide to Finding Peace, Intimacy and Validation*. Oakland, CA: New Harbinger Publications, 2006.

Gendlin, Eugene T. *Focusing*. New York: Bantam New Age Books, 1978.

Germer, Christopher K. *The Mindful Path to Self-Compassion: Freeing Yourself from Destructive Thoughts and Emotions*. New York: Guilford Press, 2009.

Gilbert, Paul. *The Compassionate Mind*. Oakland, CA: New Harbinger Publications, 2009.

Gilbert, Paul, and Chöden. *Mindful Compassion: How the Science of Compassion Can Help You Understand Your Emotions, Live in the Present, and Connect Deeply with Others*. Oakland, CA: New Harbinger Press, 2014.

Goleman, Daniel. *Emotional Intelligence: Why It Can Matter More than IQ*. New York: Bantam Books, 2005.

Goleman, Daniel, and Richard J. Davidson. *Altered Traits: Science Reveals How Meditation Changes Your Mind, Brain, and Body*. New York: Penguin Publishing Group, 2017.

Hanson, Rick. "Rick's Reflection: Brothers and Sisters." The Foundations of Well-Being. December 2017. http://beingwellinc.cmail20.com/t/ViewEmail/d/6E78008020C3BA54/8588B67B0A75880B62AF25ACF5E3F0AC.

Hanson, Rick, and Richard Mendius. *The Practical Neuroscience of Buddha's Brain: Happiness, Love and Wisdom.* Oakland, CA: New Harbinger Publications, 2009.

Hariri, Ahmad R., Susan Y. Bookheimer, and John C. Maziotta. "Modulating Emotional Responses: Effects of a Neocortical Network on the Limbic System." In *Neuroreport: For Rapid Communications of Neuroscience Research* 11, no. 1 (2000): 43–48.

Hayes, Stephen C., Victoria M. Follette, and Marsha M. Linehan. *Mindfulness and Acceptance: Expanding the Cognitive-Behavioral Tradition.* New York: Guilford Press, 2004.

Hick, Stephen F., and Thomas Bien, eds. *Mindfulness and the Therapeutic Relationship.* New York: Guilford Press, 2008.

Kabat-Zinn, Jon. *Full Catastrophe Living: Using the Wisdom of Your Body and Mind to Face Stress, Pain and Illness.* New York: Delta, 1990.

Kornfield, Jack. *The Wise Heart: A Guide to the Universal Teachings of Buddhist Psychology.* New York: Bantam Books, 2009.

Kross, Ethan, Patricia Deldin, David Gard, Jessica Clifton, and Ozlem Ayduk. "Asking 'Why' from a Distance: Its Cognitive and Emotional Consequences for People with Major Depressive Disorder." *Journal of Abnormal Psychology* 121, no. 3 (2012): 559–569.

Lal, Brij V. "Veil of Dishonour: Sexual Jealousy and Suicide on Fiji Plantations." *Journal of Pacific History* 20, no. 3–4 (1985): 135–155.

Leu, Lucy. *Nonviolent Communication. Companion Workbook: A Practical Guide for Individual, Group, or Classroom Study.* Encinitas, CA: Puddle Dancer Press, 2003.

Linehan, Marsha M. *Cognitive-Behavioral Treatment of Borderline Personality Disorder.* New York: Guilford Press, 1993.

Linehan, Marsha M. "Validation and Psychotherapy." *Empathy Reconsidered: New Directions in Psychotherapy,* edited by Arthur C. Bohart and Leslie S. Greenberg, 353–392. Washington, DC: American Psychological Association, 1997.

Lundberg, Gary B., and Joy S. Lundberg. *I Don't Have to Make Everything All Better: Six Practical Principles that Empower Others to Solve Their Own Problems while Enriching Your Relationships.* New York: Penguin Books, 1995.

Lynch, Thomas R. *Radically Open Dialectical Behavior Therapy: Theory and Practice for Treating Disorders of Overcontrol.* Oakland, CA: New Harbinger Press, 2018.

Marturano, Janice. *Finding the Space to Lead: A Practical Guide to Mindful Leadership.* New York: Bloomsbury Press, 2014.

Neff, Kristen. *Self-Compassion: The Proven Power of Being Kind to Yourself.* New York: HarperCollins Publishers, 2015.

Nhat Han, Thich. *The Heart of Buddha's Teachings.* Berkeley, CA: Parallax Press, 1998.

Nhat Hanh, Thich. *Peace Is Every Step: The Path of Mindfulness in Everyday Life.* New York: Bantam Books, 1991.

Ochsner, Kevin N., Silvia Bunge, James J. Gross, and John D. E. Gabrieli. "Rethinking Feelings: An fMRI Study of the Cognitive Regulation of Emotion." *Journal of Cognitive Neuroscience* 14, no. 8 (2002): 1215–1229.

Packer, Toni. *The Wonder of Presence and the Way of Meditative Inquiry,* Boston: Shambhala Publications, 2002.

Peters, David. "The Neurobiology of Resilience." *InnovAIT* 9, no. 6 (2016): 333–341.

Plutchik, Richard. "Perception and Action Planning." *European Journal of Cognitive Psychology* 9 (1987): 129–154.

Porges, Stephen W., Jane A. Doussard-Roosevelt, and Ajit K. Maiti. "Vagal Tone and the Physiological Regulation of Emotion." In

Emotion Regulation: Behavioral and Biological Considerations, edited by Nathan A. Fox, 167–186. Ann Arbor, MI: Society for Research in Child Development, 1994.

Ratey, John Jay. *A User's Guide to the Brain: Perception, Attention and the Four Theaters of the Brain.* New York: Vintage Books, 2001.

Roamer, Lizabeth and Susan M. Orsillo. *Mindfulness and Acceptance-Based Behavioral Therapies in Practice.* New York: Guilford Press, 2009.

Rogers, Carl R. "Evaluations of the Persona in the Social Context." *Psychology: A Study of Science*, vol. 3, edited by Sigmund Koch, 184–256. New York: McGraw-Hill, 1959.

Rogers, Carl R. *On Becoming a Person: A Therapist's View of Psychotherapy.* New York: Houghton Mifflin Company, 1961.

Rosenberg, Marshall B. *Nonviolent Communication: A Language of Life.* Encinitas: Puddle Dancer Press, 2003.

Salzberg, Sharon. *Loving-Kindness: The Revolutionary Art of Happiness.* Boston: Shambhala, 1995.

Shafir, Rebecca. "Mindful Listening for Better Outcomes." *Mindfulness and the Therapeutic Relationship,* edited by Steven F. Hick and Thomas Bien, 215–231. New York: Guilford Press, 2008.

Shafir, Rebecca. *The Zen of Listening.* Adyar, India: Quest Books; Theosophical Publishing House, 2003.

Shapiro, Shauna L. and Christian D. Izzet. "Meditation: A Universal Tool for Cultivating Empathy," *Mindfulness and the Therapeutic Relationship,* edited by Steven F. Hick and Thomas Bien, 161–175. New York: Guilford Press, 2008.

Siegel, Daniel J. *The Mindful Brain: Reflection and Attunement in the Cultivation of Well-Being.* New York: W. W. Norton and Company, 2007.

Spikins, Penny, Holly. E. Rutherford, and Andrew P. Needham, "From Homininity to Humanity: Compassion from the Earliest Archaics to

Modern Humans." *Journal of Archeology, Consciousness and Culture* 3 (2010): 303–332.

Sprecher, Susan, and Beverly Fehr. "Compassionate Love for Close Others and for Humanity." *Journal of Social and Personal Relationships* 22, no. 5 (2005): 629–651.

Suzuki, Shunryu. *Zen Mind, Beginner's Mind.* Boulder, CO: Shambhala Publications, 2011.

Taylor, Jill Bolte. *My Stroke of Insight: A Brain Scientist's Personal Journey.* New York: Viking Penguin, 2008.

Young, Shinzen. *Five Ways to Know Yourself: An Introduction to Basic Mindfulness.* 2011. https://www.shinzen.org/wp-content/uploads/2016/08/FiveWaystoKnowYourself_ver1.6.pdf

ABOUT THE AUTHOR

At this publication Corrine works with individuals, families, and organizations as DBT coach dedicated to helping people cultivate emotional balance and greater well-being. She teaches workshops on mindfulness, self-compassion, social and emotional skills, and conflict management. Since 2005 Corrine has been teaching Dialectical Behavior Therapy skills to families—an activity that never ceases to give her life meaning and joy.

Corrine was called to study psychology and spirituality upon being touched by the profound depth of suffering experienced by a loved one with a mental health disorder—someone who, but for grace and providence, could be any one of us.

www.DBTCoach.com